W9-ANU-394

BRITAIN'S
BEST-LOVED
DRIVING
TOURS

Hungry Minds, Inc.

New York, NY ■ Indianapolis, IN ■ Cleveland, OH

Written by Roy Woodcock, John McIlwain

Revised fifth edition published 2002
Revised second edition 1995, published in this format 1997
First published January 1991
Reprinted December 1997
Second edition of revised format 1999

Edited, designed and produced by AA Publishing.

© Automobile Association Developments Ltd 1997, 1999, 2002
Maps © Automobile Association Developments Ltd 1997, 1999, 2002

Ordnance Survey® This product includes mapping data licensed from Ordnance Survey® with the permission of the Controller of Her Majesty's Stationery Office. © Crown copyright 2001. All rights reserved. Licence number 399221

Mapping produced by the Cartographic Department of The Automobile Association.

All rights reserved. No part of this publication may be reproduced, stored in a retrieval system, or transmitted in any form or by any means – electronic, photocopying, recording or otherwise – unless the permission of the publishers has been obtained beforehand.

This book may not be lent, resold, hired out or otherwise disposed of by way of trade in any form of binding or cover other than that in which it is published, without the prior consent of the publisher.

The contents of this publication are believed correct at the time of printing. Nevertheless, the publishers cannot accept responsibility for errors or omissions or for changes in details given in this guide or for the consequences of any reliance on the information provided by the same. Assessments of attractions and so forth are based upon the author's own experience and, therefore, descriptions given in this guide necessarily contain an element of subjective opinion which may not reflect the publishers' opinion or dictate a reader's own experience on another occasion.

Published by AA Publishing

Published in the United States by
Hungry Minds, Inc.
909 Third Avenue, New York, NY 10022

Find us online at Frommers.com

Frommer's is a registered trademark of Arthur Frommer.
Used under license.

ISBN 0-7645-6592-3
ISSN 1520-9946

Cataloging-in-Publication Data is available from the Library of Congress.

Color separation: Daylight Colour Art, Singapore

Printed and bound by G. Canale & C. S.P.A., Torino, Italy

Right: *Woolsack Races, Tetbury, Gloucestershire*

CONTENTS

ABOUT THIS BOOK

This book is not only a practical touring guide for the independent traveller, but is also invaluable for those who would like to know more about Britain.

It is divided into 6 regions, each containing between 4 and 6 tours which start and finish in major towns and cities which we consider to be the best centres for exploration.

Each tour has details of the most interesting places to visit en route. Panels catering for special interests follow some of the main entries – for those whose interest is in history, wildlife or walking, and those who have children. There are also panels which highlight scenic stretches of road and which give details of local events, crafts and customs.

The simple route directions are accompanied by an easy-to-use map at the beginning of each tour, along with a chart showing how far it is from one town to the next in miles and kilometres. This can help you to decide where to take a break and stop overnight, for example. (All distances quoted are approximate.)

Before setting off it is advisable to check with the information centre at the start of the tour for recommendations on where to break your journey and for additional information on what to see and do, and when best to visit.

Tour Information
See pages 161–73 for addresses, telephone numbers and opening times of the attractions mentioned in the tours, including telephone numbers of tourist offices.

Accommodation
See pages 159–60 for a list of recommended hotels for each tour.

Business Hours
Banks are generally open 9am to 4pm weekdays. Some banks are open on Saturdays until noon. In Scotland, opening times differ and some banks close for lunch.

Post offices open from 9am to 5.30 or 6pm Monday to Friday and 9am to 12.30pm on Saturdays.

Shops are open from 9am to 5.30pm, Monday to Saturday. Some are also open from 10am to 4pm on Sunday.

Credit Cards
All major credit cards are widely accepted in Britain.

Currency
The unit of currency is the pound (£), divided into 100 pence. Coins: 1, 2, 5, 10, 20 and 50 pence; one and two pounds. Notes: £5, 10, 20, 50.

Customs Regulations
Visitors from EU countries are governed by EU regulations and can bring in items for their own personal use without paying duty. Visitors resident outside Europe are limited to certain duty-free allowances; check at time of purchase.

Electricity
240 volts, 50 cycles AC. Plugs are three-pin style. Electric shavers operate on 240 or 110 volts. Visitors from the US will need a transformer. Visitors from Europe, Australia and New Zealand will need an adaptor. Most hotels are fitted with special razor sockets which will take both voltages.

Embassies
Australia: Australian High Commission, Australia House, Strand, London WC2B 4LA, tel: 020–7379 4334.
Canada: Canadian High Commission, 38 Grosvenor Street, London W1X 0AA, tel: 020–7258 6600.
New Zealand: New Zealand High Commission, New Zealand House, 80 Haymarket, London SW1Y 4TQ, tel: 020–7930 8422.
US: American Embassy, 24 Grosvenor Square, London W1A 1AE, tel: 020–7499 9000.

Emergency Telephone Numbers
Police, fire and ambulance tel: 999.

Entry Regulations
Passports are required by all visitors except citizens of EU countries, who must have suitable identity documents. Visas are not required for entry into Britain by American citizens, nationals of the British Commonwealth and most European countries.

Health
Inoculations are not required by visitors for entry to Britain. Health insurance is recommended for non-EU citizens.

Motoring
For information on all aspects of motoring in Britain, see pages 158–9.

Public Holidays
1 January – New Year's Day
2 January – holiday in Scotland only
Good Friday
Easter Monday (not Scotland)
1st Monday in May – May Day
Last Monday in May – Spring Bank Holiday
1st Monday in August – Bank Holiday in Scotland only
Last Monday in August – August Bank Holiday (not Scotland)

25 December – Christmas Day
26 December – Boxing Day

Route Directions
These abbreviations are used for British roads:
A - main roads; **B** - local roads; unclassified roads - minor roads.

Telephones
Insert coins after lifting the receiver; the dialling tone is a continuous tone.
Useful numbers:
Operator – 100
Directory Enquiries – 192
International Directory
 Enquiries – 153
International Operator – 155.
  To make an international call, dial 00 (the international code), then the country code, followed by the area code and the local number.
  Country codes are:
Australia 61;
Canada 1;
New Zealand 64;
Republic of Ireland 353;
UK and Northern Ireland 44;
US 1.

Time
The official time is (GMT) Greenwich Mean Time.
  British Summer Time (BST) begins in late March when the clocks are put forward an hour. In late October, the clocks go back an hour to GMT. The official date is announced in the national newspapers and is always at 2am on a Sunday.

Tourist Offices
England; English Tourism Council, Black's Road, Hammersmith, London W6 9EL (tel: 020 8563 3000).
Scotland; Scottish Tourist Board, 23 Ravelston Terrace, Edinburgh EH4 3EU (tel: 0131–332 2433).
Wales: Wales Tourist Board, 2 Fitzalan Road, Cardiff CF2 1UY (tel: 029 2049 9909).

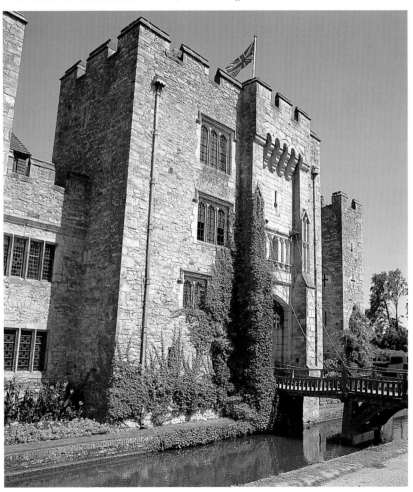

Hever Castle, Kent: Anne Boleyn's childhood home

THE WEST

The rich, rural lands of the counties from Dorset and Wiltshire westwards contain some spectacular scenery. Soft chalklands around Salisbury give way to harder and older rocks, which create the steep and dramatic hills of the Quantocks, Exmoor and Dartmoor.

An alternating sequence of cliffs and beaches forms the western coastline: there are the precipitous granite cliffs near Land's End, and stupendous sandstone cliffs on the northern fringe of Exmoor. Steep roads are an indication of the resistance of the rocks. As a contrast to hills and cliffs, the flat fenlands of the Somerset Levels stretch away from the coast.

The pretty village of Selworthy in Somerset stands on the side of a wooded hill

The Levels are dotted with dairy cattle grazing on lush green meadows, many of which, thanks to conservation techniques, still contain buttercups and other wild flowers. West Country towns are situated round the edges of the high ground and in the river valleys. Many coastal towns which grew up as fishing ports have become holiday resorts, and traffic tends to be congested during the summer. Even the M5 motorway can become crowded at peak holiday weekends.

Early settlements left their mark on this area, too: Dartmoor probably has the greatest number of relics, but more famous and popular are the sites at Glastonbury, Stonehenge and Avebury. More recent evidence of human activity can be seen in many areas of mining, which is still practised near St Austell, where china clay is obtained for the paper industry.

Copper and tin were important minerals in Cornwall from the time of the Romans until earlier this century, when richer and larger deposits in other countries made the British mines uneconomic. The history of mining can be traced in the mining museums which are among the increasing number of the southwest's indoor attractions, complimenting the scenic splendour of this part of Britain.

Penzance

The end of the railway line and the most westerly major town of England enjoys a mild climate which enables palm trees to grow along the coastline. Penzance was immortalised by Gilbert and Sullivan in *The Pirates of Penzance*. The National Trust's Trengwainton Gardens, just inland, contain magnolias and many delicate shrubs. A maritime museum and a geological museum are among the other attractions, and there is plenty of activity in the harbour. The *Scillonian* makes regular sailings to the Isles of Scilly.

St Austell

Originally noted for tin mining, St Austell has become associated with the china clay industry, which is why the landscape to the north is scarred with hollows overlooked by lunar mounds of white debris. The Wheal Martyn Museum gives a fascinating depiction of mining history. This regional market centre grew up around the Market Hall, one of many local buildings constructed from granite, and other buildings of architectural interest include the parish church, the White Hart Hotel and the Quaker Meeting House.

Lynton

Steep tree-covered cliffs make up the northern edge of Exmoor, with Lynton at the top of the slope and Lynmouth down by the sea below. The Catholic church is an outstanding building with decorative marble work, and the Lyn and Exmoor Museum has interesting displays about the area. Joining Lynton with Lynmouth is the dramatic cliff railway, built by the Victorian lawyer Sir George Newnes out of the fortune he made by publishing the famous *Sherlock Holmes* stories.

Salisbury

This ancient town was originally at Old Sarum, 2 miles (3km) to the north, where there was an Iron-Age settlement. In 1220 the foundations of the new cathedral were laid at New Sarum, now called

St Michael's Mount – a place of mystery and magic

Salisbury, and gradually the new town developed. The cathedral is beautiful, built in the shape of a double cross, with a graceful spire rising to 404 feet (123m). Among many features of interest are the Poultry Cross, St Thomas's Church, the Playhouse and the delightful River Avon.

Bridgwater

Situated on the edge of Sedgemoor, where James II defeated the Duke of Monmouth's rebellion in 1685 in the last battle fought on English soil, Bridgwater grew up as a port and still has a tidal river linking it to the sea. The church is a fine and imposing building, well worth a visit; Monmouth used the tower as a look-out while trying to locate the King's infantry. Another famous figure in the Bridgwater area was Admiral Blake, and his birthplace is now a museum which contains exhibits of his life, as well as a history of the town.

Bays,Cliffs
& Granite

Small bays, sandy beaches and steep rugged cliffs alternate around the Cornish coast on this tour, which then heads inland across undulating countryside, dotted with relics of the mining industry. Granite is everywhere, in the walls and in the villages.

3 DAYS • 158 MILES • 255KM

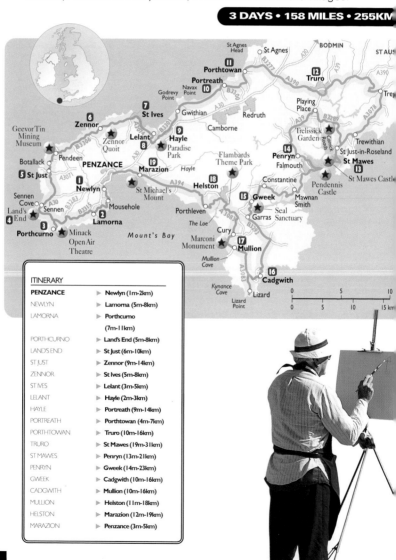

i *Station Road, Penzance*

SPECIAL TO...

A 20-minute helicopter flight from Penzance takes you to St Mary's, the largest of the Isles of Scilly. There is also a summer service to Tresco, the second largest island. Tresco has several miles of deserted golden beaches, but no roads and cars.

▶ *From Penzance, drive south along the coast for a mile (1.6km) to Newlyn, and a little further to Mousehole.*

❶ Newlyn, Cornwall
Really a suburb of Penzance, this is a lively and colourful fishing port, once famous for its artist colony. The Newlyn Art Gallery shows contemporary work.

Further along the coast is Mousehole. Pronounced 'mowzel', this delightful old fishing village consists of a semicircle of colour-washed and granite houses round its harbour. Some of the roofs are specially weighted down to combat strong sea winds. Dolly Pentreath, supposedly the last person to speak Cornish as her native language, died here in 1777.

▶ *Continue on an unclassified road to Lamorna.*

❷ Lamorna, Cornwall
Lamorna is a holiday centre. The tempting golden sand of its spectacular cove is surrounded by steep blocks of granite cliffs and rocky outcrops.

▶ *Join the B3315, then at Trethewey turn left on to an unclassified road to Porthcurno.*

❸ Porthcurno, Cornwall
Porthcurno's beach of almost-white sand is overlooked by a remarkable theatre in the cliffs. The Minack is Britain's equivalent to an ancient Greek theatre, set 200 feet (60m) above the waves. It was created by Miss

Rowena Cade, who cut it out of the cliffs in 1931. The theatre has a 16-week season, and can seat 750 on its granite terraces.

▶ *Return to the B3315 and continue for another 4 miles (6km), then join the A30 to Land's End.*

❹ Land's End, Cornwall
England's most westerly point, Land's End is 873 miles (1,405km) from John O'Groats, Scotland's most northerly town. On a fine day the Isles of Scilly, 28 miles (45km) away, can be seen, along with Wolf Rock Lighthouse and the Longships Lighthouse, only 1½ miles (2km) offshore. Land's End is the setting for wild coastal walks and amazing rock formations.

Further along is the small village of Sennen, the battle-

The end of England – the haunting majesty of Land's End

ground of the last Cornish fight against invading Danes. Sennen Cove has a good sandy beach and excellent bathing.

▶ *Continue with the A30, then left on to the B3306 for 5 miles (8km) to St Just.*

FOR CHILDREN

The legendary Last Labyrinth at Land's End is a major attraction using electronic equipment and including a life-size galleon with scrambling nets and cabins. You can also watch the glass-blower or woodcarver at work, and there is a fascinating collection of shells.

St Ives' golden beaches attract many holidaymakers in summer

copper trade, but now it is a small industrial town with a good sandy beach, though there are still a few boats to be seen in the harbour. Paradise Park, just off the road before entering Hayle, is a conservation theme park with otters and endangered species of birds. There is also a first-class falconry display.

▷ *The B3301 runs along the coast to Portreath.*

RECOMMENDED WALKS

From the B3301 it is possible to walk to Godrevy Point and Navax Point on a circular walk of 3 miles (5km).

8 St Just, Cornwall
This enchanting village and its neighbourhood are rich in anti-quities. St Just is noted for the contents of its large medieval church: a stone of the 5th or 6th century inscribed with XP, the first two letters of the Greek word for Christ, and the shaft of a 9th-century Hiberno-Saxon cross. Abandoned and ruined mines litter the countryside north of the town.

At Botallack, along the B3306, is a deep mine which extended out beneath the sea, and at the Geevor Tin Mining Museum at Pendeen, a little further on, you can take an underground tour of this working mine.

▷ *Keep going along the B3306 to Zennor.*

6 Zennor, Cornwall
Zennor, named after St Senara, is a grey stone village huddled round its restored 12th-century church in a wild, bleak land-scape. The Wayside Folk Museum, the oldest private museum in Cornwall, recaptures the flavour of this area from 3000 BC onwards, with displays on archaeology, tin mining and many other aspects of Cornish life. The writers D H Lawrence and Virginia Woolf both lived here in the 1920s. Zennor Quoit, to the southeast, is a chambered tomb from about 2000 BC.

▷ *A further 5 miles (8km) along the B3306 is St Ives.*

7 St Ives, Cornwall
St Ives was a prosperous pilchard port in the 19th century, but is now more noted for tourism, with its two fine sandy beaches and many excellent museums and galleries. The town has managed to preserve its old-world charm: quaint houses and narrow streets clus-ter round the 15th-century church. Be sure to visit the wonderful Tate Gallery, the Barbara Hepworth Museum and Sculpture Garden, and the Leach Pottery.

ⓘ *The Guildhall, Street-an-Pol*

▷ *Take the main A3074 for 3 miles (5km) to Lelant.*

8 Lelant, Cornwall
Lelant has a fine Norman and Perpendicular-style church with a 17th-century sundial, but what most people come here for is Merlin's Magic Land, a family attraction, with bumper boats, motor bikes and many other attractions.

▷ *Follow the A3074, then the B3301 to Hayle.*

9 Hayle, Cornwall
During the 18th century Hayle developed as a port for the

10 Portreath, Cornwall
Portreath's tiny harbour cottages cluster around the port and the 18th-century pier, at the foot of windswept cliffs. It is a marvel-lous place to go walking along the coast path and there are spectacular views from Reskajeage Downs, above.

▷ *Turn inland along the B3300, then left on unclassified roads for Porthtowan.*

11 Porthtowan, Cornwall
Porthtowan is a pleasant little place with a sandy beach and magnificent cliffs to north and south. If you have time, walk up on to the cliffs for fantastic views inland and over the Atlantic.

▷ *Follow unclassified roads, then the B3277 and A390 to Truro.*

12 Truro, Cornwall
Truro is a quiet town with a blend of old and new buildings. Lemon Street has many fine Georgian structures, and Walsingham Place is a beautiful early 19th-century crescent off Victoria Place. The whole town is dominated by the cathedral, which has three spires and was

built on the site of a 16th-century church. The Royal Cornwall Museum in River Street is considered the finest in Cornwall and there is also a fine art gallery and concert hall.

ℹ️ *Municipal Buildings, Boscawen Street*

▶ *Follow the **A39** eastwards, then turn right along the **A3078** for St Mawes.*

13 St Mawes, Cornwall
Smart shops and houses and many narrow old streets make this an interesting place to wander round. You should try to visit St Mawes Castle, built by

Henry VIII in the 1540s to guard the mouth of the Fal estuary. The views across Carrick Roads, a stretch of sea, to Falmouth are particularly impressive.

Trelissick Garden, north of St Mawes, boasts a fine collection of exotic plants from all over the world.

▶ *Turn north on the **A3078** then the **B3289**, using King Harry ferry, which closes before dusk, then join the **A39** and follow signs to Penryn.*

14 Penryn, Cornwall
Almost everything in Penryn is built of granite – granite buildings, a granite port and granite

blocks lying around everywhere waiting to be shipped out. The narrow streets of this old town stretch up the sides of the valley in an untidy but appealing way.

Further on is Falmouth, on one of the finest natural harbours in the world. There are beaches to the south of the town, and on the northern side of the peninsula are the docks and 18th- and 19th-century buildings. Pendennis Castle was built at the same time as its twin, St Mawes Castle, to guard the harbour entrance.

ℹ️ *28 Killigrew Street, Falmouth*

▶ *Leave Falmouth on unclassified roads passing through Mawnan Smith, Porth Navas, Constantine and Brill to Gweek.*

15 Gweek, Cornwall
This lovely little stone village with two stone bridges across the channels of the Helford River is now better known for its seal sanctuary. Along the picturesque and tranquil banks of the Helford, sick and wounded seals and birds are treated. There are displays which show the work of the centre, and a safari bus will take you round the park to see the convalescent pool and nursery and exercise areas.

▶ *Travel to Garras on unclassi-fied roads. Then take the **B3293** and unclassified roads across Goonhilly Downs, south to Cadgwith and on to Lizard Point on an unclassified road and the **A3083**.*

16 Cadgwith, Cornwall
Attractive thatched cottages clustered round the small beach and harbour create a beautiful setting for local fishermen and tourists. Sandy coves alternate with rugged cliffs along this stretch of coast, but the most dramatic feature is the noisy water of the Devil's Frying Pan, created when a vast sea cave collapsed.

Truro's cathedral was built on the site of a 16th-century church

Cadgwith, a busy fishing harbour
Opposite: Sir Francis Drake

Further on, Lizard Point is the southernmost point in England with dramatic 180-foot (55m) cliffs and a lighthouse, open to the public.

▶ *Head north from Lizard Point for 4 miles (6km) along the A3083, then the B3296 to Mullion.*

RECOMMENDED WALKS

Among the most dramatic walks is the path from Cadgwith towards Landewednack. On the west coast of the Lizard, the coast near Kynance Cove can look most romantic and appealing.

17 Mullion, Cornwall
The village of Mullion boasts a fine 14th- and 15th-century church, which contains carved oak bench-ends, well worth inspecting. The church tower is partially built of the local multi-coloured serpentine. Nearby Mullion Cove is surrounded by steep cave-pocked cliffs and has splendid views.

▶ *Drive on unclassified roads via Poldhu and Cury to the A3083 and on to Helston.*

18 Helston, Cornwall
Radio buffs should visit Poldhu Point before entering Helston, to see the Marconi Monument, which commemorates the first transatlantic transmitting station. The ancient Furry Dance takes place in Helston on 6 May, when there is dancing in the streets all day. In the past this town was a port, before the Loe Bar, a 600-foot (183m) ridge of shingle, blocked it off from the sea. Behind Loe Bar is The Loe, a pretty lake, into which, according to legend, Sir Bedivere threw King Arthur's sword Excalibur.

Nearby Flambards Village Theme Park provides entertainment for the whole family, open in the evenings in July and August. It features a Victorian village, a simulation of the World War II blitz and other themes.

▶ *Take the B3304 through Porthleven, then along the A394 to Marazion. Take an unclassified road before the bypass, into the village.*

19 Marazion, Cornwall
This ancient port is famous for St Michael's Mount, the granite island located offshore, but is a remarkable place in its own right. Cornwall's oldest chartered town, it has the safest beach in Cornwall and some of the best windsurfing in Europe. Henry III granted the town a charter in 1257 and for hundreds of years tin and copper ores were exported from here. The small town still attracts visitors, in spite of the bypass which has reduced the amount of through-traffic.

▶ *Return to Penzance via an unclassified road to the A394.*

FOR HISTORY BUFFS

St Michael's Mount is accessible by foot at low tide, and you should make time to get across to see the castle and priory, both founded by Edward the Confessor in the 11th century. This was the legendary home of the giant Cormoran, who was slain by Jack the Giant Killer.

BACK TO NATURE

The bird-watching hot spot of Marazion Marsh lies close to the sea just behind the coast road at Marazion. Autumns in previous years have produced regular sightings of aquatic warblers and spotted crakes, as well as occasional records of transatlantic vagrants such as white-rumped sandpipers and lesser yellowlegs.

Mining,
Moorland &
Legends

This tour leads through granite scenery, market towns and green river valleys, before crossing the moorland expanse of Dartmoor, with its famous ponies and notorious prison, and finally descending to the farmlands around Tavistock.

3 DAYS • 150 MILES • 240KM

ℹ️ *Bypass Service Station, St Austell*

▶ *Leave St Austell and drive 12 miles (19km) north on the A391, then cross the A389 to Bodmin.*

❶ Bodmin, Cornwall

The only Cornish town recorded in the Domesday Book, Bodmin lies on the steep southwestern edge of Bodmin Moor, which overlooks the town. The Celts, Romans and King Arthur have all had links with the town, and the parish church, the largest in Cornwall, is dedicated to St Petroc, the greatest of all Celtic saints.

Further north, just off the A389, is Pencarrow House, begun in the 1700s by Sir John Molesworth. In the grounds is an ancient Iron Age encampment, and there are walks through the flower gardens, a play area and a pets' corner.

ℹ️ *Shire House, Mount Folly Square*

▶ *From Pencarrow return to the A389. Turn left, then after half a mile (0.8km), left again on to the B3266 to Camelford.*

❷ Camelford, Cornwall

Camelford is thought by some to have been Camelot, the fabulous city of King Arthur, and Slaughter Bridge, one mile (1.6km) to the north, is said to have been Arthur's last battleground. The North Cornwall Museum contains many items of rural life in Cornwall, with sections on agriculture and slate and granite quarrying.

ℹ️ *North Cornwall Museum, The Cleese*

▶ *From Camelford continue on the B3266, turning left on to the B3314 and then almost immediately right to join the B3263 to Tintagel.*

❸ Tintagel, Cornwall

Romance and legends connect this area strongly with King

Tintagel: the Old Post Office (left); weathered cliffs and caves (below)

Arthur. The dramatic cliffs of slate on 'the Island', which is really a peninsula, have caverns and a waterfall. The 12th-century ruins of Tintagel Castle are in a spectacular setting on a wild, wind-lashed promontory. In the small town the highlight for most visitors is the Old Post Office, a small 14th-century manor house built of local slate. Excellent and beautiful walks can be found along the coast paths nearby and in the Rocky Valley, a few miles further north.

▶ *Follow the B3263 along the coast to Boscastle.*

RECOMMENDED WALKS

Trethevy car-park, north of Tintagel, is a good starting point for walks in the Rocky Valley, especially to St Nectan, for beautiful woodland scenery.

---

4 Boscastle, Cornwall
Boscastle is a picturesque harbour at the head of a deep S-shaped inlet between high cliffs. A few houses are actually built into the side of the road, and oak woods, river valleys and the sea combine to make this a classic beauty spot. The river and the tide occasionally meet with explosive collisions just beyond the outer breakwater.

▶ *From Boscastle take the B3266 and unclassified roads east across the A39 to join the A395. Turn left on to the A395 and follow it for 3 miles (5km) before branching left on to unclassified roads again through Tresmeer and Egloskerry to Launceston.*

5 Launceston, Cornwall
Launceston is an ancient town standing on the hilltop around the ruins of a castle. This was the only walled town in Cornwall and the South Gate, a narrow arch, remains.

St Thomas's Church has the largest font in Cornwall, and the Church of St Mary is famed for the carvings completely covering its external walls. A nostalgic steam railway runs into the Kensey Valley through 3 miles (5km) of glorious countryside. At the station there is a model railway and a small museum. The Tamar Otter Park and Wild Wood has peacocks and golden pheasants strutting about, and deer roam the woods.

ℹ *Market House Arcade, Market Street*

▶ *Continue eastwards on the old A30, now unclassified, then just past Lobhillcross turn right on to unclassified roads to Lydford.*

6 Lydford, Devon
Formerly a major centre for tin, this secluded village on the edge of Dartmoor is dominated by the remains of its 12th-century castle. Its old prison, a reminder

Okehampton Castle, now in ruins but open to the public

of the harsh conditions of the past, was described as 'one of the most heinous, contagious and detestable places in the realm'. Lydford Gorge, scooped out by the River Lyd is a mile (1.6km) to the southwest, where the 90-foot (27m) high White Lady Falls and Devil's Cauldron are to be found.

RECOMMENDED WALK

Follow the River Lyd into the famous Lydford Gorge, and you will see the whirlpools and tumbling water of the Devil's Cauldron.

▶ *Follow the A386 north from Lydford, then after a short stretch east on the A30 take the B3260 to Okehampton.*

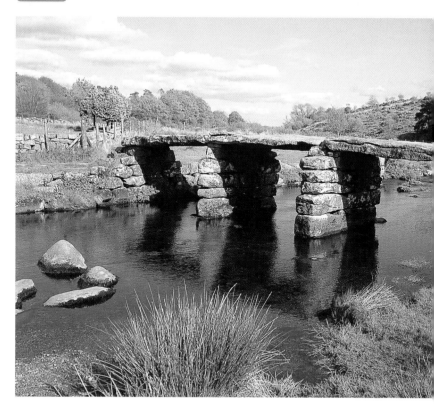

One of England's finest clapper bridges can be seen at Postbridge

7 Okehampton, Devon
Okehampton is at the foot of the highest part of Dartmoor, accessible to walkers when the army is not using the firing range. An old ruined castle, one of Devon's largest, sits on a hill to the west. The Museum of Dartmoor Life is an innovative museum portraying life in the area for hundreds of years.

Southeast of the town is Okehampton Camp, the remains of an Iron Age hill-fort on a steep ridge.

i 3 West Street

▶ *Return to the old **A30** (now an unclassified road) past Sticklepath and South Zeal. Just before Whiddon Down turn right on to the **A382** for Moretonhampstead, at which take the **B3212** to Postbridge.*

8 Moretonhampstead, Devon
Before reaching this town you will pass the remarkable Castle Drogo, a massive granite castle designed by Edward Lutyens, to the left of the road near Drewsteignton. Drive on across the heart of Dartmoor to Moretonhampstead, a small market town with some fine old buildings. At Postbridge you can see the finest of the clapper bridges. One of England's oldest man-made bridges, it was used by pack-horses to carry ore from the mines.

RECOMMENDED WALKS

From Castle Drogo a circular tour leads through the delightful village of Drewsteignton, down to Fingle Bridge and then back along the wooded valley of the River Teign.

▶ *Drive across Dartmoor for 14 miles (23km) along the B3212 to Princetown.*

9 Princetown, Devon
Princetown, the highest town in England, is noted for its prison, which was built for French prisoners-of-war brought to Dartmoor to work for Sir Thomas Tyrwhitt, who built a magnificent house near by.

FOR CHILDREN

The miniature pony centre at Moretonhampstead encourages visitors to touch the animals, and rides can be arranged on the tiny ponies. The ponies have been pure-bred in pedigrees stretching back to about 1890, and other miniature animals here include bulls, pigs, goats and harvest mice.

---

there are many older buildings – the remains of a Benedictine abbey founded in the 10th century, and 15th-century St Eustace's Church. The statue of Francis Drake is a reminder that the Elizabethan sailor was born at nearby Crowndale Farm.

[i] *Town Hall, Bedford Square*

▶ *Leave Tavistock on the A386 and just before crossing the river bridge, turn right along an unclassified road for 4 miles (6km) to Morwellham Quay.*

⑪ **Morwellham Quay,** Devon

Formerly a port, Morwellham, at 350 feet (107m) above water level, is linked to the river by a remarkable inclined plane. It was the greatest copper port in Victorian times, and the old harbour and quays have been repaired by the Morwellham Trust. Crafts and costumes of 100 years ago are on show and there are underground recon-structions of working conditions and early mining techniques.

▶ *Return to the A390 and head westwards to Liskeard.*

⑫ **Liskeard,** Cornwall

Liskeard is a small, lively town with attractive buildings includ-ing Webb's Hotel and Stuart House, where Charles I slept for a week during 1644. Relics of the past can be found at St Keyne Station on the B3254 just outside town. Fair organs, street organs and a mighty Würlitzer are on show here in Paul Corin's musical collection.

▶ *A short drive along the A390 brings you to Dobwalls.*

⑬ **Dobwalls,** Cornwall

The remarkable family theme park has eight adventure areas, with ropewalks, towers to climb and two railroads on a gauge of 7¼ inches (18cm). You can roar through tunnels and canyons on the *Queen of Wyoming*, or one of the other engines pulling the mini trains.

▶ *Continue with the A390 for Lostwithiel.*

⑭ **Lostwithiel,** Cornwall

Lostwithiel sits at the highest point reached by the tide on the River Fowey. The old bridge dates from the 14th century, and Restormel Castle, overlooking the River Fowey, is even older, having first been built as a wooden fort in the 11th century.

At Charlestown, a few miles along the road, is the Shipwreck and Heritage Centre, with an assortment of treasures from the sea bed. Outside the museum is the unspoilt harbour, which still looks much as it did in the 1790s.

[i] **Lostwithiel Community Centre, Liddicoat Road**

▶ *Return to St Austell on the A390.*

BACK TO NATURE

The wilds of Dartmoor have a surprising variety of wildlife. Cottongrass, sundew, bog asphodel and bog bean grace many of the wetter areas, and birdlife includes curlews, dunlin, lapwings, kestrels and buzzards.
In winter, look for short-eared owls, merlins and hen harriers.

SPECIAL TO...

Dartmoor and Bodmin Moor are great lumps of granite covered with boggy vegetation, heather and grasses, all of which can thrive on the acidic soils. When the minerals of granite are weathered, kaolin or china clay is often left behind. It has been quarried in this area for many years. The Wheal Martyn Heritage Centre, at Carthew, near St Austell, has a historic trail through the 19th-century clay workings.

▶ *Head west along the B3357 to Tavistock.*

FOR HISTORY BUFFS

Dartmoor is rich in prehistoric remains; Bronze Age coffins are beside the road a mile (1.6km) northeast of Princetown, along with a row of standing stones.
Two miles (3km) northwest, at Merrivale, are hut circles and one of Dartmoor's finest burial cists, while another group of Bronze Age hut circles overlooks the River Walkham at Great Mis Tor, a mile (1.6km) further northeast of Merrivale.

---

⑩ **Tavistock,** Devon

Famous for its October Goose Fair, Tavistock is also of consid-erable interest for its association with tin and copper mining. The town is largely Victorian, but

Where Exmoor
Meets the Sea

Bright bays, steep coasts, low coastlines, lonely moorland and delightful stone villages combine to make this a memorable and varied tour.

3 DAYS • 133 MILES • 214KM

Valley of the Rocks
Bristol   Channel
Exmoor Falconry and Animal Farm
Martinhoe
LYNTON
Foreland Point
1 Lynmouth
Porlock Weir
Bossington Selworthy
0   5   10 m
0   5   10   15 km
Malmsmead **2**
Oare
Porlock **3**
Luccombe
5 **Minehead**
West Somerset Railway
Watchet **6**
Blackmoor Gate **15**
E x m o o r
Exmoor Zoological Park
Simonsbath
Wootton Courtenay
Dunster
Washford
M5
Arlington Court **14**
Exford
Wheddon Cross
9
Cleeve Abbey
A361
Barnstaple **13**
Brendon Hills **7**
Elworthy
Cobbaton Combat Collection
North Molton
Winsford **8**
Wimbleball Lake
Combe Sydenham Country Park
Appledore Instow
Tapeley Park
Bideford **12**
Umberleigh
South Molton **10**
Big Sheep
Great Torrington **11**
Rosemoor

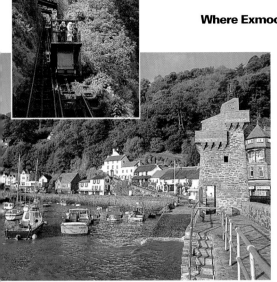

Top: Lynton's Cliff Railway
Left: the harbour at Lynmouth

tiny stream called Oare Water.

▶ *Take the unclassified road,
then join the A39 to Porlock
and eventually on to Selworthy.*

RECOMMENDED WALKS

Starting from Malmsmead, walk
upstream along Badgworthy
Water, where you might see a
dipper or a kingfisher. From the
memorial in Blackmore, walk
on to the waterslide and Lank
Combe, the probable location
of Doone Valley.

Town Hall, Lee Road, Lynton

RECOMMENDED WALK

Many footpaths lead from
Lynton, notably a coastal walk
into the Valley of the Rocks.
Take the narrow road between
the parish church and the
Valley of the Rocks Hotel, and
follow a path carved out of
solid rock on Hollerday Hill.

BACK TO NATURE

The wooded valley of
Watersmeet, near Lynmouth, is
safeguarded by the National
Trust. Along the paths, look for
the bright yellow flowers of
Welsh poppy, sometimes growing alongside clumps of the
rare Irish spurge. Woodland
birds are common and dippers
and grey wagtails have become
accustomed to human visitors.

▶ *Take the B3234, dropping very
steeply down into Lynmouth.*

❶ Lynmouth, Devon

Lynmouth is on a junction
where the East and West Lyn
meet. The 1890 cliff railway still
provides a link with Lynton by
means of two railcars; the top car
uses water ballast to haul the
other one up from the bottom.
The poet Shelley lived in
Lynmouth for a time. The River
Lyn is very strongly embanked
now and on leaving the town you
will see the gorge down which
the flood water came with such
devastation in 1952.

▶ *Leave on the A39 towards
Barnstaple, turn left on to the
B3223 signed Simonsbath and
then immediately left again up
a narrow steep road which
leads through Rockford and
Brendon to Malmsmead.*

❷ Malmsmead, Somerset

This isolated village is set in
idyllic scenery, and is reached
along narrow roads with gradi-
ents of 1 in 4. The East Lyn is a
rocky stream, and if you walk up
the valley of the tributary
Badgworthy Water, you will see
some of the best of Exmoor.
This is popularly assumed to be
Doone country, though
Blackmore, who wrote *Lorna
Doone*, always refused to say
where his tale of bandits was
actually set. R D Blackmore,
grandson of a 19th-century
rector of Oare, further on from
Malmsmead, named his characters after local people. The 500-
year-old church here was the
setting for Lorna Doone's
violent wedding. At the
Robber's Bridge further along
the road there is a picturesque
spot by the East Lyn, now only a

❸ Porlock, Somerset

Once down the notorious steep
hill, and a descent of 1,350 feet
(411m), pause to admire Porlock
Weir, a small village of thatched
cottages fringing a tiny harbour.
Culbone Church is possibly the
smallest surviving medieval
church in England, and can only
be reached on foot.

Exmoor Falconry and Animal
Farm at Bossington is a must for
family outings, with donkey
rides and a hay bounce. Just off
the A39 is Selworthy. Much of
this pretty village is owned by
the National Trust.

▶ *Return to the A39 and turn
left towards Minehead. Shortly,
turn right on an unclassified
road to Luccombe.*

❹ Luccombe, Somerset

Pause in this secluded village to
visit the fine church and
churchyard, entered through a
charming lychgate, and have a
gentle stroll past the thatched
cottages. At Wootton Courtenay,
on the road to Minehead, the
magnificent church has a
saddleback roof.

▶ *From Wootton Courtenay, turn
north to rejoin the A39 and
continue to Minehead, then
further to Dunster, just south
of the A39, up the A396.*

5 Minehead, Somerset

A large expanse of sand and an attractive harbour area have lured visitors to this bright and breezy town. Take a ride on the West Somerset Railway, which runs through 20 miles (32km) of superb scenery from the coast to the Quantocks. Just outside Minehead is Somerwest World, a large holiday camp with a cable-car, monorail and funfair.

A little further on, Dunster's Norman castle looks out over the village and at the opposite end of the main street is the Conygar Tower, built in 1775 as a land-mark for shipping. There is a 16th-century yarn market, and you can see the working water mill, on the River Avill, which dates from 1680 and still produces flour for local bakeries. Blenheim Gardens are fine to sit and relax in.

[i] 17 Friday Street

SPECIAL TO...

The Minehead Hobby Horse (or 'Obby 'Oss) procession takes place on the eve of May Day, and is said to have originated as an attempt to frighten off Danish invaders, using a strange, multicoloured beast accompanied by musicians to create a fearsome sight and sound. There is also an 'Obby 'Oss procession in Padstow.

▶ *Follow the A39, then the B3191 towards Blue Anchor and Watchet.*

6 Watchet, Somerset

Much of Watchet's early growth was due to iron mining in the Brendon Hills; paper-making is now the main industry. The poet Coleridge found the main character for his epic poem *The Rime of the Ancient Mariner* in this historic seaport.

Just outside Washford, 3 miles (5km) south of Watchet, is Tropiquaria, which has displays of fish and animals. South of Washford is Cleeve Abbey,

founded by Cistercian monks in 1198, with a well-preserved refectory, gate house and chapter house. Further along the road is Combe Sydenham Country Park, in a hidden valley on the edge of the Brendons, where there is a restored 11th-century corn mill and a deer park.

▶ *From Washford, follow the unclassified road southwards to join the B3188 via Monksilver to Elworthy, then take the B3224 west through the Brendon Hills.*

7 Brendon Hills, Somerset

These undulating slopes, where Exmoor merges into the distinc-tive patchwork of the Brendon Hills, are not high enough for moorland, but have lush fields and trees and long views across the countryside. In earlier times small mining towns grew up to work the local deposits of iron ore, but the last one closed down in 1883. You can still see Bronze Age round barrows along the Ridgeway.

▶ *Continue along the B3224, turn left on the A396 and then follow an unclassified road to Winsford.*

8 Winsford, Somerset

Winsford is one of the best centres for tourism on Exmoor, with its church standing over the village. The mysteriously inscribed Caractacus Stone, a mile (1.6km) to the south, prob-ably dates from between the 5th and 7th centuries.

▶ *From Winsford take the unclassified road to join the B3223 and continue to Simonsbath.*

9 Simonsbath, Somerset

Situated 1,100 feet (335m) above sea-level, Simonsbath is the highest village in Exmoor, in the centre of what used to be the Royal Exmoor Forest. Climb steeply out of the hamlet and on to the moors. In places the tradi-tional old Exmoor hedges block the fabulous views.

▶ *Use unclassified roads to cross the moor southwards, and join the A399, then the B3226 for South Molton.*

10 South Molton, Devon

Formerly important for the wool trade, but now a cattle market and tourist centre, South Molton is known to have existed as a Saxon colony. The square is given grandeur by the Guildhall and Assembly Rooms which overlook it, and the splendid church has a magnificent tower and a remarkable stone pulpit. On the road west, the Cobbaton Combat Collection recalls World War II with tanks, artillery and radio equipment.

[i] 1 East Street

▶ *Follow the B3227 for 15 miles (24km) to Great Torrington.*

11 Great Torrington, Devon

Great Torrington was a market town in Saxon times and the scene of fierce fighting in the Civil War. The original church was used as a gunpowder store but an explosion blew it to pieces. At Dartington Crystal you can watch fine crystal glass being blown, and just outside the town the Royal Horticultural Society has a garden at Rosemoor. The Gnome Reserve at West Putford boasts the world's largest population of gnomes.

[i] Castle Hill

▶ *Take the A386 to Bideford.*

12 Bideford, Devon

This interesting little town was a major port in the 16th and 17th centuries with a busy trade in tobacco. There is a new high bridge for the main road, but ships still move upstream to the old stone bridge across the estu-ary. The Royal Hotel, which dates from 1688, was where Charles Kingsley wrote part of his novel *Westward Ho!* Follow the old road to Barnstaple and you will pass Instow, a resort by the dunes with colourful views across to the port of Appledore.

Tapeley Park, on the way to Instow, has Italian terraced gardens and a traditional kitchen garden.

i   *The Quay, Kingsley Road*

▶ *Follow the coast road along the B3233 for 10 miles (16km) to Barnstaple.*

FOR CHILDREN

At Abbotsham, 2 miles (3km) west of Bideford, is the Big Sheep, where you can watch the free demonstration of sheep milking and sheep shearing, and have a go at spinning. Other attractions include sheep racing, a nature trail and an adventure playground.

FOR HISTORY BUFFS

Like most towns on Devon's north coast, Bideford has strong maritime traditions. It was a busy port in England in the 16th century, with many links to the East Indies and the Americas. Smuggling as well as legal trading were part of the life in this area, and some of this history can be seen in the North Devon Maritime Museum in Appledore, north of Bideford.

⓭ Barnstaple, Devon
Barnstaple is one of North Devon's major market towns. It was once a busy ship-building town and a port trading with America, but the River Taw

Quince Honey Farm, South Molton

became too silted in the 19th century. There are many fine examples of Georgian architecture. Queen Anne's Walk is a pleasant colonnade, and you can still see the Tome Stone, where merchants used to set their money to make their contracts binding. The Museum of Barnstaple and North Devon is here, at The Square. The fine long bridge over the River Taw has 16 arches and dates from the 13th century.

i   *36 Boutport Street*

▶ *Continue northwards on the A39 for Arlington.*

⓮ Arlington, Devon
Arlington Court is one of the few great houses of North Devon. Formerly the home of the Chichester family, it has been owned by the National Trust since 1949. Sir Francis Chichester, the yachtsman, is the most famous descendant of this old family. The house contains a rich collection of model ships and there are walks in the park and woods. During the summer there are horse-and-carriage rides between the house and the collection of old carriages kept in the stables.

▶ *Continue along the A39 to Blackmoor Gate.*

⓯ Blackmoor Gate, Devon
Blackmoor Gate is really a road junction, but the Exmoor Zoological Park is near by along the A399 and provides entertainment for all the family. For the next few miles the road is narrow, winding and very steep in places, with dramatic views of coastal cliffs.

There is a short stretch of toll road, before entering the Valley of the Rocks, a gorge littered with enormous slabs of granite. Walk up to the top of Castle Rock, where the vertical drop is 800 feet (244m).

▶ *Take the A399 and then an unclassified road via Trentishoe and Martinhoe back to Lynton.*

Somerset's
Hamstone Towns

Wooded hills and rich valleys combine with the mellow dignity of country towns in golden stone to make South Somerset and Dorset one of the least spoiled parts of England. Add to this a splendid sea view and you have a tour to linger long in the memory.

3 DAYS • 130 MILES • 209KM

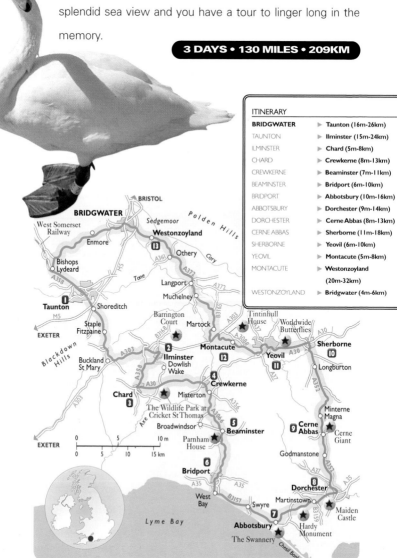

ITINERARY		
BRIDGWATER	➤	**Taunton** (16m-26km)
TAUNTON	➤	**Ilminster** (15m-24km)
ILMINSTER	➤	**Chard** (5m-8km)
CHARD	➤	**Crewkerne** (8m-13km)
CREWKERNE	➤	**Beaminster** (7m-11km)
BEAMINSTER	➤	**Bridport** (6m-10km)
BRIDPORT	➤	**Abbotsbury** (10m-16km)
ABBOTSBURY	➤	**Dorchester** (9m-14km)
DORCHESTER	➤	**Cerne Abbas** (8m-13km)
CERNE ABBAS	➤	**Sherborne** (11m-18km)
SHERBORNE	➤	**Yeovil** (6m-10km)
YEOVIL	➤	**Montacute** (5m-8km)
MONTACUTE	➤	**Westonzoyland** (20m-32km)
WESTONZOYLAND	➤	**Bridgwater** (4m-6km)

75069

---

i *50 High Street, Bridgwater*

▶ *Leave Bridgwater on an unclassified road to Enmore. Continue to Bishops Lydeard then turn left on to the A358 to Taunton.*

❶ Taunton, Somerset
As you drop steeply down from the Quantock Hills, a stunning view of the Vale of Taunton Deane opens up, with the undulating ridge of the Blackdown Hills in the distance. Taunton lies in the heart of this rich vale. The largest town between Bristol and Exeter, it has one of the biggest livestock markets in the southwest. In the Great Hall of Taunton Castle, the infamous Judge Jeffreys sent over 500 rebels to their deaths at his 'Bloody Assize'. A walk down Hammet Street gives the best view of the Perpendicular tower of 15th-century St Mary's Church. The town is a mecca for cricket lovers, and next to the County Ground is Somerset's Cricket Museum, in the 13th-century Priory Barn.

---

i *Paul Street*

SPECIAL TO...

The West Somerset Railway is the longest preserved line in Britain, running through some of the finest scenery in the West Country. Starting off at Bishops Lydeard, at the foot of the Quantocks near Taunton, it runs 20 miles (32km) down to the coastal plain and beaches of the Bristol Channel.

▶ *Leave Taunton on the B3170 heading south. Shortly after crossing the M5, turn left for Staple Fitzpaine. Continue on unclassified roads towards Buckland St Mary and the A303. Turn left on to the A303, then right on to the B3168 to Ilminster.*

❷ Ilminster, Somerset
Dabinetts, Brownsnouts, Kingston Blacks and Red Streaks are all local varieties of apples. Somerset is real cider

---

Leaving Bishops Lydeard on the West Somerset Railway
Opposite: Abbotsbury swan

country, and near Ilminster, at Dowlish Wake, are Perry's Cider Mills, where this powerful apple brew has been made for centuries. Visitors can wander through the farm to see how it is done and afterwards sample some 'scrumpy' for themselves.

Ilminster has a lovely little shopping centre, built in the local hamstone (a golden limestone). Of particular note are the pillared market house and the 15th-century minster Church of St Mary. Herne Hill is a local beauty spot and vantage point to the southwest of the town. One of the earliest National Trust properties, Barrington Court, lies to the north – an intriguing model estate with Tudor manor house and gardens.

i *Shudrick Lane*

▶ *From Ilminster go south on an unclassified road, turning left on to the A358 for Chard.*

❸ Chard, Somerset
This handsome market town astride the busy A30 claims to be the birthplace of flight. To find out why, visit the Chard Museum in High Street. Besides flight, you can find out more about blacksmiths, early funerals, historic costumes and even artificial limbs – they were invented here.

ℹ️ *The Guildhall, Fore Street*

▶ *Leave Chard on the **A30** for Crewkerne (8miles/13km).*

Parnham House, Beaminster

FOR CHILDREN

The Wildlife Park at Cricket St Thomas is set in a deep, wooded valley just off the A30 between Chard and Crewkerne. The park is home to a great variety of animals and birds – from wild deer to penguins, elephants and parrots. There are plenty of leisure park features, including a scenic railway and an adventure playground.

❹ Crewkerne, Somerset
Crewkerne is an ancient market town whose wealth was founded on minting coins, and in later centuries on flax-weaving and sail-making. It was here that HMS *Victory*'s sails were made, and more recently the sails for several contenders for the Americas Cup yacht race.

Captain Hardy, Nelson's flag captain on the *Victory*, was a pupil at the old grammar school.

▶ *From Crewkerne on the **A356**, signposted Dorchester/ Bridport, turn right on to the **A3066** for Beaminster.*

❺ Beaminster, Dorset
'The forgotten county' and 'the hidden valley' are two of the epithets ascribed to the scenery around Beaminster. This town, in the Brit Valley, is virtually unspoilt. Three fires in 200 years once rendered the town 'the pityfullest spectacle that Man can behold' but the mellow honey-coloured hamstone houses testify to the healing power of time. Most streets offer a view of the fine pinnacled tower of the golden church, built in 1503. The Tudor manor house at Parnham, near Beaminster, enjoys world renown as a centre for craftsmanship in wood, and is open to the public on certain days of the week.

▶ *Continue south on the **A3066** to Bridport.*

❻ Bridport, Dorset
In olden times, the term 'Bridport dagger' used to strike fear into the heart of many a criminal, for that was the nickname for the hangman's noose. Ropes and nets have been made here for a thousand years now, and this is still Europe's biggest netmaking centre. The unusual width of the streets allowed for rope-walks, where the flax strands were laid out to be twisted into shape. In South Street, look out for St Mary's Church with its hamstone tower and 13th-century knight's tomb.

ℹ️ *32 South Street*

▶ *Leave Bridport heading for West Bay, then turn on to the **B3157** for 8 miles (13km) to Abbotsbury.*

❼ Abbotsbury, Dorset
Abbotsbury shelters in a valley between high chalk downs and the shingle coast of Chesil Bank, that sweeps round to the 'Isle' of Portland. A long main street of thatched limestone cottages heralds your approach to the village centre, clustered round the 15th-century church and the Ilchester Arms public house. From opposite here a narrow, unsignposted road leads high up over Black Down Hill to the Hardy Monument, an obelisk commemorating Vice-Admiral Hardy. St Catherine's Chapel, built for seamen in the 15th century, looks down from its grassy knoll near by, and near the church are the remains of an 11th-century Benedictine abbey. The one surviving feature is a fine thatched tithe barn, the largest in England.

BACK TO NATURE

The Fleet is a large brackish lagoon which lies behind the shelter of Chesil Beach. Towards the western end, the swannery at Abbotsbury is worth visiting, while at the eastern end, the mudflats revealed at low tide support thousands of birds such as waders, gulls and other wildfowl. The shingle flora of Chesil Beach is worth studying, and in the heart of nearby Weymouth lies Radipole Lake, an RSPB reserve.

▶ *Leave Abbotsbury uphill on an unclassified road to Martinstown; then turn left and on to the **B3159**, then left again for Dorchester.*

8 **Dorchester,** Dorset

The county town of Dorset is in the heart of Thomas Hardy country and is still the busy market town portrayed in *The Mayor of Casterbridge*. Hardy's statue stands near the top of High West Street. Founded as *Durnovaria* by the Romans in AD 70, Dorchester has many fine Georgian buildings. Judge Jeffreys was sent here by King James to punish rebels after the Battle of Sedgemoor in 1685. At Old Crown Court, six local farmworkers were sentenced in 1834 to be transported to Australia for forming a trades union: they became known as the Tolpuddle Martyrs. There are numerous sites of interest, including the floor of a Roman town house and Maumbury Rings, a Roman amphitheatre. The town boasts three museums: the Dinosaur

Museum; the Military Museum, which is the unlikely location for Hitler's desk; and the Dorset County Museum.

ℹ️ *Unit 11, Antelope Walk*

FOR HISTORY BUFFS

Maiden Castle, 2 miles (3km) southwest of Dorchester, is the finest prehistoric hill-fort in Britain. The massive oval earthworks can be seen for miles around. Three huge ditches were dug by Iron Age men to protect some 5,000 inhabitants. Archaeological excavations have revealed a history stretching back to the Stone Age, and among the finds have been the skeletons of 34 people.

▶ *From Dorchester head north on the **A352** for Cerne Abbas.*

9 **Cerne Abbas,** Dorset

Before entering Cerne Abbas, as you pass through Godmanstone,

The Giant of Cerne Abbas

look out for the smallest pub in England, the Smith's Arms, just 20 by 10 feet (6 by 3m). Cerne Abbas itself is a charming village and its main source of interest is not difficult to spot. Cut into the steep chalk hillside behind the village, the Cerne Giant, a wellendowed figure 180 foot (55m) high, is a fertility symbol dating from Roman times.

▶ *Continue north on the **A352** for Sherborne.*

10 **Sherborne,** Dorset

Sherborne claims, with some justification, to be one of the most beautiful towns in England. Set in a gentle valley among wooded hills, it has a charming stone-built centre. Two kings of Wessex were buried in Sherborne's Saxon abbey, the mother cathedral of the Southwest until 1075. Sherborne Old Castle dates from the 12th century, and Sherborne New Castle was built by Sir

Walter Raleigh in the 1590s. It was here that Sir Walter was 'extinguished' by a servant who first saw him smoking the tobacco he brought back from the New World.

At Compton House near by is Worldwide Butterflies, where exotic butterflies can be seen in 'tropical' surroundings. You can also see Britain's only silk farm, where silk for many royal wedding dresses was made.

ⓘ *3 Tilton Court, Digby Road*

▶ *Leave Sherborne on the **A30** heading west for Yeovil.*

⓫ Yeovil, Somerset
Yeovil is a thriving industrial and administrative centre, nationally known for its gloves and helicopters. It suffered disastrous fires in 1499, 1623 and 1640, and during World War II air raids destroyed many of its oldest

Below: the charming hamstone town of Montacute
Right: Wells Cathedral's clock

buildings. One to survive was the 14th-century stone church, impressive for its simplicity and size.

ⓘ *Petter's House, Petter's Way*

▶ *Leave Yeovil on the **A30** and turn right on to the **A3088**, turning left for Montacute.*

⓬ Montacute, Somerset
This is yet another delightful hamstone village. In a corner of the square is the entrance to its showpiece, Montacute House, a splendid Tudor mansion in formal, landscaped gardens. It was built by Sir Edward Phelips, chief prosecutor of Guy Fawkes in 1605.

Although on a smaller scale than Montacute, nearby Tintinhull House attracts many visitors each year.

▶ *From Montacute take the **A3088** to Stoke-sub-Hamdon, then the **A303** and right on to the **B3165**. Join the **A372** heading for Westonzoyland.*

RECOMMENDED WALKS

There are several enjoyable walks from Montacute, notably the woodland Ladies' Walk, or the paths that lead to the folly of St Michael's Hill near by.

⓭ Westonzoyland, Somerset
Westonzoyland's 100-foot (30m) church tower looks boldly over Sedgemoor, once covered by sea and now a vast expanse of fenland – the largest wetland of its type anywhere in Britain. A map in the church porch will show you how to explore the historical connection, for near here the last battle on English soil was fought. A granite monument on this quiet open land is all that marks the spot for posterity.

▶ *From Westonzoyland continue on the **A372** for 4 miles (6km) to Bridgwater.*

Hills & Vales
of West Wessex

From Wiltshire's gentle valleys and downlands to the rugged hills and expansive wetlands of Somerset, the Wessex scenery constantly changes. This tour takes in one of Britain's finest cathedrals, one of Europe's loveliest gardens and the world's most famous prehistoric temple.

3 DAYS • 137 MILES • 221KM

Built for ceremonies long forgotten, Stonehenge remains a mystery

☐ *Fish Row, Salisbury*

▶ *Leave Salisbury on the **A345** signed Amesbury and in 1 mile (1.6km) reach Old Sarum.*

❶ Old Sarum, Wiltshire

Iron Age men, Romans, Saxons, Danes and Normans in turn chose this windy hilltop for their settlements. Within a huge circular mound are the foundations of the Norman cathedral and castle that once stood here. Bishops Osmund and Roger built the cathedral, but cathedral life wasn't easy, and castle and clergy did not get on. In 1220 the bishop chose a new site in the valley, known today as Salisbury, and materials from the demolished cathedral were then used for Salisbury's new glory.

▶ *Continue on the **A345**, then take the first left on to unclassified roads for the Woodfords. In 5 miles (8km) reach Amesbury and 1 mile (2km) further north on the **A345** is Woodhenge. Return to the*

A303 *and head west signed Honiton, then right on to the* **A360** *to Stonehenge.*

❷ Stonehenge and Woodhenge, Wiltshire

A henge is a prehistoric monument, usually of religious significance. Woodhenge, the neolithic precursor of Stonehenge, had six concentric rings of timber posts, surrounded by a ditch. The holes marking the site are now marked by concrete posts.

At Stonehenge huge stones 15 to 20 feet (4.5 to 6m) high have been the subject of enormous speculation. Is it a temple for Romans or Druids? How were 26-ton stones brought here? One thing is certain – the axis is aligned with the midwinter and midsummer sun; perhaps this revered monument is a giant calendar.

▶ *From Stonehenge continue on the **A360**, turning left on to the **B390** just past Shrewton. On reaching the **A36** turn right, then right again after 1 mile (1.6km) on to the **B3414** to Warminster.*

❸ Warminster, Wiltshire

Warminster was formerly a wool town and corn market; today it is the home of the Army School of Infantry and the REME (Royal Electrical and Mechanical Engineers) workshops. Four miles (6km) to the west is Longleat, seat of the Marquess of Bath and nationally famous as a wildlife park.

☐ *Central Car Park, Warminster*

▶ *Take the **A350** for Westbury. Leave by the **A3098** for 7 miles (11km) to Frome.*

RECOMMENDED WALK

Westbury's White Horse, cut into the chalk escarpment of Salisbury Plain in the 18th century, is said to replace one carved in AD 879 to commemorate King Alfred's victory over the Danes at Ethandun. Climb from the church at Bratton on the B3098, east of Westbury, or drive up to Westbury Hill, turning right from the B3098, just before the cemetery.

gral shops, and St John's Church.

Three miles (5km) from Frome, on the A361, is Nunney, with its romantic moated 14th-century castle.

> ☐ *The Round Tower, Justice Lane*

▶ *Leave Frome to join the A361 for Shepton Mallet, 11 miles (16km), then by the A371 to Wells (6 miles/10km).*

SPECIAL TO...

The Royal Bath and West Show is held at the end of May and attracts huge crowds from far and wide to the showground near Shepton Mallet, 11 miles (16km) from Frome.
As well as the agricultural activities, attractions include aerobatics, showjumping and motorcycle displays.

---

4 Frome, Somerset

'Friendly Frome' (say Froom), on the River Frome, is an attractive market town which grew rich on trade in woollen cloth. Its steep narrow streets are scattered with medieval and Tudor buildings. Cheap Street, with its ancient shops and leat gutter is a must, as are the 1726 Blue House, the bridge with its inte-

5 Wells, Somerset

Wells is England's smallest city, lying in the shadow of the Mendip Hills, and gets its name from the springs that bubble in to a pool in the bishop's garden. The splendid cathedral was begun in the 12th century and finished in the 15th, and its astronomical clock in the north transept is one of the oldest

cathedral clock-faces in Britain. South of the cathedral is the moated Bishop's Palace, where the swans used to ring the bell by the bridge for food.

St Cuthbert's Parish Church in High Street is the largest in Somerset, with a 122-foot (37m) tower.

> ☐ *Town Hall, Market Place*

FOR CHILDREN

Stalactites and stalagmites, soaring caverns and bottomless pits are all to be found at Wookey Hole Caves near Wells, first inhabited 50,000 years ago. On the surface, visitors can walk around a mill which still produces watermarked paper from rags, distort themselves in the mirrors of the old fairground and change new pence for old to play original one-arm bandits at the Penny Pier Arcade.

▶ *Leave Wells on an unclassified road to Wookey Hole, and shortly after the Wookey Hole Caves fork right for Priddy, then left on the B3135 for Cheddar (5 miles/8km).*

Elizabethan Longleat House, seat of the Marquess of Bath

BACK TO NATURE

Ebbor Gorge, on the route between Wookey Hole and Priddy, is thought by many to be the loveliest and most unspoilt Mendip gorge.

6 Cheddar, Somerset

The rugged grandeur of Cheddar Gorge unfolds slowly and magically as you descend a meandering road. Cliffs tower to a height of 450 feet (137m) here, and the 'Beware of falling rocks' sign is no idle warning. Climb the 274 steps of Jacob's Ladder at the south end for the best views, or rest in the Garden of Fragrance, especially created for the blind. At the bottom of the gorge, Gough's and Cox's Caves offer a chance to go subterranean in search of the lost Yeo.

Cheddar would not be Cheddar without its cheese, but the product outgrew the place and has largely gone elsewhere. A 1990 replica of a 1920s factory shows how it used to be made.

ⓘ   *The Gorge*

FOR HISTORY BUFFS

Axbridge, near Cheddar, is a fine example of a close-knit, winding medieval town. The jewel is King John's Hunting Lodge, at the corner of High Street and The Square. This handsome three-storeyed building has nothing to do with either King John or with hunting, but has been exquisitely restored by the National Trust, and now houses the Axbridge Museum, open on summer afternoons.

▶ *Leave Cheddar on the B3151 for Glastonbury (12 miles/9km).*

7 Glastonbury, Somerset

Said to be the 'cradle of English Christianity', Glastonbury is a town steeped in Christian and Arthurian legends. The focal point is the ruined abbey, which may have originated in the 1st century, but was sacked at the Dissolution in 1539. Joseph of Arimathea is reputed to have come here as a missionary in AD 63, and a thorn in the Abbot's kitchen is said to derive from his wooden staff, which turned into a thorn bush. The chapel on the Tor dates from AD 179. Through the ages, writers have speculated that this is the site of Avalon, King Arthur's final resting place. The chalice which Christ used at the Last Supper is said to be beneath the Chalice Spring on the Tor. Of particular note in the town are the Abbey Barn, now housing the Somerset Rural Life Museum, the fine 14th-century George and Pilgrims Hotel, and The Tribunal, once a courthouse and now a museum.

ⓘ   *The Tribunal, 9 High Street*

▶ *Leave Glastonbury on the A361 and in 7 miles (12km)*

turn left on to the **A37**, then right on to the **A371** signposted Castle Cary. Shortly, fork left on to the **B3081** for Bruton, (4 miles/6km).

8 Bruton, Somerset

Little Bruton, on the River Brue, has a charm of its own. Be sure to explore The Bartons, narrow alleys leading down to the river, which is crossed by an unusual packhorse bridge. St Mary's Church, with its twin towers, is particularly fine, and prominent in the town is King's School, established in the 16th century. The tall building on the hill as you leave is the Bruton Dovecote, formerly belonging to the abbey which once existed here.

▶ *Leave Bruton by the B3081, signposted Wincanton. In Redlynch turn left at the*

Nature tamed: the classical order and opulence of Stourhead

crossroads and in 3 miles (5km) right, and shortly right again to join the **B3092** to Stourhead (½mile/1km).

9 **Stourhead,** Wiltshire

Henry Hoare, an eminent banker, decided to landscape his Palladian Wiltshire home, Stourhead, in the grand manner. He began in 1740 by damming springs of the Stour to create a sweeping lake with wooded islands. This is one of the finest gardens in the world, now in the care of the National Trust. An unmistakable landmark on the border of the Stourhead estate is Alfred's Tower, a triangular brick structure 160 feet (49m) high, built in 1772. It marks the spot where King Alfred rallied his troops to fight the Danes in AD 879.

▶ Leave Stourhead on the **B3092** for Mere (2 miles/3km). Take the **B3095**, then turn left on to the **B3092** to Gillingham (2½ miles/4km), then Shaftesbury (3 miles/5km) via the **B3081**.

10 **Shaftesbury,** Dorset

Perched on a hill 700 feet (213m) above sea-level, the pretty town of Shaftesbury commands marvellous views across Dorset's Blackmoor Vale. The local history museum near St Peter's Church contains the Byzant, a strange ornamental relic, formerly carried by towns-folk in a ceremony confirming their rights to draw water from wells at the foot of the hill.

☐ *8 Bell Street*

▶ Leave Shaftesbury on the **A30** signposted Salisbury. In 6 miles (10km) turn left for Ansty and Tisbury. Continue north, then turn right on the **B3089** at Fonthill Bishop. In 2 miles (3km) turn at Chilmark to Fovant (3 miles/5km). Go left on the **A30** to Wilton.

11 **Wilton,** Wiltshire

In Saxon times, Wilton was capi-tal of Wessex. Thousands now flock here each year to visit Wilton House, built in the 1540s and remodelled by Inigo Jones

Shaftesbury's most famous street, cobbled Gold Hill

in the 17th century. The Double Cube Room, now restored, is especially ornate. There is a world-famous collection of paintings by Rubens, Van Dyck and Tintoretto, among others.

▶ Leave Wilton by the **A36** for Salisbury (4 miles/6km).

SCENIC ROUTES

On the B3151 south of Cheddar, it is worth stopping as you approach Wedmore to look back over Sedgemoor, one of England's few wetlands, stretching away to the marvel-lous backdrop of the Mendip limestone ridge.
As you ascend the steep hill to enter Shaftesbury, look back over the rich farmland of Dorset's lovely Blackmoor Vale, with the wooded ridge of Stourhead and Alfred's Tower beyond.

THE SOUTH & SOUTHEAST

Despite being well populated, the five counties of Surrey, Sussex, Kent, Hampshire and Dorset have retained large areas of rich farmland, commons and heaths and forested areas. Perhaps the most famous area is the New Forest in Hampshire, much of which is heathland; 'forest' was originally a term for hunting ground.

Architectural styles are especially distinctive in the Weald of Sussex and Kent, where tile-hung houses can be seen in many villages, as well as thatched houses and oasthouses – though most of these are now residences, having ceased production of beer from locally grown hops. Further west is Hardy Country: many of Dorset's attractive towns and villages can be related to the writings of Thomas Hardy and his views of life in the 18th century.

The scenery varies from gentle, undulating landscapes to steep escarpments on the edges of the North and South Downs and dramatic coastal cliffs, notably at Beachy Head, where the South Downs reach the sea. At the foot of the white cliffs of Dover, where the North Downs reach the coast, the Channel Tunnel dives beneath the sea on its way to France.

The historic West Gate, Canterbury

Seaside resorts such as Bournemouth and Folkestone attract large numbers of visitors, especially in the summer months and at weekends, although many of the beaches are not very sandy in the south-eastern part of England.

Religion plays an important part in the life of this region, where Winchester and Canterbury are at opposite ends of the Pilgrim's Way. Fine cathedrals can be seen in both these towns, and a great many impressive churches are hidden away in small villages. These were often financed from agricultural profits and competition was fierce, with villages trying to outdo their neighbours with bigger or better churches. Near the chalk hills, many of these churches are built of this soft rock, but are faced with a layer of resistant flint.

Winchester

There is so much to see in this City of Kings that it is worth taking a guided walking or driving tour. Winchester is a place of history and legend. The Round Table in the castle's Great Hall is actually a medieval creation which celebrates the King Arthur legend. From here you can walk past the old Butter Cross in the centre of town and make a diversion to the fine cathedral – before taking a look at the statue of King Alfred, which recalls Winchester's past status as his kingdom's capital.

Bournemouth

This town developed along with the Victorian enthusiasm for the seaside, when a few rich families built villas on what used to be a fairly desolate heath. An attractive beach stretches for miles along the coast, and windsurfing, swimming and boating are popular. There are beautiful gardens to visit with subtropical vegetation which thrives in the mild climate. Quiet, wooded walks can be taken in the steep valleys called chines, which slope down from the cliff tops to the shore.

Royal Tunbridge Wells

This spa town has been a fashionable market and trading centre for many years; even in the 17th century, the Pantiles was an established shopping centre. The town first developed as a spa when its chalybeate spring was discovered in 1606; it can still be seen, in Bath Square. The surrounding countryside consists of miles of common, on which stand the spectacular High Rocks.

New Alresford's ancient fulling mill on the River Alre

Canterbury

Canterbury's cathedral dominates the landscape for miles around, but there is much more to see in this ancient city, often thought of as the birthplace of English Christianity. A walk round the streets is a walk through history, and a visit to the Canterbury Heritage Museum is a good way to start a tour. The city walls, St Martin's church, the ruins of St Augustine's Abbey, the Royal Museum and the Old Weavers' House are among the buildings you must not miss. There are also modern entertainments, including two theatres and an excellent pedestrianised area for shopping.

A Journey
Across the Weald

Over undulating

3 DAYS • 122 MILES • 197KM

sandstone hills, through the orchards of the 'Garden of England', and the once vast Forest of Anderida, this is an area of delightful villages, superb castles and immaculate gardens. Church spires and towers and tile-hung Wealden houses all add to its beauty, as the buildings and countryside compete with each other to provide the most delightful views.

ITINERARY		
ROYAL TUNBRIDGE WELLS	▶	Penshurst (7m-11km)
PENSHURST	▶	Hever (6m-10km)
HEVER	▶	Limpsfield (10m-16km)
LIMPSFIELD	▶	Sevenoaks (9m-14km)
SEVENOAKS	▶	Ightham (6m-10km)
IGHTHAM	▶	Mereworth (6m-10km)
MEREWORTH	▶	Lamberhurst (14m-23km)
LAMBERHURST	▶	Cranbrook (10m-16km)
CRANBROOK	▶	Tenterden (11m-18km)
TENTERDEN	▶	Northiam (8m-13km)
NORTHIAM	▶	Bodiam (5m-8km)
BODIAM	▶	Burwash (10m-16km)
BURWASH	▶	Rotherfield (13m-21km)
ROTHERFIELD	▶	Royal Tunbridge Wells (7m-11km)

i   *The Old Fish Market, The
Pantiles, Royal Tunbridge Wells*

▶ *Leave Tunbridge Wells on the
A264, then take the B2188
north to Penshurst.*

❶ Penshurst, Kent

Penshurst is a small village with
stone houses and a magnificent
church, but the main attraction is
14th-century Penshurst Place,
one of the outstanding stately
homes of Britain, set in superb
Tudor gardens. The famous
chestnut-beamed Great Hall
dominates the manor with its
medieval splendour, and its scale
and grandeur are almost beyond
belief. It also houses a fascinating toy museum. The
Elizabethan poet, Sir Philip
Sidney, was born here in 1554,
and the Sidney family still lives
in the manor. The family
became Earls of Leicester, and
the village has the original
Leicester Square – named after a
favourite of Elizabeth 1. The
Church of St Michael the
Archangel dates from the 13th
century and contains impressive
memorials to the Sidney family.

▶ *Take the road past the church
and follow the B2176, B2027
and unclassified roads for 6
miles (10km) to Hever.*

❷ Hever, Kent

Hever is best known for its
associations with Anne Boleyn,
Henry VIII's second wife. The
village inn is called King Henry
VIII, and the fine church has a
memorial to Sir Thomas Bullen,
Anne's father, who is buried
here. Hever Castle was the
family home, and it was here
that Henry VIII courted her.
This fine, moated manor house
was acquired by William Waldorf
Astor in 1903, who did much
work restoring it. He created the
modern lake and superb Tudor-
style gardens, including a
spectacular Italian Garden, and
built a mock-Tudor village
behind the house. The house
itself contains a superb collection of furniture and paintings,
and the Tudor Long Gallery

features a fascinating exhibition
of scenes from the life and times
of Anne Boleyn.

Just east of Hever is
Chiddingstone. The entire
village is owned by the National
Trust, including Chiddingstone
Castle, a late 18th-century
Gothic manor house. The main
street is lined with beautifully
preserved half-timbered 16th-
and 17th-century houses. The
Chiding Stone, after which the
village is named, is a piece of
local sandstone where nagging
wives were publicly chided by
the village population.

Three miles (5km) west of
Hever is Edenbridge. The 16th-
century Crown Hotel is note-
worthy. The 13th-century
church here has a massive tower
which is crowned with a spire of
a later date.

Near by, at Haxted, is a late
16th-century watermill, which is
currently undergoing renovation
and is expected to reopen to the
public in 2001.

▶ *From Haxted Mill take unclassified roads north to Limpsfield.*

The gardens at Penshurst Place
Left: General Wolfe, Westerham

❸ Limpsfield, Surrey

This small town nestles at the
foot of the North Downs in
wooded countryside. The
composer Frederick Delius is
buried among the yews in the
churchyard here.

A little further is the village of
Westerham. General Wolfe, who
beat the French in Quebec in
1759, was born here. His
boyhood home, 17th-century
Quebec House, is near the
green. Near by is Squerryes
Court, a William and Mary
manor house built in 1681 and
owned by the Warde family for
over 250 years. Wolfe received
his commission here, and a room
is set aside for Wolfe memorabilia. The house also contains
fine paintings, tapestries and
furniture, and the magnificent
garden has lakes, spring flowers
and shrubs. There is a statue of
Wolfe in the High Street, and on
the tiny green one of Sir
Winston Churchill, who lived at
Chartwell, just south of town,

from 1924 until his death. The house is filled with reminders of the great statesman, from his hats and uniforms to gifts presented by Stalin and Roosevelt. There are paintings of Churchill and also many works by Churchill himself. An exhibition gives visitors an insight into his life during his years at Chartwell, and his studio is arranged with easel at the ready.

Chartwell was Winston Churchill's country home until his death

RECOMMENDED WALKS

Many excellent walks can be found near Titsey, to the north of Limpsfield, southwards towards Edenbridge along the Vanguard Way, and east and west along the North Downs Way, which follows much of the old Pilgrim's Way from Winchester to Canterbury, giving fine views of southern England.

▶ Follow the **A25** to Sevenoaks.

⬛ Sevenoaks, Kent

The traditional seven fine oaks which gave the town its name were reduced to only one in the great storm of October 1987, but new trees have been planted. Sevenoaks is notable for Knole, which dates from 1456 and is the largest private house in England. Thomas Sackville, the 1st Earl of Dorset, was granted the house by Elizabeth I. Set in a wide-rolling deer park, it contains an important collection of 17th-century furniture, fine staircases and fireplaces, two state beds of James II and galleries hung with original tapestries. Beer has been brewed in the area for centuries, and you can also sample one of the wines from an increasing number of local vineyards.

ℹ️ *Buckhurst Lane*

▶ *Leave Sevenoaks on the **A225**, and rejoin the **A25** to Ightham.*

⬛ Ightham, Kent

Visiting Ightham is like stepping back in time. Ightham Mote is an unspoilt, medieval, moated manor house surrounded by beautiful Wealden scenery. Undisturbed by time, the great hall, chapel and crypt have survived in fine condition. There are many fine old half-timbered medieval buildings in the village, including an oast house and the Old Coaching Inn. The Church of St Peter is mainly 14th- and 15th-century and contains some splendid stained glass and several brasses and sculptures.

▶ *Continue east on the **A25**, which joins and becomes the **A20**. Turn south on to the **B2016** to the turning east for Mereworth.*

⬛ Mereworth, Kent

This is the heart of the 'Garden of England'. The unusual church was rebuilt in 18th-century neo-classical style, like nearby Mereworth Castle, and has a remarkable large steeple. The castle was built in the early 18th century as a copy of the Villa La Rotunda, near Vicenza in Italy. It has the appearance of

an ancient temple, and contains some impressive ceiling paintings, as well as period furniture designed by William Kent. The present village was built by Lord Westmoreland, who destroyed the original in order to use the site for the extravagant and exotic castle.

On the road to Lamberhurst you will pass the Hop Farm Country Park at Beltring, well worth a visit. The farm has the finest collection of Victorian oast houses in the world, now turned into craftsmen's workshops and a hop museum, recapturing the life of hop farmers in the past.

▶ *From Mereworth return to the **B2016** via the **A26**. Continue south on the **B2016**, **A228**, **B2160** and **A21** for 14 miles (23km) to Lamberhurst.*

⬛ Lamberhurst, Kent

This village was the centre of the Wealden iron industry and at one time produced railings for St Paul's Cathedral in London. The Owl House is a small timber-framed 16th-century house, a former haunt of wool smugglers. Surrounding it are 13 acres (5 hectares) of gardens offering romantic walks with spring flowers, azaleas, rhododendrons, roses, shrubs and ornamental fruit trees. The lawns lead to lovely woodlands of oak and birch, and informal sunken water gardens.

Bayham Abbey, 2 miles (3km) west of the village, is said to be the most impressive group of monastic remains in Kent, with church, monastery and a former gatehouse all well preserved. Set in the wooded Teise Valley, the ruins date back to the 13th century.

The beautiful gardens at Scotney were carefully planned in the 19th century around the remains of the old, moated Scotney Castle. There is something to see at every time of year, with spring flowers followed by gorgeous rhododendrons, azaleas and a mass of roses, and then superb autumn

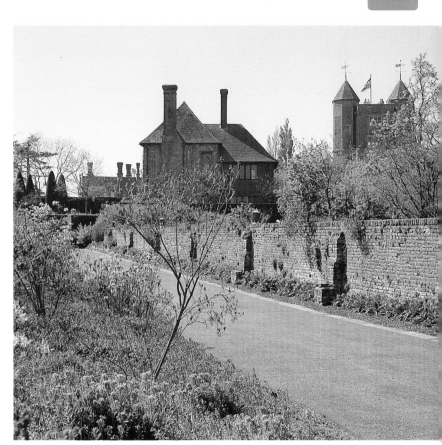

The gardens at Sissinghurst

BACK TO NATURE

South of Goudhurst is Bedgebury Pinetum, an attractive place to visit at any time of the year. It is set in a big park surrounding a Louis XIV-style mansion. Rhododendrons and azaleas are specialities, but there are numerous varieties of fungi and conifers. The mansion is now a girls' school, but most of the park is open. The Pinetum contains a nationally important collection of pine trees – several of the plants came originally from Kew Gardens, but the Forestry Commission now manages these woodlands. Bird-watchers come to Bedgebury, especially during the winter months, to see interesting species such as hawfinch, crossbill and firecrest.

colours. Open-air opera performances are given in mid-July.

▶ *Continue southeast on the A21, taking the unclassified road on the left after 1½ miles (2km), through Kilndown to the A262 and Goudhurst. About 1½ miles (2km) after Goudhurst, turn right on to the B2085, then left to Cranbrook on meeting the A229.*

8 Cranbrook, Kent
Cranbrook is a pleasant town with many 18th-century buildings. In the centre is Union Mill, the finest working smock windmill in England. Often called the 'Capital of the Weald', Cranbrook was built from the profits of the wool trade in the 15th century. The fine medieval church, 'the Cathedral of the Weald', has a porch built in 1291,

and the local museum recaptures much of the history of the area.

Three miles (5km) from the town is Sissinghurst Castle. The popular and colourful gardens were created in the 1930s by Vita Sackville-West and her husband, Sir Harold Nicolson. Derelict buildings and wild vegetation were transformed into this beautiful series of gardens with orchards, herbs and the famous 'white garden' where only white or grey flowers grow. Visitors can look at the quaint tower room where Vita wrote her novels.

i *Vestry Hall, Stone Street, Cranbrook*

▶ *Continue on the A262, then the A28 to Tenterden.*

9 Tenterden, Kent

Described as the 'Jewel of the Weald', the centre of this Wealden market town is dominated by the marble tower of St Mildred's Church. It is worth the climb up the tower because of the fine views across the Weald and, on a clear day, as far as France. The high street has shops and houses, many with original Georgian fronts. William Caxton, the father of English printing, is believed to have been born in Tenterden, and at the western edge of the town is the William Caxton Inn. Pub signs are often quite revealing about the past, and near the church is the Woolpack Inn, a reminder that much of the town's wealth came from sheep during the 15th and 16th centuries.

Woollen cloth was traded overseas, using Small Hythe as a port. It is difficult to visualise this countryside location, now far removed from the sea, as a thriving port and shipbuilding centre.

Dame Ellen Terry lived in Smallhythe Place, an early 16th-century timbered harbour master's house, from 1899 until she died in 1928, and the house is open to visitors during the summer months. Spots Farm, at Small Hythe, has 20 acres (8 hectares) of vineyards you can walk through, as well as an amazing herb garden containing

A stretch of line on the Kent and East Sussex Railway, Tenterden

SPECIAL TO...

Tenterden is the main station for the Kent and East Sussex Steam Railway, and it handles thousands of passengers every year. A stretch of the line from Tenterden through the beautiful Rother Valley was reopened in 1974 by volunteer steam enthusiasts. An extension was opened to Northiam in 1990, making a total journey of 7 miles (11km), but the highlight for steam lovers is the thrill of the engine working hard to climb the steep hill into Tenterden.

over 500 varieties, possibly the largest collection in the UK.

ℹ️ *Town Hall, High Street*

▶ *Follow the **A28** for 8 miles (13km) to Northiam.*

10 Northiam, East Sussex

The gnarled old oak tree on the village green achieved fame when Elizabeth I dined beneath it in 1573, while on her way to Rye. She is said to have taken her shoes off during the occasion and left them to the villagers when she continued her journey.

Great Dixter, half-a-mile (1km) away, is a large manor house dating back to the 15th century with a half-timbered and plastered front. The house was enlarged and restored by Sir Edward Lutyens in 1910. Its gardens are specially noted for their clematis.

▶ *Return towards the main road, taking the narrow road, first on the right, and follow country lanes to Bodiam.*

11 Bodiam, East Sussex

Bodiam Castle, on the edge of the village, is a magnificent moated fortress, built in the 1380s to stop French raiders coming up the Rother Valley. The castle survived the French, who did not attack, but could not survive Cromwell's armies, who destroyed it. The outside walls are still intact, but it is now an empty shell. Life in a medieval castle is shown on a video, and there are 'Activity Days', when school children can dress up in medieval costumes for living history lessons. It was voted one of the top six castles for children in 1989, and in May it hosts a longbow competition.

Five miles (8km) southwest of Bodiam is Robertsbridge. Its half-timbered and weather-boarded cottages, a feature of the area, line the High Street, and it is the home of Gray-Nicolls, makers of cricket bats since 1875. A mile (1.6km) east, a no-through road leads to the ruins of a Cistercian abbey, founded in 1176.

▶ *Follow the unclassified road past the station to Etchingham, then the A265 to Burwash.*

12 Burwash, East Sussex
Burwash is an outstandingly attractive village of 16th- and 17th-century houses. Inside St Bartholomew's Church is a cast-iron grave slab which is thought to be the oldest in the country.

Bateman's, half-a-mile (1km) away, was the home of Rudyard Kipling from 1902 until 1936, providing the inspiration for much of his work. His study has been kept as it was during his lifetime, and the enormous 10-foot (3m) long desk has a few untidy pieces left standing on it. Much of the neighbourhood is featured in his novel *Puck of Pook's Hill*. Upstream there is a watermill which has been restored to working order, and

near by is the waterdriven turbine Kipling had installed in 1902 to provide his house with electricity.

▶ *Take the A265, turning right on to the A267 past Heathfield. Turn left on to unclassified roads shortly after Five Ashes and follow signs to Rotherfield.*

13 Rotherfield, East Sussex
On the edge of the Ashdown Forest, Rotherfield sits in the heart of beautiful countryside. It is a delightful place to stop off and walk about. There is a fine church dedicated to St Denys, which contains 13th-century wall-paintings including Doom, and St Michael weighing souls, and in the east window is some splendid stained glass by Edward Burne-Jones and William Morris.

▶ *Return via unclassified roads to the A26. Turn right and return to Tunbridge Wells.*

FOR HISTORY BUFFS

The 'Heart of Kent' was formerly a vast forest, and the abundance of oak in medieval times gave rise to the characteristic timber-framed and half-timbered houses of the area. The houses often included a central hall and projecting upper storeys.

SCENIC ROUTES

The roads leading into Mereworth, Lamberhurst, Scotney and Bodiam are particularly memorable. The combination of villages, old Wealden buildings, hills, valleys and woods create a picturesque landscape. Villages such as Ightham are very photogenic, as are the North Downs.

Bodiam Castle's moat could not protect it from Cromwell's army

From
Cathedral to Cliffs

2/3 DAYS • 107 MILES • 172KM

ITINERARY		
CANTERBURY	▶	Chartham (4m-6km)
CHARTHAM	▶	Wye (8m-13km)
WYE	▶	Ashford (5m-8km)
ASHFORD	▶	Rye (20m-32km)
RYE	▶	New Romney (13m-21km)
NEW ROMNEY	▶	Lympne (9m-14km)
LYMPNE	▶	Folkestone (8m-13km)
FOLKESTONE	▶	Hawkinge (3m-5km)
HAWKINGE	▶	Dover (9m-14km)
DOVER	▶	St Margaret's at Cliffe (4m-6km)
ST MARGARET'S AT CLIFFE		
WALMER	▶	Sandwich (6m-10km)
SANDWICH	▶	Wingham (6m-10km)
WINGHAM	▶	Canterbury (6m-10km)

Cathedral and castles, steep cliffs and miles of flat marshes are part of this drive, which also takes in green countryside, old oast houses and thatched cottages, with a new view every few minutes.

i *34 St Margaret's Street, Canterbury*

BACK TO NATURE

Stodmarsh National Nature Reserve lies a few miles to the east of Canterbury. Vast reed-beds and areas of open water attract huge numbers of wild-fowl. Reed warblers, Cetti's warblers and bearded tits can be found in the winter, some-times in the company of short-eared owls.

▶ *Take the* **A28** *to Chartham.*

1 Chartham, Kent
The valley of the Great Stour, with gravel pits and small lakes, is noted for fishing and bird life, and Chartham is a well-known angling centre. St Mary's Church dates from the 13th century and has one of the oldest sets of bells in the country. There is a beautiful garden centre near Chartham.

Further along is Chilham, where the village square is set at the gateway to Chilham Castle, built for Henry II in 1174. The castle is not open to the public, although on rare occasions events are held in the grounds. The village has quaint pubs and antique shops. The church has a stone and flint tower, and the largely unspoilt houses around the square are of Tudor and Jacobean style.

▶ *From Chilham return to the* **A28***, travel south for 2 miles (3km) then turn off on to unclassified roads to Wye.*

2 Wye, Kent
This village, in its rural setting, is the location of the famous Agriculture School of London University, housed in a college first set up in the mid-15th century by John Kempe, a native of the town, who became Archbishop of Canterbury. The town is also the location of 18th-century Olantigh Hall, with gardens occasionally open to the public.

Picturesque timbered Chilham
Left: Dover Castle and Pharos

▶ *Return to the* **A28** *for 5 miles (8km) to Ashford.*

3 Ashford, Kent
This old market centre for Romney Marsh and the Weald of Kent is now a thriving shopping and touring centre. Medieval, Tudor and Georgian houses still survive and the 14th- and 15th-century parish church retains much of its old character.

Godinton House, northwest of town, was built in the 17th century. The rooms are full of Chippendale and Sheraton furniture, and there is fine topiary work in the garden.

i *18 The Churchyard*

▶ *Follow an unclassified road, then the* **A259** *across Romney Marsh to Rye.*

4 Rye, East Sussex
Rye is one of the Cinque Ports, a group of maritime towns which

41

were originally responsible for providing ships and men to guard against invasion. At one time Rye was almost encircled by the sea, but the harbour silted up in the 16th century and the water receded. In the winter, when mists roll in across the countryside, Romney Marsh can be sinister and mysterious – a fitting background to tales of the infamous parson and smuggler, Dr Syn.

i *The Heritage Centre, Strand Quay*

▶ *Head back on the* **A259** *to East Guldeford, then take an unclassified road through Camber to Lydd to join the* **B2075** *to New Romney.*

5 New Romney, Kent
Another ancient Cinque Port, now inland from the sea, New Romney was destroyed in 1287 by a violent storm which changed the course of the River Rother. The Romney, Hythe and Dymchurch narrow gauge railway opened in 1927, with locomotives and carriages which are one-third full size. Toys and models can be seen at New Romney station.

Getting up steam on the Romney, Hythe and Dymchurch Railway

i *Town Hall House, 35 High Street*

FOR HISTORY BUFFS

There are as many as **74** Martello towers along the south coast. A noted survivor is at Dymchurch, near New Romney. Martello towers were built to resist an invasion by Napoleon which never happened. Many were used to control smuggling. The Dymchurch tower has been fully restored and has one of the original 24-pounder guns on the roof.

▶ *Take the* **A259** *again, then unclassified roads for 9 miles (14km) to Lympne, then via the* **B2067** *to the* **A261** *which leads eastwards to Hythe.*

6 Lympne, Kent
The 11th-century castle at Lympne (pronounced *Lim*) stands on top of a cliff which was once a coastline. Below the castle (not open to the public) extensive remains of a Roman fort can be seen.

Just outside town is Port Lympne Wild Animal Park, set in 300 acres (121 hectares) of gardens surrounding a mansion. East of Lympne is Hythe,

another Cinque Port which is now a popular seaside resort and the terminus for the Romney, Hythe and Dymchurch Railway. The town has several historic buildings and summer boating along the old Royal Military Canal.

i *Red Lion Square, Hythe*

▶ *Follow the* **A259** *from Hythe to Folkestone.*

7 Folkestone, Kent
The harbour of this resort handles cross-Channel ferries, and still has a fishing fleet and a fish market. The Museum and Art Gallery in Grace Hill has displays on the town's maritime history, and at South Quay, *U475,* or *The Black Widow* as she is better known, is a Russian submarine which you can explore. Spade House was the former home of the author H G Wells. The Leas, a wide grassy promenade along the cliff top, has fine views and provides an excellent walk through wooded slopes down to the beach.

i *Harbour Street*

FOR CHILDREN

The Rotunda Amusement Park in Folkestone is open seven days a week throughout summer. Ride on the southeast's only log flume or have a gentle round of crazy golf. There are indoor amusements, and on Sundays there is a huge outdoor market.

▶ *Head inland along the* **A260** *as far as Hawkinge.*

8 Hawkinge, Kent
Set in the heart of the Downland west of Hawkinge is the Kent Battle of Britain Museum, which conjures up visions of World War II. It houses the largest collection of fragments of British and German aircraft involved in the fighting.

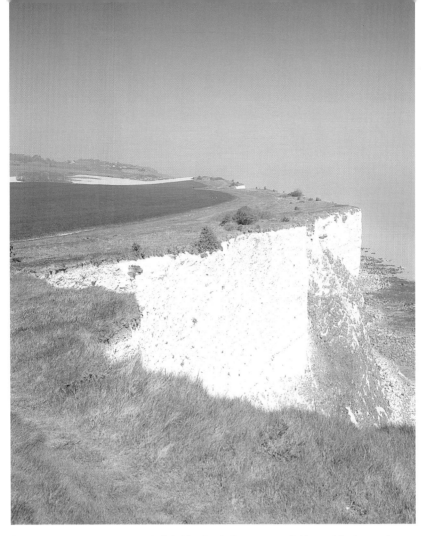

Take unclassified roads east-wards from Hawkinge, eventually running south on to the A256 for Dover.

⑨ Dover, Kent

Dover, famous for its White Cliffs, was the chief Cinque Port. It was known to the Romans as *Dubris*, and the Painted House, discovered in 1970, dates from about AD 200. Among the paintings are several references to the theme of Bacchus, the god of wine. More recent is the Old Town Gaol, which has been restored to show the dismal conditions of Victorian prison life. On Snargate Street you can see the Grand Shaft, a 140-foot (43m) staircase cut into the white cliffs,

built in Napoleonic times as a short cut to the town for troops stationed on the Western Heights. The views across to France can be best seen from Dover Castle, which overlooks the town. The Pharos, a Roman lighthouse, stands within its walls near the fine Saxon Church of St Mary de Castro.

[i] *Townwall Street*

Take the A258, then an unclassified road to St Margaret's at Cliffe.

⑩ St Margaret's at Cliffe, Kent

The flint-faced church in the upper part of this village is typical of chalkland buildings.

St Margaret's Bay is a popular start for cross-Channel swimmers

Massive chalk cliffs dominate the scene, and sheltered beneath them is the Pines Garden, created in the 1970s with trees, shrubs, a lake and waterfall, and a statue of Sir Winston Churchill.

Three miles (5km) further is Ringwould, which has another fine church, with an attractive 17th-century tower. Bronze Age barrows can be seen at nearby Free Down, and at Kingsdown there is a lot of flint, both on the buildings and on the shore.

Rejoin the A258, then take an unclassified road from Ringwould to Walmer.

Sandwich is one of the oldest
Cinque ports
Opposite: Winchester's Round Table

1 Walmer, Kent

Henry VIII built the castle here, along with over 20 other forts to defend the coast of southeast England. This fine coastal fortress, shaped like a Tudor rose, has been transformed into an elegant stately home with beautiful gardens, and is the official residence of the Lord Warden of the Cinque Ports. Lord Wellington was Warden from 1829 to 1852, and his famous boots are on display.

Further on, Deal Castle, also built by Henry VIII, is in the shape of a six-petalled flower, and tells the full story of the Tudor castles in the exhibition room. The Time Ball Tower, which used to give time signals to shipping is a unique four-storey museum of time and maritime communication on the sea front. The museum in St George's Road has a collection of old photographs, model sailing ships and maps.

i | *Town Hall, High Street, Deal*

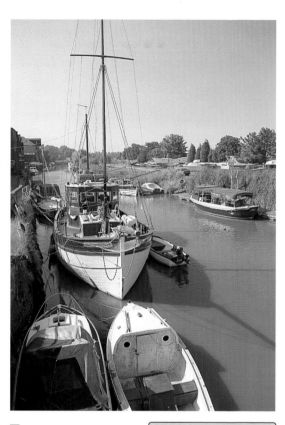

i | *The Guildhall, Market Square*

▶ *Follow the **A257** taking a detour through the village of Ash to Wingham.*

13 Wingham, Kent

This picturesque village contains a magnificent church with a green spire, caused by oxidisation. The Bird Park has cockatoos, macaws, owls and waterfowl, all with plenty of flying space, as well as rare farm animals and pets. Valuable research work takes place here to help endangered species, and to overcome man's destruction of natural habitats. A little further out of town is the village of Littlebourne. Fruit and hops are grown around here, and there is an ancient thatched barn near the flint-faced church.

▶ *Continue along the **A257** to Canterbury (6 miles/10km).*

RECOMMENDED WALKS

The North Downs Way can provide a long walk; there are clearly marked trails from Dover to Deal along the coast, or along an inland route. The route from Deal to Sandwich on the coast or inland will provide fabulous views.

▶ *Take the **A258** to Sandwich.*

12 Sandwich, Kent

The oldest of the medieval Cinque Ports, Sandwich is separated from the sea by 2 miles (3km) of sand dunes. Its white windmill dates from about 1760, and now houses a folk museum with domestic and farming exhibits. Sandwich golf course, between the town and Sandwich Bay, is a world-class championship course.

SCENIC ROUTES

Romney Marsh and the Downs are a delight, and the inland countryside, with fields, orchards and crops, is very attractive. Along the coast there are dramatic cliffs and sea views between Folkestone, Dover and Sandwich.

SPECIAL TO...

The original Cinque Ports were Hastings, Romney, Hythe, Dover and Sandwich, with Rye and Winchelsea. They were given charters by Edward I in 1278 and were really trading and fishing ports which worked together to defend the coast and fight sea battles. In return they were granted royal charters and privileges.

The Downs &
Valleys of Hampshire

The Hampshire Downs provide a gentle interlude between harsh sandy heaths near London and the valleys of the Southwest. From Winchester this tour takes you through lush valleys to panoramic views of where battle fleets throughout history set sail.

1/2 DAYS • 99 MILES • 158KM

ITINERARY	
WINCHESTER	▶ **Stockbridge (9m-14km)**
STOCKBRIDGE	▶ **Middle Wallop (6m-10km)**
MIDDLE WALLOP	▶ **Mottisfont (12m-19km)**
MOTTISFONT	▶ **Romsey (4m-6km)**
ROMSEY	▶ **Marwell (11m-18km)**
MARWELL	▶ **Bishop's Waltham**
	(4m-6km)
BISHOP'S WALTHAM	▶ **Portsdown Hill**
	(10m-16km)
PORTSDOWN HILL	▶ **Hambledon (10m-16km)**
HAMBLEDON	▶ **Queen Elizabeth Country**
	Park (7m-11km)
QUEEN ELIZABETH	▶ **New Alresford**
COUNTRY PARK	**(18m-29km)**
NEW ALRESFORD	▶ **Winchester (8m-13km)**

Statue of King Alfred, who made Winchester his capital

FOR HISTORY BUFFS

Danebury Iron Age Hillfort, on the route between Stockbridge and Middle Wallop, is a fine example of a Celtic settlement. There is a small display to illustrate the historical background, and at Andover, a few miles away, the Museum of the Iron Age gives the history of the Celts at Danebury, using sound effects, replica excavations, models and dioramas.

i The Guildhall, The Broadway, Winchester

▶ *Leave Winchester on the B3049 heading west for 9 miles (14km) to Stockbridge.*

❶ **Stockbridge,** Hampshire
A curious 'one-horse' town unique in Hampshire, Stockbridge has a straight main street backed by water-meadows. Before the railways, Welsh cattlemen stopped here with their herds on the way to the great fairs at Farnham and Maidstone. On the north side of High Street, beyond the distinctive porch of the Grosvenor Hotel, is a charming Edwardian garage, a relic of the days of running boards and red flags. Stockbridge has several good antique shops, and exceptional crafts and fishing shops.

Outside the town to the east, Stockbridge Down, above your road of entry, is a downland nature reserve and is home to many rare flowers and butterflies. Marsh Court, on the back road to King's Somborne, was designed by Lutyens and is partly built of chalk blocks.

RECOMMENDED WALKS

Houghton, on the route south of Stockbridge, is a pretty village on the Test, where the river is at its clearest and most beguiling. Two of Hampshire's major footpaths intersect here. The Clarendon Way, which runs between Salisbury and Winchester, meets rolling downland and lovely woods to east and west; and the Test Way, stretching 50 miles (80km) from the downs to Southampton Water, follows the old 'sprat-and-winkle' railway line along the valley between bursting hedgerows and rippling water.

▶ *Leave Stockbridge by the A30, then turn right signed Danebury Hillfort and in 2½ miles (4km) turn left on to the A343 for Middle Wallop.*

❷ **Middle Wallop,** Hampshire
The Wallops, Over, Middle and Nether, take their name from the brook which links these three pretty villages. Built as a wartime RAF base, where 'Cat's Eyes' Cunningham led his nightfighters into battle, the airfield is now the home of the Army Air Corps, and pilots train here in attack, reconnaissance and transport. Inside the modern Museum of Army Flying are many aircraft and ancient balloons, the world's first helicopter, a Tiger Moth and airworthy Sopwiths from World War I, as well as cockpits to clamber into, videos and displays.

▶ *From Middle Wallop take the road through Nether Wallop to join the A30 heading back towards Stockbridge. Just before Stockbridge turn right and follow the unclassified road through Houghton to Mottisfont, a total distance of 12 miles (19km).*

❸ **Mottisfont Abbey,** Hampshire
You will find no abbey here, but there is an elegant National Trust property in tree-lined grounds by the River Test; the original priory was converted after the Dissolution. Of special note is Rex Whistler's blue drawing room, with its visual tricks. Gardeners will appreciate the fine old roses here, and it is worth seeking out the 'font', a tamed spring of clear water. If this gives you a thirst, have lunch or tea at the village post office, where you can sit outside under the spreading walnut tree.

This is the heartland of the trout fishing for which the Test is world-famous, and the area is

The 12th-century church is all that remains of Romsey Abbey

jealously guarded, with barbed-wire fences protecting anglers' huts and benches by private manicured paths.

▶ Return to the **A3057** and drive for 3 miles (5km) to Romsey.

4 Romsey, Hampshire
A few years ago, travellers here were greeted at every turn by notices reading 'You're in the Strong Country'. Strong's brewery is no more: the waft of hops last drifted here in 1981, and the malthouse you see ahead has other uses, but lots of good things survive in this lively little place.

Its greatest treasure is the 12th-century abbey, a fine

unspoiled Norman church, which only escaped the ravages of the Dissolution when the townspeople bought it for £100. Buried within is Earl Mountbatten of Burma, who lived at Broadlands. This imposing 18th-century mansion gives on to Capability Brown lawns sweeping down to the Test. Another former owner, Lord Palmerston, still keeps an eye on Romsey from his perch in Market Square. Traffic is poorly managed here, so it is worth parking at Broadlands and walking into town. Children should enjoy the Rapids leisure pool, with its giant flume and swirling water; and if you visit in November, go to Saddler's Mill, where Test Valley salmon perform gymnastic feats to reach their spawning grounds upstream.

☐ *I Latimer Street*

BACK TO NATURE

The Hillier Gardens and Arboretum, set in 160 acres (65 hectares), is a unique array of hardy plants, trees and shrubs from all over the world, situated just off the A3090 between Ampfield and Braishfield, near Romsey. The famous nursery firm, founded by Sir Harold Hillier in 1953, is based at Ampfield House near by, and for a small charge members of the public can enjoy a quiet and gentle stroll in beautiful surroundings. The rhododendrons and azaleas are particularly spectacular in season, and there is something of interest all year round.

The Museum of Army Flying, Middle Wallop

▶ Leave Romsey on the **A3090** heading east. Shortly after Ampfield, turn right at the Potters Heron signed

Chandlers Ford. Cross the **B3043** and drive along Hocombe Road. At a T-junction turn left over the flyover towards Otterbourne. On entering the village turn right on to an unclassified road, cross the River Itchen and the **A335** (dogleg right and left) and proceed along Church Lane, turning at its end on to the **B3354**. Turn left on to the **B2177**, then left for Marwell.

8 Marwell Zoo, Hampshire
Set in the 100-acre (40-hectare) park of a Tudor hall, this is one of the biggest zoos in Britain. The approach here is modern, and the animals enjoy considerable freedom. Marwell's biggest claim to fame is the work done here for animal conservation – rescuing threatened species, breeding from them and return-

ing them to the wild. You might bump into a scimitar-horned oryx or perhaps a Przewalski's horse, both snatched from imminent extinction. Children will particularly enjoy patting pot-bellied pigs in their own farmyard! Also recommended are Marwell's Wonderful Railway and the licensed Treetops restaurant.

i *Marwell Zoo Park, Colden Common*

▶ Return to the **B2177** and continue to Bishop's Waltham.

9 Bishop's Waltham,
Hampshire
As you approach, tall flint ruins on the right give a clue as to how

FOR CHILDREN

Paultons Park, off the M27 at Ower near Romsey, is a family leisure park offering a wealth of entertainment and activity for children. Set in 140 acres (56 hectares) of beautiful parkland, Paultons grows every year as features are added; it is now the second-largest attraction in the South. A giant adventure playground, an astra glide, bumper boats, pirate ship, flying saucer, train rides and a pets' corner are just a few of the experiences to be had, along with a trip to Wind in the Willows.

the town got its name. For 400 years, Bishops of Winchester lived here in a splendid palace, built in 1135, and all but destroyed by Cromwell's troops. Little remains except the walls of the great hall, but the site is open to the public. In the town centre, shops and houses span eight centuries of architecture, many hiding salvaged palace beams. Look out for the Bishop's Mitre in the Square, last remnant of the Market Hall. The town's history is charted in the small museum in Brook Street.

Four miles (6km) to the south of Bishop's Waltham, on the A334, is the elegant Georgian town of Wickham, birthplace of William of Wykeham, founder of Winchester College and Chancellor of England. As you leave on Bridge Street, watch for the Chesapeake Mill, built in 1820 from the timbers of a captured American Man o' War, the *Chesapeake*.

Peaceful Southwick, further on, is where Eisenhower made his 1944 headquarters at Southwick House. In the village he and Montgomery met world leaders and planned the world's greatest seaborne invasion.

▶ *From Southwick take the Porchester road to Portsdown Hill.*

7 **Portsdown Hill,**
Hampshire
The view from Portsdown's chalk heights is one of the finest in Britain. Ahead is Portsmouth and its spreading harbour, home of the Royal Navy, and beyond is the Isle of Wight. In between lies Spithead, where naval fleet reviews take place and, further west, the Solent, now a yachtsman's paradise. Portchester's 3rd-century Roman castle, Nelson's flagship, Victoria's beloved Osborne House and the homes of Charles Dickens and Lord Tennyson are all within sight of Portsdown.

For a fascinating look at history, trek down the tunnels in one of 'Palmerston's follies'.

These were giant forts built by the Prime Minister in the 1850s to guard the Solent against the French. Fort Nelson is open to the public.

▶ *From Portsdown Hill take the A3 heading northwards, and at Waterlooville turn on to the B2150 through Denmead to Hambledon.*

The Bat and Ball at Hambledon is full of cricketing memorabilia

8 **Hambledon,** Hampshire
The cause of Hambledon's worldwide fame lies 2 miles (3km) from its pretty Georgian centre on the Clanfield road. In front of the Bat and Ball pub, a granite monument stands near a thatched hut and beautifully mown sward of grass.

For sporting people the world over, this is a shrine, for it was here on Broadhalfpenny Down that Hambledon got its title 'the cradle of cricket'. It was in Sussex that shepherds first played the game, but here rules were established and skills honed. Nyren, landlord of the Bat and Ball in 1760, was the manager of the village team which, in its day, beat All England – and his victuals were

equally good. Players, we are told, 'struck dismay into a round of beef' and his punch was 'such that would have made a cat speak'!

▶ *Leave Hambledon on an unclassified road, passing through Clanfield, then follow Petersfield signs to join the A3. In a mile (1.5km) turn off for*

Queen Elizabeth Country Park.

9 **Queen Elizabeth Country Park,** Hampshire
Set in a deep valley, with steep downland on either side, this is the ideal place to leave the car and stretch your legs. On one side, dense woodland stretches upward; on the other, smooth grassland, speckled with sheep, climbs impressively to the viewpoint on Butser Hill.

Butser Ancient Farm is a reconstruction of real Iron Age farm remains. Here, visitors can walk freely round the huts and pens, finding out for themselves in a unique and graphic way what life was like in the prehistoric age. The Park Centre, with café and shop, organises a host of activities – pony trekking, grass skiing and guided walks are

The Iron Age reconstructed at Butser Ancient Farm
Right: Swan Green, Lyndhurst

daily occurrences, and there are annual 'specials', among them sheep events and in July, the Hampshire Country Park Show.

ⓘ *Queen Elizabeth Country Park, Gravel Hill, Horndean*

▶ *Rejoin the A3 towards Petersfield, shortly turning left via unclassified roads to East Meon and West Meon. Turn right on to the A32, then left at traffic lights on to the A272 signposted Bramdean. In 4 miles (6km) go right (B3046) through Cheriton to New Alresford.*

🔟 **New Alresford,** Hampshire
Alresford (pronounced Orlsford) is a town rich in history. Built in the 13th century by the Bishops of Winchester as a wool centre, it annually played host to 200,000 sheep, from medieval times to as recently as 1972. The best way to sample its charm is to descend picturesque Broad Street, turning left into Ladywell Lane to the ancient mill on the River Alre, where woollen cloth was

fulled – that is, cleaned and thickened – returning to the town centre via The Dean.

Alresford's main attraction is its elegance, and everywhere there are small clues to the town's chequered history. For instance, the steep pitch of the tiled roofs hint at previous thatching. The town was ravaged by a series of fires between the early 15th century and 1689, which spread quickly

---

SPECIAL TO...

Starting from Alresford and running 10 miles (16km) to Alton through peaceful agricultural scenery, the Watercress Line, a preserved steam railway, is a golden chance to enjoy train travel of days gone by. Volunteers do most of the restoration work, and West Country Pacific carries out most of the mechanical work on this line.

If you want to see how abandoned hulks from Welsh scrap yards are transformed into gleaming and steaming leviathans, stop off at Ropley, where the main restoration work is carried out.

---

along the thatch, but the practice continued despite an edict from Winchester banning it.

▶ *Leave Alresford on the B3046 then turn left on to the B3047. In 6 miles (10km) cross the A33 at Kings Worthy and return to Winchester.*

SCENIC ROUTES

Two stretches on the route epitomise the English village scene at its best. The Wallop brook idles past the thatched cottages of Middle and Nether Wallop between the A343 and the A30.

Cheriton, on the B3046 south of Alresford, is similarly lovely. Look out as you leave it for some really unusual cottages. Hampshire's gentle valley scenery can be seen to advantage south of Stockbridge.

After threading your way from Houghton across the Test's many rippling carrier streams, there are delightful views from the A3057 across lush water-meadows with cornfields and wooded ridges beyond.

1/2 DAYS • 105 MILES • 168KM

SALISBURY

Whitsbury
Rockbourne
Damerham
Roman Villa ★
Cranborne
Fordingbridge
🔟
Brook
Rufus Stone ★
SOUTHAMPTON
Minstead
Moyles Court ★
Bolderwood
Lyndhurst 9️⃣
Beaulieu
Hinton Martell
Ringwood 2️⃣
New Forest
Rhinefield 4️⃣
National Motor Museum
Beaulieu
8️⃣
Exbury 7️⃣
Wimborne Minster 🔢
Brockenhurst
Boldre
Bucklers Hard 6️⃣
BLANDFORD FORUM
Sopley
Boldre
Lymington
Exbury Gardens
Lepe Country Park
Poole
5️⃣
Christchurch 1️⃣
DORCHESTER
Mudeford
The Solent
BOURNEMOUTH
Hengistbury Head

ITINERARY		
BOURNEMOUTH	▶	**Christchurch** (5m-8km)
CHRISTCHURCH	▶	Ringwood (10m-16km)
RINGWOOD	▶	Bolderwood (10m-16km)
BOLDERWOOD	▶	Rhinefield (4m-6km)
RHINEFIELD	▶	Lymington (8m-13km)
LYMINGTON	▶	**Bucklers Hard** (8m-13km)
BUCKLERS HARD	▶	Exbury (6m-10km)
EXBURY	▶	Beaulieu (4m-6km)
BEAULIEU	▶	Lyndhurst (7m-11km)
LYNDHURST	▶	Fordingbridge (14m-23km)
FORDINGBRIDGE	▶	**Wimborne Minster** (20m-32km)
WIMBORNE MINSTER	▶	**Bournemouth** (9m-14km)

Ancient Hunting Ground of Kings

A combination of seashore, downland and forest should satisfy the appetite of those who like their terrain varied but not too rugged. On the way are picturesque towns and villages reflecting 1,500 years of history, peaceful trout streams flowing south to the sea and, at the heart of the tour, the New Forest, an ancient hunting ground of kings.

Native ponies in the New Forest

i *Westover Road, Bournemouth*

▶ *Leave Bournemouth on the A35 and head east for 5 miles (8km) to Christchurch.*

❶ Christchurch, Dorset
Formerly Twineham, this town was one of Alfred the Great's walled strongholds against the Danes, between the Rivers Avon and Stour. The walls have long gone, and dominating the busy centre now is the fine 12th-century priory church, the reason for the town's change of name. Legend has it that a beam, cut too short, was lengthened and positioned overnight by a mystery workman, thought to have been Christ. Within easy reach are the museum, art gallery and ancient Place Mill on the Quay.

i *23 High Street*

FOR CHILDREN

Try a spot of crab fishing at Mudeford, near Christchurch. You will need some simple equipment – a line or string – and a hook is optional: you can tie the bait on instead. The shops on the quayside should have all the necessities. Station yourself by the rails near the shops and have a go.

RECOMMENDED WALKS

One different option from the many forest walks on the tour is to sample the seaside breezes at Mudeford. Take the little ferry across the mouth of the harbour, and walk along the beach to Hengistbury, which rises steadily to over 120 feet (36m) – a gentle round trip of 2 to 3 miles (3 to 5km).

▶ *Take the B3347 to Ringwood.*

❷ Ringwood, Hampshire
Upstream on the Avon lies this unassuming bustling market town. The trout fishing is good

through open heaths and lovely woods to high parts of the Forest, past the spot where naturalist Eric Ashby makes his fascinating films of the badgers, foxes and other creatures that thrive here. If you want to walk you are spoiled for choice: forest tracks with shafting sunlight to your right, high sandy ridges with panoramic views and open heathland to your left.

☐ *The Furlong*

▶ *Leave Ringwood by the **A338** signed Salisbury, then turn right in 2 miles (3km) on to an unclassified road and continue east for about 5 miles (8km) before going under the **A31** for Bolderwood.*

❸ Bolderwood, Hampshire
Here, in the heart of the New Forest, the Forestry Commission has created three waymarked walks of different lengths among the trees, which range from native oak and beech to foreign wellingtonia. A leaflet helps you identify them as you walk. There are many deer in the New Forest, but normally only the silent, the patient or the fortunate see them – except at the Bolderwood Deer Sanctuary, where a sighting is guaranteed; bring your binoculars. Near by is a memorial among the pines dedicated to Canadian fliers serving at Stony Cross who were killed in the war.

The ponies which wander in parts of the Forest are not wild, but belong to Commoners, people living in the Forest with rights to graze animals (and to an annual ration of free cordwood for their fires). Look out for the brand mark of the owner; every autumn the ponies are rounded up and rebranded, and surplus ponies are sold at the Beaulieu Road sales. Feeding the ponies is illegal.

You might like to stop at the Knightswood Oak, reputedly the oldest in the Forest (600 years old) and 21 feet (7m) round. In the snake pit at Holidays Hill (on the A35, just east of your

crossing point), the less squeamish can get a close-up look at the native vipers and adders.

▶ *From Bolderwood follow an unclassified road southeast across the **A35** to Rhinefield.*

❹ Rhinefield, Hampshire
Towering above you are some of the tallest conifers in Britain – Douglas firs, redwoods and spruces – planted in 1859 as an approach to Rhinefield hunting lodge, now demolished. Behind the drive, on either side, are attractive mixed woodlands of oaks, beeches and pines, through which runs the 1½-mile (2km) Tall Trees nature trail.

Rhinefield House, nearby, is a hotel housed in a bizarre Victorian creation that is half-castle, half-house. You can have a meal or afternoon tea here.

Brockenhurst is a lively and prosperous village, popular as a centre for New Forest camping and touring. Within the shadow of the Norman/Early English church lie the bones of Brusher Mills, New Forest character and killer of snakes.

▶ *From Brockenhurst turn right on to the **A337** for Lymington.*

❺ Lymington, Hampshire
Signs of Lymington's early prosperity as a salt town, spa and seaport can still be seen in the charming houses which line the quay and the wide High Street climbing the hill. The town enjoys a different sort of maritime wealth these days: it has become a popular yachting centre. The Isle of Wight car ferry snakes down the Lymington River through serried masts of luxury yachts. Two buildings of particular note here are Pressgang Cottage, by the quay; and Georgian St Thomas's Church at the top of High street, unusual for its cupola.

☐ *New Street*

▶ *Leave Lymington by the **B3054** signed Beaulieu and*

here, and the town has many attractive Georgian and Queen Anne houses, with a splendid Early English parish church near the bypass. Near by, on the A31, is the Avon Forest Park, with many acres of contrasting meadow, heath and moorland. From Ringwood you can take in the New Forest, which spreads east and north. A narrow road between old gravel pits, converted into reservoirs, brings your first taste of the Forest at Moyles Court. The manor house, now a school, was the home of Alice Lisle, who sheltered the rebellious Duke of Monmouth's men, and was sentenced to death by Judge Jeffreys. The route winds

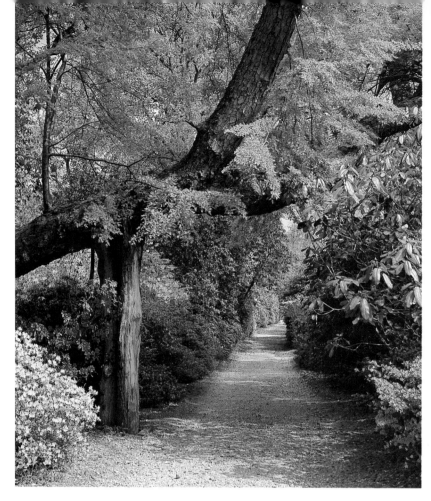

in 6 miles (10km), just before Beaulieu, turn right for Bucklers Hard.

BACK TO NATURE

Pennington and Keyhaven Marshes are reached by walking along the sea wall from the car park at Keyhaven, a few miles southwest of Lymington. There are good views across the saltmarsh at low tide and over the pools and marshes inland from the wall. Waders and wildfowl are abundant during the winter and, in summer, several species of terns as well as black-headed gulls grace the area.

6 Bucklers Hard, Hampshire

When you leave your car on the edge of Bucklers Hard, prepare to step back in time. Little has changed here since 1800, when this was one of Britain's shipbuilding centres. Three of the ships which fought under Nelson at Trafalgar were built here. Twin rows of shipbuilders' cottages, carefully preserved, slope down to the water, where the slipways were. Some are open for the public to view, and a Maritime Museum tells the story of this unique place.

► *From Bucklers Hard turn right for Exbury.*

7 Exbury, Hampshire

The name of de Rothschild is synonymous with wealth, and at Exbury House, home of the banking family, no expense was spared to create the magnificent 200-acre (81-hectare) woodland garden, which is open to the

Exbury Gardens are famous for their rhododendrons and azaleas

public. Crowning glories here are the displays of rhododendrons and azaleas, best seen in late spring.

Beside the waters of the Solent, Lepe Country Park offers a chance to picnic or walk the shore, with lovely views across to the Isle of Wight. To the east is the Spithead shore near Portsmouth; ahead, Cowes and Osborne, Queen Victoria's final home; and to the west, Yarmouth, Hurst Castle and the open sea. Half a mile (1km) of crumbling concrete marks the point where D-Day's Mulberry Harbour was made. Evenings can be particularly lovely here, and big ships describe wide arcs as they follow the deep water out to sea.

▶ *Return to Beaulieu.*

8 Beaulieu, Hampshire
Charming Beaulieu, with its pond and river, is the setting for a world-famous museum. The National Motor Museum stands in the grounds of 13th-century Beaulieu Abbey, home of the Montagus, which retains much beauty despite the destruction wrought after the Dissolution. A monorail winds through the 3rd Baron Montagu's modern showcase for over 250 vintage cars

Beaulieu – home of Lord Montagu and his National Motor Museum

and motorcycles. The collection includes record breakers *Bluebird* and *Thrust 2*, and there are many other attractions in the grounds.

| *i* | John Montagu Building

▶ *Take the B3056 to Lyndhurst.*

9 Lyndhurst, Hampshire
Open roads through rolling gorse heathlands bring you to Lyndhurst, the 'capital' of the New Forest, a busy tourist town in the summer. Alice Hargreaves (née Liddell), the original Alice of Lewis Carroll's *Alice in Wonderland*, is buried in Lyndhurst churchyard. At Queen's House the Verderers, guardians since Norman times of Commoners' rights, hold their

bi-monthly ancient court on Mondays. They employ agisters to patrol the forest daily, often on horseback, to supervise and control animals grazing on the 90,000 acres (36,423 hectares). Forest ponies have their tails cut specially to indicate their own agister. The New Forest Museum offers an insight into the fascinating history and traditions of the popular area.

| *i* | New Forest Museum and Visitor Centre

▶ *Leave Lyndhurst on the A337 signposted Cadnam. In 2 miles (3km) turn left through Minstead, then left, immediately left and immediately right to cross the A31 to Brook, then keep left on the B3078 for Fordingbridge.*

10 Fordingbridge, Hampshire
The comfortable little town of Fordingbridge, on the River Avon, had a quiet time in the 1970s and '80s, but is now coming to life again, with new shops opening and industries arriving. Stand on the old bridge and look for trout or pike. On this spot, during the time of William the Conqueror, a guard was posted to arrest New Forest deer poachers on their only escape route to the west. The fine medieval parish church stands on the Alderholt road.

▶ *Leave Fordingbridge heading northwest and follow unclassified roads to Rockbourne. Turn southwest through Damerham and Cranborne, and on to Wimborne Minster.*

11 Wimborne Minster, Dorset
On the way to Wimborne Minster, you pass through Rockbourne, with its pretty Tudor and Georgian cottages by a stream. To the south of the village is the excavated site of a Roman villa, open to the public. Wimborne Minster itself, though medieval in its street pattern, is no sorry relic of a bygone age. It has a Town Trail which explores its rich heritage of fine medieval and Georgian buildings – details obtainable from the Information Bureau. Central to it all is the Minster, of Saxon origin and curiously chequered in grey and brown stone. After all the history, you might want to browse through the hundreds of stalls at Wimborne's huge weekend market, or visit the model town on King Street.

| *i* | 29 High Street

▶ *Leave by the B3078 crossing the A31 and immediately bear left via Canford Magna to join the A341 and the A347 to Bournemouth.*

FOR HISTORY BUFFS

King William II (Rufus or red-haired), son of the Conqueror, fully deserved the fate which met him while out hunting in the New Forest in August 1100. An arrow, supposedly fired by a companion, missed the stag and mortally wounded him. But questions remain. Was it an accident? Was it Sir Walter Tirel who fired the arrow, and then fled to France? Or was it the mysterious Purkes, who took the body to Winchester? You can visit the site of the king's death, marked by the Rufus Stone in a glade just off the A31 near Minstead.

WALES & THE MARCHES

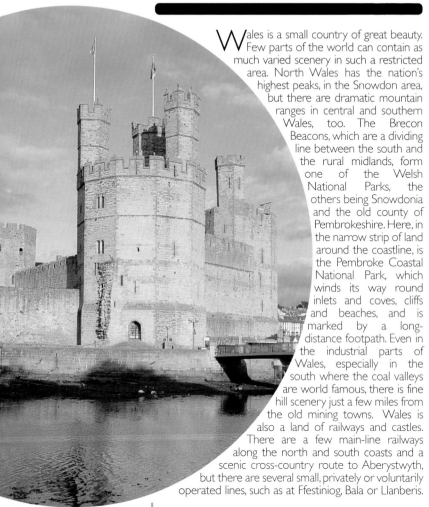

Wales is a small country of great beauty. Few parts of the world can contain as much varied scenery in such a restricted area. North Wales has the nation's highest peaks, in the Snowdon area, but there are dramatic mountain ranges in central and southern Wales, too. The Brecon Beacons, which are a dividing line between the south and the rural midlands, form one of the Welsh National Parks, the others being Snowdonia and the old county of Pembrokeshire. Here, in the narrow strip of land around the coastline, is the Pembroke Coastal National Park, which winds its way round inlets and coves, cliffs and beaches, and is marked by a long-distance footpath. Even in the industrial parts of Wales, especially in the south where the coal valleys are world famous, there is fine hill scenery just a few miles from the old mining towns. Wales is also a land of railways and castles. There are a few main-line railways along the north and south coasts and a scenic cross-country route to Aberystwyth, but there are several small, privately or voluntarily operated lines, such as at Ffestiniog, Bala or Llanberis.

Caernarfon Castle, begun during Edward I's conquest of Wales

Wales has a long history of rebellion and conflict, and centuries of struggle against English rule have left a legacy of imposing fortresses. Caernarfon is probably the outstanding example, built to mark Edward I's conquest of the north. Penrhyn, near Bangor, is really a stately home, providing an ornate illustration of the wealth generated by the North Wales slate industries – for a few, at least.

The Welsh coastline has several popular resorts with sandy beaches, but for quieter attractions venture inland, where the wild landscape is sparsely populated. Wales is a walkers' paradise, and wherever you are you will find walks of all distances to suit all tastes. You should leave the car whenever possible, to enable you to appreciate the landscape to the full.

Chepstow

This is a border town which has grown up at a crossing point of the River Wye and is now located conveniently close to the M4. There was an Iron Age as well as a Roman settlement near here, but the town was really created by the Normans. They began to build the castle in 1067, and it still dominates the town from its site over the River Wye. The museum opposite the castle describes the history of the town throughout the ages, and St Mary's parish church is worth a visit.

Tenby

Described as 'the Jewel in the Crown of the Welsh Riviera', Tenby's narrow streets and tiny shops are huddled within medieval town walls. This is one of Britain's finest historic towns, containing over 300 buildings of special architectural or historic interest. The picturesque harbour has long been a hub of activity, and there are regular sailings to Caldy Island. Fine sandy beaches and excellent walking provide an abundance of holiday entertainment for young and old.

Aberystwyth

Aberystwyth, the largest town and principal shopping centre of mid Wales, is set in the middle of glorious Cardigan Bay, into which flow the rivers Ystwyth and Rheidol. The ruined castle, built by Edward I, overlooks the small harbour in the Rheidol Estuary, and on a hill above the town is the modern campus of the University College of Wales, which includes the National Library of Wales, housing early Welsh manuscripts. The narrow-gauge Vale of Rheidol Railway line runs to the deep gorge of Devil's Bridge, and at the northern end of the beach and promenade the longest electric cliff railway in Britain climbs to the top of Constitution Hill.

Barmouth

Situated where the mountains meet the sea, this is one of the most picturesque resorts on Cardigan Bay. It has a fine golden beach and a small harbour busy with pleasure craft and fishing boats. Visit the Royal National Life-boat Institution Museum and two other buildings which re-create the history of this area: Tŷ Crwn, the old lock-up for drunken seamen, and Tŷ Gwyn y Bermo, a restored 15th-century building. After exploring the town you could take a walk alongside the estuary to take in the lovely coastal scenery all around.

Bangor

This ancient town, surrounded by water and high mountains in an area of great natural

Beddgelert is a beautiful wooded village set deep in the heart of the Snowdonia National Park

beauty, is a long-established religious centre: the present cathedral was built on the site of a monastery founded in AD 525 – earlier than the cathedral in Canterbury. The northern college of the University of Wales is based here, on a high ridge overlooking the city. Bangor sits on the Menai Strait, and you can see the island of Anglesey from its restored pier, or cross the Strait on Telford's Menai Bridge or the later Britannia Bridge. The Bangor Museum and Art Gallery traces life in Wales from prehistoric times; and on the outskirts of town is the magnificent Penrhyn Castle.

2/3 DAYS • 172 MILES • 277KM

Castles on the
Welsh Marches

This route passes through the Wye and Usk Valleys. The castles built along the Welsh borders are testaments to a turbulent age, when this was an area of constant fighting between the Normans and the Welsh.

The River Wye, from Symonds Yat
Left: Hay Cinema bookshop

▷ Drive north on the **A466** to Monmouth.

❶ Monmouth,
Monmouthshire

Monmouth was an old Roman settlement, but its main growth came after 1066, and in 1673 the 1st Duke of Beaufort built Great Castle House on the site of the old Norman castle. Near Agincourt Square, dominated by the 18th-century Shire Hall, is a statue of C S Rolls, of Rolls Royce fame, whose family lived near here. East of town is Kymin Hill, where the Naval Temple commemorates British admirals. The walk up to it from the town follows the line of Offa's Dyke Long Distance Footpath.

i Shire Hall, Agincourt Square

FOR HISTORY BUFFS

Tintern Abbey, just off the road to Monmouth in the Wye Valley, was a Cistercian foundation in 1131 which survived until the Dissolution of the Monasteries under Henry VIII. The abbey church has survived almost intact, and the ruins of many monastic buildings can still be seen.

▷ Take the **A4136**, then turn left on to the **B4228** just past Staunton. Bear left on to the **B4432** after a further ½ mile (1km) to Symonds Yat.

❷ Symonds Yat,
Herefordshire

The scenery of the Wye Valley is among the finest in Britain and Symonds Yat is a particularly impressive beauty spot, above the deep gorge. The river flows for 4 miles (6km) in a large meander before returning to within 400 yards (365m) of the same point. An AA viewpoint on the summit at 473 feet (144m) affords magnificent views.

▷ Continue north via an unclassified road, turning right on to the **B4227** to Goodrich.

❸ Goodrich, Herefordshire
Imposing Goodrich Castle is a red sandstone ruin which Cromwell lost to the Royalists

---

FOR CHILDREN

As you enter the Jubilee Maze at the Museum of Mazes in Symonds Yat, you will be met by a maze man, wearing Victorian boating costume. There are 12 routes to the centre, where the Temple of Diana awaits you. Evening illuminations create a labyrinth of eerie shadows. The museum tells the history of mazes, and of magic spells and witchcraft.

---

during the Civil War, but then battered with a mortar which fired 200lb (90kg) shots. This dramatically situated castle had a moat which was excavated from solid rock, and you can still look down the 168-foot (51km) well in the courtyard.

▶ *Cross the River Wye and take the B4234 to Ross-on-Wye.*

4 Ross-on-Wye,
Herefordshire
The splendid 208-foot (63m) spire of St Mary's Church rises high above the roofs of this attractive town. Interesting old streets spread out from the market-place, with its 17th-century red sandstone Market Hall. Notable features include several ancient alms houses and 16th-century Wilton Bridge.

⒤ *Swan House, Edde Cross Street*

▶ *Leave on the A49, then the B4521 Abergavenny road to Skenfrith.*

5 Skenfrith, Monmouthshire
Skenfrith Castle was built as one of a group of three castles, along with Grosmont and White, to guard the Marches against Welsh uprisings. Its remains include a

central keep enclosed by a four-sided curtain wall and a moat. A small stone village clusters round the castle, with a quaint little 13th-century church and a mill with a working water-wheel.

▶ *Continue along the B4521, then turn north on to the B4347 to Grosmont.*

6 Grosmont,
Monmouthshire
Set on a hillside by the River Monnow, Grosmont is the site of another Norman fortress, taken and re-taken several times during the Welsh uprisings of the 13th to 15th centuries. The castle ruins can be reached by footpath from the town. Grosmont's 13th-century parish church is noted for its huge but crude effigy of an armoured knight. At Abbey Dore, further along the road, the abbey remains include a vast, atmospheric church, tucked away in the Golden Valley.

▶ *Follow the B4347, then the B4348 through the Golden Valley and on to Hay-on-Wye.*

7 Hay-on-Wye, Powys
Hay stands high above the southern bank of the River Wye.

Hay Castle was built by the Marcher Lord William de Braose.

Folk hero Owain Glyndŵr destroyed its castle during the 15th century, but the keep, parts of the walls and a gateway remain. The town's cinema has become the biggest second-hand book shop in the world; in fact the whole town seems to be taken up with second-hand books.

⒤ *Oxford Road*

▶ *Head southwest for 8 miles (13km) along the B4350 and A438 to Bronllys.*

8 Bronllys, Powys
From Bronllys there are clear views of the Brecon Beacons ahead and the Black Mountains, which dominate the scenery to the left. The 12th-century church, now rebuilt, has a very odd detached tower, and a stone-built Malt House is still in excellent condition and contains its original equipment. Bronllys Castle is half a mile (1km) along the A479.

▶ *From Bronllys take the A438, the A470 and the B4602 to Brecon.*

9 Brecon, Powys

Brecon is a pure delight, encircled by hills at the meeting point of the Rivers Usk and Honddu. The cathedral, originally the church of a Benedictine priory, dates mainly from the 13th and 14th centuries, and Brecon Castle is now in the grounds of the Castle Hotel. The County Hall houses the Brecknock Museum, with its wealth of local history, and the South Wales Borderers Army Museum has relics ranging from the Zulu War in 1879 to World War II and later. East of town is the terminus of the Monmouth and Brecon Canal, and to the south is the Brecon Beacons National Park. The Mountain Centre, off the A470, west of the little village of Libanus, is an ideal starting point for exploring the Park.

i   *Cattle Market Car Park*

SPECIAL TO...

Brecon's Brecknock Museum has a superb display of Welsh lovespoons, traditional gifts of betrothal which were carved out of single pieces of wood. From the 17th to the 19th centuries the lovespoon developed into complex and intricate works of art, with keys, bells and other motifs worked into the design.

▶ *Continue southwards along the A470 then take unclassified roads northwards to Pontsticill.*

RECOMMENDED WALKS

A good starting point for walking on the Brecon Beacons is at Storey Arms on the A470, which is at 1,425 feet (427m) above sea-level and gives the shortest route to Pen y Fan, the highest point in the Beacons. Be sure to take an OS map, food supplies and weatherproof clothes, even in fine weather.

---

10 Pontsticill, Mid Glamorgan

Walking and boating are major attractions in this area; or you could have a journey on the steam train of the Brecon Mountain Railway, which runs for 4 miles (6km) up the valley, through splendid scenery.

▶ *Take unclassified roads to Talybont-on-Usk.*

11 Talybont-on-Usk, Powys

This delightful little village is now a tourist centre, especially for walkers and outdoor activities; there is an Outdoor Pursuits Centre in the old railway station. The 18th-century Monmouth and Brecon Canal, which passes through the village, was built to carry coal and iron ore. It eventually closed in 1962, but was reopened by volunteers in 1970 for use by pleasure craft.

▶ *Follow the B4558 to Llangynidr, then the B4560 and an unclassified road to Crickhowell.*

12 Crickhowell, Powys

The name of this little market town is derived from the Iron Age fort Crug Hywel (Howell's Cairn). The town grew up around Alisby's Castle, which was captured and destroyed in 1403 by Owain Glyndŵr, and is now a picturesque ruin. The River Usk is crossed by an old bridge, dating from the 17th century, which appears to have 13 arches on one side but only 12 on the other – the result of 19th-century alterations.

▶ *Take the A40 to Abergavenny.*

13 Abergavenny, Monmouthshire

At the edge of the Brecon Beacons National Park Abergavenny, the 'Gateway to the Vale of Usk', is overlooked by the Sugar Loaf mountain, 1,955 feet (596m) high, and Ysgyryd (Skirrid) Fawr, 1,595 feet (488m). Its ruined castle was founded in 1090. Impressive buildings in the town include the stone tythe barn, and the red

Working a lock on the Brecon and Monmouth Canal

sandstone Lloyds Bank. St Mary's Church is built on the site of a former Benedictine priory.

i   *Swan Meadow, Monmouth Road*

▶ *Continue along the A40 to Raglan.*

14 Raglan, Monmouthshire

One of Britain's finest ruins is 15th-century Raglan Castle which was actually built as a fortified manor. The keep is outside the main castle and Parliamentary troops overcame the Royalists here during the Civil War, by approaching from the opposite side. The castle houses an exhibition on the history of Raglan.

▶ *Follow an unclassified road south to Usk.*

15 Usk, Monmouthshire

Usk is a small market town on the site of an ancient Roman settlement, *Burrium*. Visit the church to see the remarkable restored Tudor rood screen; and, at the other end of the town, the Gwent Rural Life Museum, in

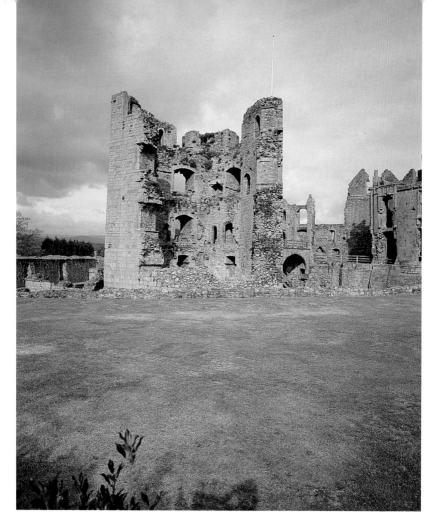

Raglan Castle was the last to fall to Cromwell in the Civil War
Right: Dylan Thomas's writing shed, Laugharne

an old stone malt barn, which is crammed with exhibits about life in the area. Usk Castle is privately owned but you can visit the ruins of the Priory next to the church.

▶ *Cross the river and continue along unclassified roads for 8 miles (13km) to Caerleon.*

16 Caerleon, Gwent

One of the four permanent Roman legions in Britain was based here, and parts of the Roman city of *Isca* are displayed in an excellent exhibition room. The major find has been the

amphitheatre outside the city walls. This oval earth mound seated 5,000 people, and is the only fully excavated amphitheatre in Britain. The Legionary Museum has more information and relics from the barracks.

▶ *Take the B4236, then an unclassified road to join the A48 for Penhow.*

17 Penhow, Gwent

The oldest inhabited castle in Wales is Penhow Castle, which is perched on a hillside above the main road. Now privately owned, it is open to the public and is an excellent example of the smaller type of fortified manor house.

Three miles (5km) further is Caerwent, on the site of *Venta*

Silurium, the only walled Roman civilian town in Wales. Remnants of the wall and mosaic pavements can still be seen. Caldicot Castle Countryside Park, 2 miles (3km) away, surrounds the 12th-century castle.

▶ *Continue straight along the A48 to Chepstow.*

BACK TO NATURE

The Forest of Dean is an excellent area for the bird-watcher. Woodpeckers, tits and nuthatches can be seen, and pied flycatchers are often spotted at the RSPB's Nagshead reserve, where nest boxes encourage the species.

The Pembroke
Coast National
Park

2 DAYS • 137 MILES • 219KM

The county of Pembrokeshire has a magnificent coastline. The inland scenery, though less dramatic, is enhanced by pretty villages and several fine castles.

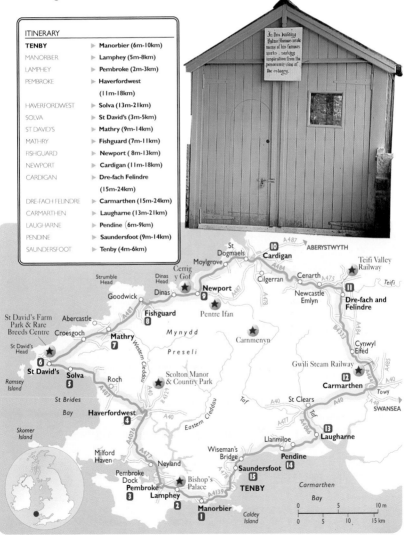

In this building Dylan Thomas wrote many of his famous works - seeking inspiration from the panoramic view of the estuary.

ℹ️ *The Croft, Tenby*

▶ *Leave Tenby on the A4139 and then turn left on to the B4585 to Manorbier.*

1 Manorbier, Pembrokeshire
The medieval traveller and scholar, Gerald of Wales (Giraldus Cambrensis), was born here in 1147 and described it as the 'pleasantest spot in Wales'. There is a castle dating from Gerald's time, which gives an impressive view out to sea from the ramparts. The sandy beach has rocky pools, and is a perfect playground for the children.

▶ *Return to the A4139 for 5 miles (8km) to Lamphey.*

2 Lamphey, Pembrokeshire
The romantic ruins of a 13th-century Bishop's Palace lie to the northeast of Lamphey. The Palace, with its ornate parapets, fishponds and notable 16th-

Tenby Harbour overlooks two bays

century chapel, was built as a country retreat for the Bishops of St David's.

▶ *Continue for another 2 miles (3km) along the A4139 to Pembroke.*

3 Pembroke, Pembrokeshire
This ancient town was built around the great 12th- to 13th-century fortress of Pembroke Castle, the largest castle in the area, and the birthplace of Henry Tudor. It still has its fine round keep, and beneath the castle is a huge natural cavern known as The Wogan. There is also a new interpretative centre with a Pembroke Yeomanry exhibition.

Pembroke still retains some of its original town wall, and has an interesting Museum of the Home where you can view objects that have been part of everyday life over the past 300 years.

ℹ️ *Visitor Centre, Commons Road*

▶ *Take the A477, then join the A4076 to Haverfordwest – 11 miles (18km).*

4 Haverfordwest, Pembrokeshire
The 12th-century castle on the hill high above the town is now a ruin. There is more history next door at Castle House, location of the Town Museum. The town is cut in two by the River Cleddau.

ℹ️ *Old Bridge*

FOR CHILDREN

Scolton Manor, 4 miles (6km) northeast of Haverfordwest, is set in magnificent grounds where there is plenty to keep children occupied: nature trails, guided walks, an adventure playground and play area, exhibitions and, in the summer months, a vintage car rally and model aircraft show.

▶ *Head northwest along the A487 to Solva.*

5 Solva, Pembrokeshire
Solva's old port still has warehouses and a restored lime kiln, and is a favourite sailing spot. Some of its cottages and merchants' houses have been converted to craft shops with a good range of high-quality individualistic products. Visit Middle Mill, a woollen mill specialising in carpets, tapestry and floor rugs.

▶ *Keep on along the A487 for 3 miles (5km) to St David's.*

6 St David's, Pembrokeshire
The city of St David's – the smallest in Britain – was founded on the site of an early Christian community, and is dominated by the cathedral and the graceful, walled Bishop's Palace. Also in the city is the Oceanarium, a purpose-built sea aquarium, and the Marine Life Centre, where over 70 species of local marine creatures can be seen. St David's Farm Park and Rare Breeds Centre is a working farm where you can observe the day-to-day routine.

ℹ️ *City Hall*

BACK TO NATURE

St David's Head has some superb coastal scenery and a wonderful display of coastal heathland flowers. Look for ling, bell heather and dwarf gorse growing alongside thrift and sea campion. For the best views of seabirds, visit Stackpole, or better still Skomer Island, a few miles off the coast and reached by ferry from Martin's Haven. Puffins, razorbills, kittiwakes, lesser black-backed gulls and choughs all put on a fine display.

SPECIAL TO...

A boat trip around Pembrokeshire's offshore islands with the Thousand Islands Company at St David's takes you on a 50-mile (80km) voyage past the highest sea cliffs in Wales, the longest sea caves and the largest grey seal colony, on Ramsey Island. The boat speeds over strong tidal currents in the narrows between the islands, including the notorious Bitches of Ramsey Sound, with its 20mph (32kph) tidal current.

St David lies buried in the town which bears his name

RECOMMENDED WALKS

Walk from St David's cathedral to the coast at Whitesand Bay. If you wish to add 2 miles (3km) and double the length of this walk, go north and do a round tour of St David's Head.

▶ *Turn northeastwards, still on the A487 to Mathry.*

7 Mathry, Pembrokeshire
This little village overlooks the Western Cleddau source stream. Mountain bikes can be hired for rides into the Preseli Hills, from where 33 dolerite stones were transported to Stonehenge. Northwest of Mathry is Abercastle, where there is a burial chamber with a 16-foot (5m) capstone resting on three of its original seven supports.

▶ *Continue along the A487 to Fishguard.*

8 Fishguard, Pembrokeshire
Fishguard has two parts. Upper Fishguard stands back from the sea, and from it the road falls

steeply to Lower Fishguard, a quaint and largely unspoilt town. There are many ancient links with boating here. The July Fishguard Music Festival is another attraction.

For a windblown and bracing day, take a return trip on the ferry to Rosslare, across the Irish Sea. Tregwynt Woollen Mill, at St Nicholas, is a working mill open to the public, which produces traditional Welsh weaves.

[i] *The Square*

▶ *Head east to Newport, still travelling on the* **A487**.

9 Newport, Pembrokeshire
Just outside the town is the Pembrokeshire Candle Centre, where you can see handmade candles being produced, and the Mini Museum, next door, has displays on the history of candle making. The remains of Newport's 12th-century castle can still be seen.

One and a half miles (2.5km) west of town is Cerrig y Gof, a group of burial chambers forming a circle. Pentre Ifan Cromlech lies 2 miles (3km) southeast of Newport.

▶ *Turn left along unclassified roads through Moylgrove and St Dogmaels, then take the* **B4546** *to Cardigan.*

The Ship Inn, Fishguard

10 Cardigan, Ceredigion
St Dogmaels Abbey, just outside Cardigan, was founded in 1115, and the ruins include large fragments of the north and west walls standing almost to their original height. One of Cardigan's most striking architectural features is the ancient bridge, which spans the River Teifi, but little now remains of Cardigan Castle, where the first National Eisteddfod took place in 1176. The magnificent towers of Cilgerran Castle, best reached from along the A484, overlook the gorge of the Teifi just upstream from the town. Watch out for the coracle demonstrations in the Welsh Wildlife Centre, and there is a coracle centre and mill at Cenarth, a few miles along the A484.

[i] *Theatr Mwldan, Bath House Road*

▶ *Follow the* **A484***, then turn right along an unclassified road to Dre-fach and Felindre.*

11 Dre-fach and Felindre, Carmarthenshire
Just before the turning to Dre-fach and Felindre, a left turn leads to the Teifi Valley Railway at Henllan, where tiny engines pull the trains along a narrow-gauge railway. The Teifi valley has long been a woollen producing area, and the Museum of the Welsh Woollen Industry is in the village. There are still a few

small mills in the area where you can see the cloth being made. The original mill building has an exhibition showing the processes involved in cloth-making, and there are spinning and weaving demonstrations.

▶ *Continue south along unclassified roads to join the* **B4333***, then the* **A484** *to Carmarthen.*

12 Carmarthen, Carmarthenshire
Carmarthen is believed to be the oldest town in Wales, and the birthplace of Merlin. Remains of Roman occupation include an amphitheatre site. The Gwili Steam Railway at Bronwydd opened in 1860, but closed in 1973 when the milk traffic was transferred to road tankers, was reopened by volunteers in 1978 and now operates for 1.6 miles (2.5km) from Bronwydd Arms to Llwyfan Cerrig, following the course of the River Gwili. A nature trail has been developed

at Llwyfan Cerrig and there is also a children's activity area.

i **Lammas Street**

▶ *Go west along the A40, turning left at St Clears to join the A4066 for Laugharne.*

🔞 Laugharne,
Carmarthenshire

Laugharne had a strong influence on Dylan Thomas, and the town hall, clock tower and many of the people became part of *Under Milk Wood*. Thomas moved into the Boathouse with his family in 1949 and along the path to it is 'The Shack', which became his workshop. The Boathouse is now a museum, Dylan Thomas is buried in the local churchyard and there is a festival of his work every third year in July. The castle by the sea was built in the 12th century, but the present building is mainly Tudor.

▶ *Follow the A4066 to Pendine.*

🔟 Pendine, Carmarthenshire

Pendine is best noted for its golden sand, on which Sir Malcolm Campbell and others made land speed record attempts. Amy Johnson took off from here in 1933 for the start of her epic transatlantic flight. Nowadays the beach is used for bathing and fishing, and there are beautiful cliff walks near by.

▶ *Take the B4314, then unclassified roads to Saundersfoot.*

🔟 Saundersfoot,
Pembrokeshire

This 19th-century fishing port and coal port has become a family holiday centre with three sandy beaches, rock pools and a

Gwili Steam Railway, Bronwydd Arms Station

sheltered harbour. Boats are available for fishing and pleasure trips. The village is in a sheltered valley, and there are good walks along the coast.

i **The Barbecue, Harbour Car Park**

▶ *Drive south along the B4316, then the A478 back to Tenby.*

SCENIC ROUTES

There are superb views of the coastline on the route from Pendine to Saundersfoot.

FOR HISTORY BUFFS

Ancient settlements were numerous in the Preseli Hills and elsewhere in southwest Wales; among the important Bronze Age relics are those at Carnmenyn. An ancient route known as the Great West Road passes a pile of rocks called Mynachlog Ddu; the bluestone which is also found at Stonehenge.

Land of Rivers
& Mountains

From the sandy beach of Borth and the muddy estuary of the Dyfi, this drive takes you through the man-made scenery of Llyn Clywedog – a striking contrast with the wild hills all around. There are rivers and waterfalls, wooded valleys and wide rolling hills.

2 DAYS • 128 MILES • 206KM

Rock-hopping at Aberystwyth
Left: carving, Strata Florida Abbey

ⓘ *Terrace Road, Aberystwyth*

▶ *Follow the coast northwards for 6 miles (10km) along the A487 and the B4572 to Borth.*

❶ Borth, Ceredigion

Three miles (5km) of sand can be found just to the north of this small village, which consists mainly of one street of cottages. Brynllys Farm near by demonstrates organic farming methods; there are nature walks here, and an information centre explains the farm's policies. Strong boots or wellingtons are advisable.

▶ *Head inland along the B4353, then turn left on to the A487 at Tre'r-ddol and follow it through to Machynlleth.*

SPECIAL TO...

Ynyslas is the area of sand dunes to the north of Borth which blocks off much of the Dyfi estuary from the sea. Behind the dunes is an expanse of reclaimed marsh; this area is now a major nature reserve. Ferries used to run across the estuary to Aberdyfi, and remains of a refuge tower can still be seen, where passengers could wait if they became stranded by the incoming tide.

---

❷ Machynlleth, Powys

On the way to Machynlleth, visit the village of Furnace. The large barn-like building beside the A487 gives Furnace its unusual name. This is an historic metal smelting site, dating from the 17th century when silver refining took place here. The water-

---

wheel has been restored and you can see the magnificent waterfall that once supplied its power.

Machynlleth itself is the chief market town of the Dyfi Valley and gained fame in the 15th century as the seat of Owain Glyndŵr's short-lived Welsh parliament. The Owain Glyndŵr Centre houses an exhibition of his campaigns. The Centre for Alternative Technology, to the north of the town, is a fascinating place to visit. Here you can see a Green Community at work, using windmills, solar panels and water-driven machinery. There is an ecological maze to explore, a children's play area and a restaurant.

ⓘ *Canolfan Owain Glyndŵr*

BACK TO NATURE

The Glaslyn Nature Reserve, off the road between Machynlleth and Llanidloes, contains heather moorland and blanket bog, together with small areas of scree, crag, rough grass and narrow river valley. Breeding birds include pipits, wheatears, ring ouzel and red grouse, and red kites, peregrines and merlins are sometimes seen.

▶ *Leave on the A489, then take the unclassified road south-eastwards to join the B4518 and on to Llyn Clywedog.*

❸ Llyn Clywedog, Powys

This reservoir, built between 1964 and 1968, has the highest concrete dam of its kind in Britain – 237 feet (72m) high – and holds up to 11,000 million gallons (50,000 million litres) of water behind it. There are excellent views of the surrounding hill country from the dam and Glyndŵr's Way and other waymarked walks follow the Clywedog valley.

Four miles (6km) further is Llanidloes, the first town on the River Severn, and there are several interesting buildings along its tree-lined streets. The most famous is the 16th-century half-timbered Old Market Hall, with its open ground floor – one of the last of its kind in Wales.

[i] *Town Hall, Great Oak Street, Llanidloes*

▶ *Drive southwards along the **A470** from Llanidloes for 15 miles (24km) to Rhayader.*

RECOMMENDED WALKS

Llanidloes is a marvellous centre for walking with Owain Glyndŵr's Way and the Cross Wales Walk both passing through the town. Shorter walks include Allt Goch, which takes less than an hour and gives excellent views over the town and the Severn valley.

---

❹ Rhayader, Powys

This small market town on the River Wye is an ideal centre for visiting the 'Lakeland of Wales'. The lakes are the reservoirs of the Elan valley, which provide Birmingham with its water supply. Pony trekking and

Newbridge on Wye

angling are particularly popular here. Although Rhayader is now a peaceful little town, it has had its share of excitement in the past. The 19th-century Rebecca riots, protesting against toll gate impositions, centred around the town, and the castle was destroyed during the Civil War. At the Welsh Royal Crystal Glass Factory you can watch the art of glass-blowing, and there are numerous craft shops and a pottery. Gigrin Farm, ½ mile (1km) to the south, offers a farm trail of nearly 2 miles (3km) in beautiful surroundings, and there are pets and a children's playground.

[i] *Leisure Centre, North Street*

BACK TO NATURE

The Elan Valley Visitor Centre, near Rhayader, organises guided walks for bird-watchers. Golden plover, ring ouzel and dunlin nest near by, and there are red grouse and a few merlins up on the moors. Dippers, grey wagtails and a flashing blue kingfisher may be seen on the streams, and the rare red kite floats around overhead.

▶ *Follow the **A470** to Newbridge on Wye.*

❺ Newbridge on Wye, Powys

The 'new' bridge of the town's name was built in 1910 to replace an old wooden structure. The church was founded in the late 19th century by the Venables family, who own Llysdinam Hall. There is a Field Study Centre in the Hall's grounds belonging to the University of Wales' Institute of Science and Technology.

▶ *Continue southwards on the **A470** to Builth Wells.*

❻ Builth Wells, Powys

Builth Wells was one of a string of Welsh spa towns which drew crowds of health-seeking Victorians, but it was an important centre long before that. The castle was built in Norman times by James de San George, who was also responsible for Harlech, Caernarfon, Beaumaris and Conwy castles. The Wyeside Arts Centre provides a fine selection of entertainment throughout the summer with films, exhibitions and theatre. Just outside town, in the village of Llanelwedd, is the Royal

Welsh Showground, which hosts the Royal Welsh Agricultural Show in July.

ℹ️ *Groe Car Park*

▶ *Take the **A483**, then turn left along unclassified roads at Garth to Llanwrtyd Wells.*

7 Llanwrtyd Wells, Powys
The smallest town in Britain, Llanwrtyd Wells is on the River Irfon. Traces of its Victorian grandeur recall the town's heyday, when travellers flocked here to sample its sulphur water – and traces of its odour remain along the river. The Abergwesyn Pass, which leads over the mountain from Llanwrtyd, has some of Wales' finest scenery.

▶ *Drive northwards into the hills along an unclassified road to Abergwesyn, 5 miles (8km).*

8 Abergwesyn, Powys
The road that crosses the mountains from Abergwesyn to Tregaron is one of Britain's most spectacular routes. It was originally a drovers' route, along which cattle were taken to the markets of the Midlands and London in the 18th and 19th centuries. The views around the Devil's Staircase, a steep and tortuous zigzag section of the road, are particularly impressive.

▶ *Take the mountain road to Tregaron.*

9 Tregaron, Ceredigion
Tregaron is a small, Welsh-speaking community, famous as the birthplace of outlaw Twm Sion Catti, and of Henry Richard, the 'Apostle of Peace' who founded the Peace Union, forerunner of the League of Nations.

Cors Caron, the Red Bog

At the foot of steep hills, and at the southern end of a great expanse of bog, Tregaron is a popular pony trekking centre.

The often bleak and misty marshland, Cors Caron, was formerly a lake fed by the River Teifi, and is now a National Nature Reserve, with restricted public access. At the Kite Centre there is a small museum of local history, and information on the rare Red Kite.

▶ *Follow the **B4343** for 10 miles (16km) to Pontrhydygroes and the **B4574** to Cwmystwyth, 4 miles (6km) further.*

10 Pontrhydygroes,
Ceredigion
The village of Pontrhydygroes grew around the lead-mining industry and is now a quiet

Devil's Bridge straddles the lovely Mynach Gorge

Rheidol Railway climbs 680 feet (207m) in the 12 miles (19km) from Aberystwyth along a breathtakingly scenic route to terminate at Devil's Bridge Station.

▶ Take the **A4120** northwards to Ponterwyd.

12 Ponterwyd, Ceredigion
This small cluster of houses round a craggy gorge featured in the writings of 19th-century traveller George Borrow, whose book *Wild Wales* relates his stay at the village inn, now the Borrow Arms. A mile west of the village is the Llywernog Silver Lead Mining Museum and Caverns and there are fine views stretching to Cardigan Bay from Nant-yr-Arian Visitor Centre, further along the road.

FOR CHILDREN

Gold, silver, lead and copper were mined from the rocks of the Cambrian Mountains in former centuries, and many of the relics of these days can still be seen. The Llywernog Silver Lead Mining Museum and Caverns near Ponterwyd has many old machines, some of which have been restored to make a fascinating working museum. You can try your hand at panning for gold and working the hand pumps, and visit the underground drift mine, with its floodlit cavern.

community set among wooded hills. The surrounding area was part of the Hafod estate in the 18th century, where Thomas Johnes began the task of afforesting the land. Further along, Cwmystwyth is another old mining settlement; the mines here were once worked by the Romans and the monks of Strata Florida Abbey.

▶ Head northwest along the **B4574** for another 4 miles (6km) to Devil's Bridge.

11 Devil's Bridge, Ceredigion
The River Mynach meets the River Rheidol here to create spectacular falls over 300 feet (91m) high. Three bridges were built across the chasm, one above the other, and Devil's Bridge is the earliest one, probably the 12th-century work of the monks from nearby Strata Florida Abbey. The higher bridges date from 1753 and the early 20th century. Ninety-one steep steps, called Jacob's Ladder, lead down to the river. The narrow-gauge Vale of

FOR HISTORY BUFFS

On the road from Tregaron to Pontrhydygroes you will pass the ruins of the Cistercian Strata Florida Abbey, founded in 1164. It was here, in 1238, that Llywelyn the Great gathered all the Welsh princes to swear allegiance to his son Dafydd. The abbey fell into disrepair after the Dissolution, but the magnificent Norman arch still remains.

▶ Head west along the **A44** back to Aberystwyth.

SCENIC ROUTES

Just before descending into Borth there are fine views of the sandy coast with the estuary and hills beyond. There are magnificent hill views all around Clywedog; as well as on the minor roads near Abergwesyn and the B4574 near Cwmystwyth.

Water, Water
Everywhere

Follow the magnificent coastline with glorious sandy beaches before turning inland and heading into the hills. Tumbling rivers and large lakes are constant companions from Trawsfynydd as far as Corris, and man-made features include dams and a huge nuclear power station.

2 DAYS • 150 MILES • 244KM

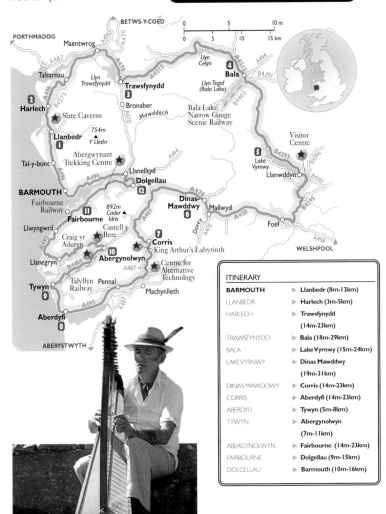

ITINERARY		
BARMOUTH	▶	Llanbedr (8m-13km)
LLANBEDR	▶	Harlech (3m-5km)
HARLECH	▶	Trawsfynydd (14m-23km)
TRAWSFYNYDD	▶	Bala (18m-29km)
BALA	▶	Lake Vyrnwy (15m-24km)
LAKE VYRNWY	▶	Dinas Mawddwy (19m-31km)
DINAS MAWDDWY	▶	Corris (14m-23km)
CORRIS	▶	Aberdyfi (14m-23km)
ABERDYFI	▶	Tywyn (5m-8km)
TYWYN	▶	Abergynolwyn (7m-11km)
ABERGYNOLWYN	▶	Fairbourne (14m-23km)
FAIRBOURNE	▶	Dolgellau (9m-15km)
DOLGELLAU	▶	Barmouth (10m-16km)

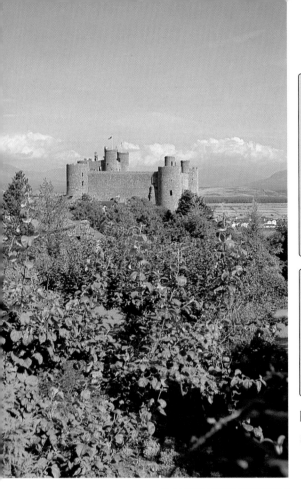

Magnificent Harlech Castle

ℹ️ *The Old Library, Barmouth*

▶ *From Barmouth follow the A496 north to Llanbedr.*

❶ Llanbedr, Gwynedd
At Llanfair, just to the north of Llanbedr on the A496, are the exciting old slate caverns, where you can walk through the old workings and see the enormous Cathedral cavern, but be sure to wear warm clothing, as the temperature inside is normally 10°C (50°F) or below.

▶ *Continue along the A496 to Harlech.*

❷ Harlech, Gwynedd
Harlech Castle is one of the most magnificently sited of Welsh castles, looking out over Cardigan Bay. It was built in the

BACK TO NATURE

Shell Island, also known as Mochras, near Llanbedr, is not really an island but a peninsula with sand dunes and sandy beaches covered with shells – more than 200 varieties are believed to have been found. It is a great place for birds, including terns and shelduck, and waders such as sandpipers, dunlin, oystercatchers and gulls, and there is a great selection of flowers – over 170 species have been seen in the summer, including a few orchids.

13th century by Edward I to subdue the Welsh but was captured by Owain Glyndŵr in 1404. Harlech's theatre presents a varied programme throughout the year and there are plenty of interesting craft shops in town.

FOR CHILDREN

King Arthur's Labyrinth at the Corris Craft Centre in Machynlleth, offers a wonderfully atmospheric interpretation of the legends of King Arthur which is sure to appeal to children (and a lot of adults, too). The stories are recounted while you are transported on a boat journey through caverns deep under the Welsh Mountains.

RECOMMENDED WALKS

Stroll through Llanbedr village and then follow the north side of the Artro estuary to the coast at Llandanwg, where there is a small medieval church which is often half covered with wind-blown sand.

ℹ️ *Gwyddfor House, High Street*

▶ *Keep on along the A496, then turn off right on to the A487 for 2 miles (3km) before joining the A470 for Trawsfynydd.*

❸ Trawsfynydd, Gwynedd
The lake here is a man-made reservoir which provided cooling water for the decommissioned nuclear power station. Nature trails have been created around the lake, and there is excellent fishing. To the south along the A470 is the Rhiw Goch Ski Centre at Bronaber, where all-year skiing is possible.

▶ *Drive into the hills along the A4212 to Bala.*

❹ Bala, Gwynedd
Situated at the top of Llyn Tegid (Bala Lake), the largest natural lake in Wales, Bala has become a great water sports centre. Sailing, windsurfing, fishing and canoeing all take place on the River Tryweryn. The other big lake near by is Llyn Celyn, a man-made reservoir, which supplies Liverpool

with some of its water and is a popular trout-fishing lake. The Bala Lake Narrow Gauge Scenic Railway runs 4½ miles (7km) to Llanuwchllyn through splendid scenery. Bala was the home of the Methodist cause and has retained much of its Welsh character and culture.

☐ *Penllyn, Pensarn Road*

▶ *Leave Bala on the B4391, then follow the unclassified road southwards over the hills and on to the B4393 to Lake Vyrnwy.*

5 Lake Vyrnwy, Powys
This vast reservoir was created in the late 19th century to supply Liverpool with water; the village of Llanwddyn was levelled to make way for it and rebuilt on higher ground. The lake and the surrounding woodlands are now a reserve of the RSPB. There is a small visitor centre, and nature trails and hides are provided to enable you to view the wildlife in the area, which includes red squirrels, polecats and badgers.

▶ *Continue along the B4393, then turn right on to a minor road to join the B4395. Turn right again on to the A458 through Mallwyd, then head north on the A470 to Dinas-Mawddwy.*

6 Dinas-Mawddwy, Gwynedd
This little village is an ideal base for outdoor holidays in the area. Meirion Mill Shop, an outlet for clothing and other crafts, is based at the old woollen mill. Pottery and slate goods are available as well as woollens, and the old railway line is a good place for a stroll.

▶ *Continue along the A470 and then left on the A487 for 14 miles (23km) to Corris.*

7 Corris, Gwynedd
Corris is an old slate mining village with a new centre for traditional industries, where

tourists can watch craftsmen at work. There is also a Railway Museum and, to the south, at the disused Llwyngwern Quarry, is the Centre for Alternative Technology (see page 69).

☐ *Craft Centre*

▶ *Drive southwards along the unclassified road on the eastern side of the river through Esgairgeiliog. Turn right on to the B4404, join the A487 for a short distance, then turn right on the A493 to Aberdyfi.*

8 Aberdyfi, Gwynedd
Sailing boats have now replaced the cargo ships that once traded at this harbour on the sheltered Dyfi Estuary. There is a fine sandy beach along the coast, and you can take a ferry trip across to Ynyslas, with its vast expanse of sand dunes and marshland. The

Dinas Mawddwy is an ideal base for exploring the area

town achieved fame in the song *The Bells of Aberdyfi*; ghostly church bells are said to ring from an ancient town which was completely flooded by the sea.

☐ *The Wharf Gardens*

▶ *Drive north along the A493 for 5 miles (8km) to Tywyn.*

9 Tywyn, Gwynedd
There are miles of golden sandy beaches at this popular seaside resort which is excellent for surfing and sailing. St Cadfan's Church dates back to Norman times and houses St Cadfan's Stone, a 7-foot (2m) monument some 1300 years old. The inscriptions on it are thought to be the oldest known writing in Welsh. Tywyn is famous for the

Dolgellau is situated in an area of outstanding scenery
Right: the Ffestiniog Railway

Talyllyn Railway, which runs inland for 7 miles (11km).

ℹ️ **High Street**

> ### SPECIAL TO...
>
> The Talyllyn Railway, which runs inland from Tywyn to Nant Gwernol, was built in 1865 to handle slate traffic. This was the first railway in the world to be taken over by a voluntary preservation society, and it is now operated as a tourist attraction.

▶ *Leave Tywyn on the **A493**, but turn inland along the **B4405** to Abergynolwyn.*

🔟 **Abergynolwyn,** Gwynedd
Two miles (3km) west of Abergynolwyn, along an unclassified road, is the romantic ruin of Castell y Bere, built by Llywelyn the Great in the 13th century. Further still is Craig yr Aderyn (Bird Rock), thought to be the only inland nesting place of cormorants in Britain, but also the home for choughs, kestrels and feral goats.

▶ *Take an unclassified road heading westwards through Llanegryn back to the coast, then the **A493** to Fairbourne.*

⓫ **Fairbourne,** Gwynedd
Fairbourne is a popular holiday base with a sandy beach and miles of safe swimming, where windsurfing is a great attraction. So, too, is the Fairbourne Railway which was built in the 1890s as a horse-drawn tramway. It was later converted to steam and now runs 1½ miles from Fairbourne to the end of the peninsula. The main line Cambrian coast railway also runs through here.

▶ *Rejoin and continue along the **A493** to Dolgellau.*

⓬ **Dolgellau,** Gwynedd
Dolgellau has always been a major route centre and is still an important regional capital and market centre. Tourism has replaced its main industry, flannel-weaving, and all that remains of this former occupation are the ruins of the fulling mills on the banks of the River Aran. Pony trekking is popular, and ponies can be hired at the Abergwynant Trekking Centre, west of town. Walking is also popular, and there are strenuous walks up to the summit of Cader Idris, as well as gentle strolls. A delightful route near by is the Torrent Walk, from Brithdir to the falls of the Afon Clywedog.

ℹ️ **Tŷ Meirion, Eldon Square**

▶ *Join the **A470** to Llanelltyd, then turn left on to the **A496** back to Barmouth.*

> ### FOR HISTORY BUFFS
>
> Dolgellau is built on the site of an ancient settlement among green hills. Three Roman roads met here, and it remained an important centre for the Welsh people throughout the Middle Ages. The Welsh leader Owain Glyndŵr signed his alliance with Charles VI, the King of France, here.

Quarries, Castles & Railways

From Bangor make a brief visit to the island of Anglesey before heading down the coast to Caernarfon and then inland to Snowdonia. The hills are scarred with quarries in places, but still create an overpoweringly beautiful backdrop.

2 DAYS • 113 MILES • 180KM

ITINERARY		
BANGOR	▶	**Menai Bridge (3m-5km)**
MENAI BRIDGE	▶	**Caernarfon (9m-14km)**
CAERNARFON	▶	**Llanrug (4m-6km)**
LLANRUG	▶	**Llanberis (4m-6km)**
LLANBERIS	▶	**Beddgelert (14m-23km)**
BEDDGELERT	▶	**Porthmadog (8m-13km)**
PORTHMADOG	▶	**Portmeirion (3m-5km)**
PORTMEIRION	▶	**Blaenau Ffestiniog**
		(12m-19km)
BLAENAU FFESTINIOG	▶	**Betws-y-Coed (12m-19km)**
BETWS-Y-COED	▶	**Llanrwst (4m-6km)**
LLANRWST	▶	**Tal-y-Cafn (7m-11km)**
TAL-Y-CAFN	▶	**Colwyn Bay (7m-11km)**
COLWYN BAY	▶	**Llandudno (6m-10km)**
LLANDUDNO	▶	**Conwy (5m-8km)**
CONWY	▶	**Llanfairfechan (7m-11km)**
LLANFAIRFECHAN	▶	**Bangor (8m-13km)**

ⓘ *Town Hall, Bangor*

▶ *Drive along the **A5122** for 3 miles (5km) to Menai Bridge.*

❶ Menai Bridge, Gwynedd
Menai Bridge takes its name from the suspension bridge built by Telford between 1819 and 1826 high above the Menai Strait. Nowadays, traffic on the busy A5 uses Stephenson's Britannia Bridge, whose original tubular structure was rebuilt after a fire in 1970, with a road deck above the railway.

From a lay-by on the A545 beyond Menai Bridge, there are superb views of both bridges, with the mountains of Snowdonia beyond. In Menai Bridge itself is the Tegfryn Art Gallery, which features the work of contemporary Welsh artists.

▶ *Follow the **A4080** to the **A5**, recross the Menai Strait on the Britannia Bridge, then on to the **A487** to Caernarfon.*

❷ Caernarfon, Gwynedd
The airport south of Caenarfon is a great all-weather attraction. It used to be a RAF camp during World War II, and is now a hands-on museum, where you

Thomas Telford's graceful suspension bridge over the Menai Strait

can climb into exhibits, touch the controls and use a flight simulator. You can also have a flight over Caernarfon Castle or round Snowdon. In 1969, Prince Charles was invested in the castle, following a tradition set by Edward I, whose first-born son was presented to the people as the Prince of Wales. Inside the castle you can see the investiture robes, and an explanation of the history of the castle and surrounding area, as well as the Museum of the Royal Welch Fusiliers.

Just outside the town, at Segontium, are the remains of a fine Roman fort which served as an important outpost of the Empire for three centuries.

ⓘ *Oriel Pendeitsh, Castle Street*

▶ *Take the **A4086** eastwards and turn on to an unclassified road to Llanrug.*

❸ Llanrug, Gwynedd
The lived-in castle at Bryn Bras, to the south of Llanrug, has spacious lawns, tranquil woodland walks and excellent mountain views. This neo-Norman building on the fringe of Snowdonia was built in the 1830s on the site of an earlier castle, and the majestic gardens are worth visiting in their own right.

▶ *Return to and continue along the **A4086** to Llanberis.*

❹ Llanberis, Gwynedd
At Llanberis you can take a 40-minute trip in a narrow-gauge train along the shores of Llyn Padarn, in the Padarn Country Park. The famed modern pump storage hydro scheme is close by at Dinorwic.

Dolbadarn Castle is in the town, and less than a mile (1.6km) from the High Street is Ceunant Mawr, one of the most impressive waterfalls in Wales. The most popular footpath up Snowdon starts here, as does the Snowdon Mountain Railway, the only public rack-and-pinion railway, which climbs 3,000 feet (915m) to the summit in less than 5 miles (8km). Each train can take a maximum of 59 passengers and will normally not run with fewer than 25. Services depend on demand and weather conditions, which can be very harsh at the top of Snowdon, even when Llanberis is pleasant and sunny. The views can be superb.

ⓘ *41a High Street*

▶ *Leave on the **A4086**, then turn right on to the **A498** for 14 miles (23km) to Beddgelert.*

RECOMMENDED
WALKS

From Llanberis, walk around
the eastern end of Llyn Padarn
at the foot of the Dinorwic
quarries, then along the northern side of the lake. Visit the
Welsh Slate Museum and pass
through the woods and via the
tramway bridge, before going
round the western end of the
lake and back into Llanberis.

5 **Beddgelert,** Gwynedd
The grave of Gelert is one of the
saddest memorials you are likely
to see. According to legend,
which may actually be a 19th-
century invention, Gelert was a
faithful wolfhound killed by
Prince Llywelyn, who thought it
had killed his son, when in fact
the dog had saved him from a
wolf. Just outside this small town
is the award-winning Sygun
Copper Mine, where you can
explore the tunnels of a 19th-
century mine which was once
one of the world's major copper
producers. A guided tour will
take you past veins of ore
containing gold, silver and other
metals. From Beddgelert the
drive takes you through the
picturesque Pass of Aberglaslyn.

[i] *Tourist Association, Ael-y-Bryn*

▶ Follow the **A498** southwards
to Porthmadog.

6 **Porthmadog,** Gwynedd
Porthmadog was the creation of
William Alexander Madocks,
who hoped to benefit from the
tourist traffic to Ireland; in fact,
the town made its money from
slate. The Ffestiniog Railway,
which runs through magnificent
scenery to Blaenau Ffestiniog,
once carried the slate here to be
shipped abroad, and is now a
major tourist attraction. It uses
horseshoe bends and a complete
spiral at one point to gain height.
Porthmadog also has the little
Welsh Highland Railway, and a
Motor Museum next to the
Porthmadog Pottery.

Italian-style Portmeirion

[i] *Station Yard*

▶ Drive along the **A487** before
turning right on to an unclassified road to Portmeirion.

7 **Portmeirion,** Gwynedd
This Italianate garden village,
surrounded by woods and
beaches, was created by the
Welsh architect Sir Clough
Williams-Ellis. Portmeirion was
used as the setting for the 1960s
cult television series *The
Prisoner*, and now produces a
distinctive range of colourful
pottery.

FOR CHILDREN

Padarn Country Park is open
all year round and has picnic
spots, boats for hire, a slate
museum and a deserted village.
You can ride on the narrow-
gauge railway running along the
shore of Llyn Padarn and walk
along the nature trail or the
archaeological trail, by the lakeside or in the woodlands.

▶ Return to and take the **A487**
eastwards, turning left on to
the **A496** at Maentwrog.
Shortly turn right on to the
B4391 which joins the **A470**
at Ffestiniog. Turn left on to the
A470 and continue to
Blaenau Ffestiniog.

8 **Blaenau Ffestiniog,**
Gwynedd
Blaenau Ffestiniog depended
for its livelihood on the slate
quarries, until demand for slate
fell away. Now visitors can get
first-hand experience of the slate
miners' working conditions at
the Llechwedd Slate Caverns,
where the Deep Mine tour will
take you down on Britain's
steepest passenger incline. The
Miners' Tramway is a guided rail
tour of an 1846 route, through a
chain of enormous caverns first
opened to the public in 1972. A
modern industry is established
at Tan-y-grisiau, where hydro-
electricity is produced in a
pumped storage scheme. Drive

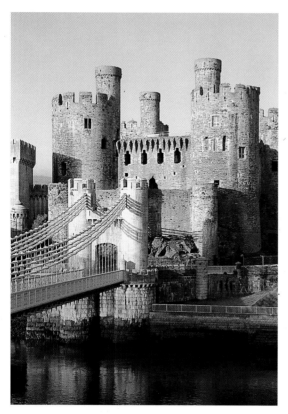

Set on a rock above the town, Conwy Castle is an imposing sight

bridge was designed by Inigo Jones in 1636, and the Gwydir Chapel contains the coffin of Llywelyn, Prince of Wales. Take a tour around the Trefriw Wells Roman Spa, where the water has been used as an aid to healthy living since Roman times, and is said to ease rheumatism and nervous tension. At the Trefriw Woollen Mills, you can see bedspreads and tweeds being manufactured, using electricity generated from the River Crafnant.

> **FOR HISTORY BUFFS**
>
> Trefriw has been known for its spa water since the 1st century, when Roman soldiers tunnelled into the Allt Coch mountains to reach the source. The water is rich in chalybeate; at the Victorian Pump House you can enjoy a sample of the water, which is said to help eliminate fatigue, nervous tension, stress, lumbago and anaemia.

▶ *Continue along the A470 to Tal-y-Cafn.*

⓫ Tal-y-Cafn, Gwynedd
The 80-acre (32-hectare) garden at Bodnant is claimed to be one of the finest gardens in the world. Now owned by the National Trust, it is located in the beautiful Conwy Valley, with views out to the Snowdon mountains. Throughout the year visitors can find much of interest, with native and exotic trees and flowers, and there is a nursery where plants are propagated.

▶ *Keep going along the A470 and then the A547 to Colwyn Bay.*

⓬ Colwyn Bay, Clwyd
Colwyn Bay is a lively seaside town, which grew in the late 19th century as a result of the arrival of the railway, and the pier, promenade and many hotels and shops date from this period. The town is famous for its parks and gardens. The

up the mountain road to the Stwlan Dam for the remarkable view along the Vale of Ffestiniog. The Ffestiniog Railway runs through 13½ (22km) scenic miles to Porthmadog, and the more energetic can visit the Rhiw Goch dry ski slope at Trawsfynydd Holiday Village.

ℹ *Unit 3, High Street*

▶ *Continue along the A470 to Betws-y-Coed.*

❾ Betws-y-Coed, Gwynedd
Betws-y-Coed is a popular inland resort set among forested land and magnificent mountains. The River Conwy is met by three tributaries here, and there are numerous bridges, waterfalls, and river pools with walks and

play areas for children. Upstream are the Swallow Falls, one of the most famous of all tourist attractions in North Wales, and downstream is Fairy Glen, a much photographed and painted beauty spot. Back in the centre of the small town, there are many interesting shops and a craft centre. The 14th-century Church of St Mary has a Norman font and an effigy of the great-nephew of Llywelyn the Great. There is also a Motor Museum here.

ℹ *Royal Oak Stables*

▶ *Leave Betws-y-Coed on the A5, shortly turning right on to the B5106 and follow it north for 4 miles (6km) to Llanrwst.*

❿ Llanrwst, Gwynedd
This historic market town is set in a delightful landscape of hills, forests, rivers and lakes. The

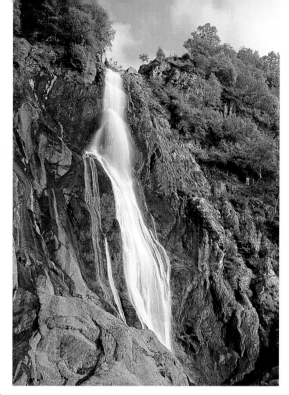

The impressive Aber Falls

Welsh Mountain Zoo has chimpanzees, free-flying eagles, a sea lion display and jungle adventure land. Other wild animals, though less lively, can be seen in the Dinosaur World in Eirias Park, which contains the largest collection of model dinosaurs in the British Isles.

ℹ️ *Prince's Drive*

▶ *Follow the **B5115** coast road for 6 miles (10km) to Llandudno.*

🔢 Llandudno, Gwynedd
St Tudno gave his name to the town in the 5th century, and a church still stands on the site of his cell. The town is the largest holiday resort in Wales, with two excellent sandy beaches situated between the headlands of Great Orme and Little Orme. The Great Orme Country Park can be reached on the Great Orme Tramway, which has been taking passengers up to the top of the 679-foot (207m) summit since 1902. The energetic can enjoy the artificial ski slope and the 2,300-foot (700m) toboggan run, and there are fun rides for the children. Llandudno retains some of its Victorian elegance while catering for modern visitors. Lewis Carroll was a visitor, and Alice Liddell, for whom he wrote *Alice in Wonderland*, stayed here. A White Rabbit statue recalls Carroll's connections with the town, and there is an Alice exhibition in The Rabbit Hole, on Trinity Square.

ℹ️ *1–2 Chapel Street*

▶ *Drive south along the **A546** for 5 miles (8km) to Conwy.*

🔢 Conwy, Gwynedd
Conwy's castle dominates the town, and inside it is a model of the castle and town as they were in the 14th century. This ancient city still has its complete medieval walls, and you can take a pleasant stroll along the ramparts. There are three remarkable bridges crossing the river, including the Conwy Suspension Bridge, designed and built by Thomas Telford in 1826 and renovated in 1990. The smallest house in Britain, a mere 6 feet (2m) wide and 10 feet (3m) high, stands on the quay. There is a Butterfly House in Bodlondeb Gardens, where exotic varieties fly freely around in a natural environment.

ℹ️ *Conwy Castle Visitor Centre*

▶ *Head west along the **A55** to Penmaenmawr and further along to Llanfairfechan.*

🔢 Llanfairfechan, Gwynedd
Penmaenmawr has one of the finest beaches in North Wales, stretching between two granite headlands, and this is a fun holiday centre for the children. Further along, at Llanfairfechan, there is a sandy beach and beautiful inland scenery. There are excellent walks near by, notably up to the Aber Falls, 3 miles (5km) west of the town. The village of Aber was once the location of the palace of the Welsh king, Llywelyn the Great.

▶ *Keep on along the **A55** before turning right on to the **A5122**, passing Penrhyn Castle on the return to Bangor.*

BACK TO NATURE

The shores of the Menai Strait harbour a rich variety of marine creatures, best looked for at low tide among the seaweeds. This abundance of life supports thousands of birds; waders such as redshanks, dunlins and curlews can be seen feeding alongside gulls and wigeon, and you can scan the open water for divers, grebes and cormorants.

SPECIAL TO...

Contained in the 840 square miles (2,175sq km) of the Snowdonia National Park are mountain peaks over 3,000 feet (915m) high, as well as miles of coastline and sandy beaches, and old mines and quarries, museums, castles and railways add further interest to this remarkable area.

CENTRAL ENGLAND & EAST ANGLIA

This large area of England stretches from the Welsh Borders to the North Sea, and covers a great variety of scenery: volcanic peaks in Shropshire; the steep scarp of the Cotswolds; the lowlands of East Anglia, and the flat Fens near King's Lynn.

The Fens and East Anglia are rich agricultural lands, growing potatoes, sugar beet and flowers and large expanses of prairie-like wheat fields. Further west, in the cattle country of Shropshire and Gloucestershire, the climate is wetter and the countryside takes on a patchwork appearance – in marked contrast to the open landscapes of Norfolk, Suffolk and Lincolnshire. On the higher lands of the Cotswolds, a golden, mellow stone is used to build walls and houses, giving a gentle beauty to farmland, villages and towns. Grand mansions such as Blenheim Palace and imposing churches have been built out of the Cotswold limestone, as have some of the Oxford colleges. Fine churches are characteristic of this area and are generally the result of wealth earned from the sale of wool.

Timber-framed house, Saffron Walden

The Cambridge colleges include some of the most impressive buildings in England, but perhaps the most dramatic sight on this flat landscape is Ely cathedral, which can be seen from many miles away. Other striking landmarks on the fenlands are the windmills, which were once vitally important means of pumping away surplus water.

From Lincoln the landscape changes as the tour moves into Robin Hood country, where a considerable expanse of forest has survived. There are also areas of forest to be seen on the Shrewsbury tour which follows the trail of industrial development, visiting Ironbridge, the birthplace of the 'industrial revolution'. After tracing the achievements of industry you can celebrate a literary genius at Stratford, on the Gloucester tour, where visitors from all over the world make their pilgrimage to the birthplace of William Shakespeare.

Lincoln

Lincoln's triple-towered cathedral dominates the city and the surrounding countryside, from its site on a limestone ridge overlooking the River Witham. A fascinating collection of old buildings can be seen in the cathedral close, including the old tithe barn and the Bishop's Palace and the 11th-century castle sits high on the city's steep hill. Other attractions include the Museum of Lincolnshire Life and the City and County Museum.

King's Lynn

This historic port and market town grew up in the 'Lin', a marshy area alongside the River Ouse along which ships travelled, bringing wealth into the town. Warehouses and merchants' houses can be seen today, but particularly notable features include the amalgam of buildings forming the Guildhall; the 1683 Custom House, standing alone alongside the quay; and the 12th-century St Margaret's Church.

Ipswich

There has been a settlement here since the Stone Age, but the port's real development started with Anglo-Saxon settlers in the 7th century. Cardinal Wolsey was born here in 1475. Industry has contributed much to the growth of this important regional and shopping centre, and there are some fine old buildings, such as the 16th-century Ancient House and the Custom House. The Ipswich Museum and the Wolsey Art Gallery are both worth a visit.

Oxford

Oxford is a captivating place. Its ancient university buildings in their mellow stone have a tranquil dignity, despite being within walking distance of the busy shopping centre. Magdalene, built in the 15th century, is a particu-

King's College Chapel, Cambridge

larly beautiful college. The 17th-century Ashmolean is Britain's oldest museum and the Bodleian Library, begun in 1598, contains over 5 million books. There are countless other collections and museums and a walk through the streets or along the Cherwell or Thames will convey the city's unique charm.

Gloucester

The Romans built the fortified port of Glevum here to aid their attack on Wales; a small part of the wall survives, and there are many more relics to be seen in the City Museum. Gloucester's cathedral is one of the finest in the world, with a massive nave and 14th- to early 15th-century cloisters. The port has declined in recent years, but be sure to visit the National Waterways Museum in the Llanthony Warehouse.

Shrewsbury

Shrewsbury, on the River Severn, is bordered by parkland and crossed by many bridges. The red sandstone castle guards a narrow strip of land leading into the original town, where there are many fascinating buildings including Rawley's Mansion and the Lion Coaching Inn, as well as a good selection of modern shops. The famous Shrewsbury School, where Charles Darwin was a pupil, looks down on the town and the river.

Through Fen,
Forest &
Farmland

2 DAYS • 122 MILES • 196KM

This is a tour through history and legend, visiting the land of Robin Hood, one of England's most famous folk heroes. It crosses the edge of the fenland region of Britain, taking in the great ducal estates of Nottinghamshire – Clumber Park, Thoresby Hall and Welbeck Abbey – as well as the ancient woodlands of Sherwood Forest.

ITINERARY		
LINCOLN	▶	**Bardney (10m-16km)**
BARDNEY	▶	**Woodhall Spa (9m-14km)**
WOODHALL SPA	▶	**Heckington (16m-26km)**
HECKINGTON	▶	**Sleaford (5m-8km)**
SLEAFORD	▶	**Leadenham (9m-14km)**
LEADENHAM	▶	**Newark-on-Trent**
		(10m-16km)
NEWARK-ON-TRENT	▶	**Southwell (8m-13km)**
SOUTHWELL	▶	**Edwinstowe (16m-26km)**
EDWINSTOWE	▶	**North Leverton**
		(18m-29km)
NORTH LEVERTON	▶	**Dunham Bridge**
		(7m-11km)
DUNHAM BRIDGE	▶	**Lincoln (14m-23km)**

One of the Spitfires housed in the old RAF station at Coningsby

ⓘ *9 Castle Hill; 21 Cornhill, Lincoln*

▶ *From Lincoln take the B1190 east to Bardney.*

❶ Bardney, Lincolnshire
A small fen town on the River Witham, Bardney is dominated by its sugar beet factory, which was opened in 1927. The town's appearance is more practical than beautiful, but some fine examples of Georgian buildings can be seen among the Victorian houses. Bardney Abbey, dating from the 7th century, was destroyed by Vikings and refounded in 1087. Ethelred the Unready built Tupholme Abbey, 2 miles (3km) beyond the river bridge, and restoration work is being carried out here.

BACK TO NATURE

Chamber's Wood, near Bardney, is a Forestry Commission oak woodland which is particularly good for the bird-watcher, especially in the spring when everything is singing. Look for several species of tits as well as chaffinches, woodpeckers, nuthatches and treecreepers. Interesting flowers include giant bellflowers and lilies of the valley.

▶ *Continue along the B1190, then just after Bucknall turn south on to unclassified roads to Woodhall Spa.*

❷ Woodhall Spa, Lincolnshire
This inland watering place was once famous for its natural springs and has a pump room built in the 19th century after the discovery of medicinal waters. Today it is best known for its championship golf-course. The 60-foot (18m) Tower on the Moor is thought to have been erected by the builders of Tattershall Castle, further south, whose fine keep is a relic of the castle built in 1440 by Ralph Cromwell, one of the richest men in the kingdom. He also built a magnificent collegiate church, in which perpetual prayers for his soul were to be said. There are excellent views from the castle looking across the low countryside as far as Lincoln and Boston. The only working fen steam engine in the country is at near by Dogdyke Pumping Station, worth a visit.

▶ *From Tattershall take the A153, the B1395 at North Kyme, and in a short distance turn right on to an unclassified road, crossing the A17 into Heckington.*

❸ Heckington, Lincolnshire
The flat, exposed landscape round Heckington is an ideal location for a windmill, and

there has been one on the same site since 1830. The Friends of Heckington Windmill have fully restored the present mill, which is the only eight-sailed windmill still working in the country, and was used for drainage as well as grinding corn. The Information Centre next door to it is in the Pearoom, which until the 1960s was used for sorting pea seeds. One of the pubs in the village, the Nag's Head, claims that Dick Turpin, the infamous highwayman, once stayed there. The magnificent decorated cruciform church dates from the 14th century.

ⓘ *The Pearoom Craft Centre, Station Yard*

▶ *Follow the B1394, then the A17 to Sleaford, entering the town on the B1394.*

❹ Sleaford, Lincolnshire
Sleaford is a small town set on the River Slea and the partly navigable Sleaford Canal. St Denys' Church, which dominates the town, has a 144-foot

The keep of Tattershall Castle
Opposite: Robin Hood and Little John, Sherwood Visitor Centre

(44m) solid stone spire, one of the oldest in the country, and its window tracery is exceptionally fine. The Black Bull Inn's sign dates from 1689 and illustrates the old sport of bull-baiting, which continued in these parts until 1807. The mounds beside Castle Causeway are all that remains of the 12th-century castle, where King John was taken ill with a fatal fever on the night after losing his crown jewels while crossing the Wash.

[i] *Money's Yard, Carre Street*

RECOMMENDED WALKS

Pleasant walks in the Sleaford area include the Culverthorpe Walk, starting from a lakeside picnic site southwest of Sleaford, and the Blankney Walk to the north of Sleaford, near the B1188.

▶ *Take the **A15** north to rejoin the **A17** and continue to Leadenham.*

5 **Leadenham,** Lincolnshire
This little village grew up along the line of limestone hills called Lincoln Cliff, which stretches from near Humberside as far south as Grantham. It is worth visiting just for the lovely church spire, but there are many attractive stone houses and the Old Hall is built entirely of golden-coloured stone.

▶ *Follow the **A17** to Newark-on-Trent via the village of Coddington.*

6 **Newark-on-Trent,**
Nottinghamshire
The sign on the edge of the town reads 'Historic Newark-on-Trent', and this is certainly a treasure house of history. The ruined 12th-century castle is where King John died in 1216, and is opposite the Ossington, a Victorian flight of fancy.
    Travellers have been passing through the town for centuries:

the Roman Fosse Way and the Great North Road intersect near by, and the River Trent has been canalised here. The cobble-stoned market-place, the scene of Prime Minister William Gladstone's first major political speech, still survives, and you cannot miss the massive 252-foot (77m) spire of St Mary Magdalen, which is 30 feet (9m) higher than the total length of the church.

[i] *The Gilstrap Centre, Castlegate*

FOR HISTORY BUFFS

Lady Godiva of Coventry fame and wife of Earl Leofric of Mercia, was the first official owner of the town of Newark, and presented it to the monastery of Stow, further down the River Trent. In the next century Newark was owned by the Bishop of Lincoln, who used the stone to rebuild the wooden castle. The new version was destroyed by Oliver Cromwell's troops.

▶ *Take the **A617** and the **A612** west to Southwell.*

7 **Southwell,**
Nottinghamshire
Visitors to this market town are taken by surprise as the spires of the magnificent Minster suddenly come into view above the rolling countryside. This 12th- and 13th-century building, with a Romanesque nave and transept, is the mother church of Nottinghamshire and replaced an earlier Saxon church. Charles I spent his last few hours of freedom at the Saracen's Head Inn, just along the road, and another famous visitor, the poet Lord Byron, often stayed at Burgage Manor near by – Byron wrote the well-known epitaph for the local carrier, John Adams, who died of drunkenness:
    John Adams lies here, of the parish of Southwell,
    A carrier who carried his can to his mouth well.

He carried too much, and he carried so fast,
    He could carry no more – and so was carried at last.

SPECIAL TO...

The spires of Southwell's Norman Minster are visible for miles around. It was built during the 12th century and contains early English Gothic as well as Norman architecture, which has survived turbulent times: during the Civil War, Cromwell's soldiers stabled their horses in the nave. The octagonal Chapter House is a unique feature, dating from the 13th century, with twin Norman towers.

▶ *Take the **B6386** to Oxton, then the **A6097** north which becomes the **A614**, and finally turn left on to the **B6034** to Edwinstowe.*

8 Edwinstowe,
Nottinghamshire

Edwinstowe is an old colliery village, and it was at St Mary's Church that Maid Marian is said to have married Robin Hood. The massive and ancient Major Oak, named after Major Rooke, a local 18th-century antiquary, is claimed to be the oldest tree in the forest. Near by is the Sherwood Visitor Centre, where there are walks, nature trails, exhibitions and amusements. Sherwood Forest Village, just down the road, is a holiday complex with indoor facilities.

i *Sherwood Information Centre, Church Street*

▶ *Return via the **A6075** to the **A614** heading north then turn right on to unclassified roads passing Bothamsall, then along the **B6387** crossing the **A1** to the **A638** to Retford. Take unclassified roads east from Retford to North Leverton.*

9 North Leverton,
Nottinghamshire

Dutch-style houses give this village a flavour of Holland, which fits in well with the flat, fenland landscape. A windmill, three storeys high and still in working order, stands above the plain, but is dwarfed by the vast cooling towers of the power station to the north along the Trent valley. Further south is the village of Rampton, surrounded by rich farmland criss-crossed with drainage ditches, used to reclaim the area from marshland.

FOR CHILDREN

Sundown Adventureland is a children's theme park on the road from North Leverton to Rampton. Its many attractions include a pirate ship, Noah's ark, a miniature farm with pets and farm animals, and there are secret passages to explore in a Tudor village.

Lincoln's majestic cathedral soars above the rooftops of the town

▶ *Continue south along unclassified roads then join the **A57** to Dunham Bridge.*

10 Dunham Bridge,
Nottinghamshire

Prepare to pay when you cross the River Trent, as a toll is levied here – a rare occurrence on British roads. The A57 out of Dunham runs alongside a major drainage ditch which dates from Roman times. Further along, Doddington brings you back into Lincolnshire. The landscape round here has been drained and cultivated for hundreds of years, and this delightful village has a fine Elizabethan hall as its focal point, with impressive ceramics, and a medieval scold's bridle is among many other curiosities.

▶ *Return to Lincoln on the **B1190**.*

Fen, Farm
& Coast

Through flat fields and across the

2 DAYS • 151 MILES • 242KM

fenland, you are drawn to the magnificence of Ely's cathedral, then on to the undulating ground of rural Norfolk. The farming landscape continues to the coast, before ending with lavender and a royal residence.

BURNHAM

Above: Thetford Forest gives way to natural woodland

ET

[i] The Custom House, Purfleet Quay, King's Lynn

▶ Take the **A47** to Wisbech, entering via the **B198**.

1 Wisbech, Cambridgeshire
Wisbech is at the centre of a rich flower- and fruit-growing area. It was once only 4 miles (6km) from the sea, but due to land reclamation is now 11 miles (17km) inland. The Wisbech and Fenland Museum illustrates local history. Near by is the Aviation Museum, containing an interesting but rather morbid exhibition of aircraft equipment recovered from crashes in the area. The church has two naves, and a Braille Plan for blind visitors in the garden. The Brinks, two rows of houses along the River Nene, are among the finest examples of Georgian architecture in England, and Peckover House contains fine panelling and furniture; in its garden is the ginkgo, or maidenhair tree – the tallest in the land until a storm took away the top.

[i] 2–3 Bridge Street

▶ Follow the **A1101**, then the **A1122** to Downham Market.

2 Downham Market, Norfolk
There has been a settlement in this area since Roman times. Denver Sluice, 2 miles (3km) away, is where the River Great Ouse and the Old and New Bedford Rivers are regulated in order to prevent flooding. The most interesting building in the town is the Church of St Edmund, with its Early English tower.

▶ Leave Downham Market eastwards to join the **A10** then turn south and follow to Ely.

3 Ely, Cambridgeshire
Ely ('Eel Island') refers to the staple diet of the Saxons who once lived here. The Fens cathedral city is still a small market centre with ancient buildings and medieval gateways but has a busy quayside. It was founded as a religious community in the 7th century, and during the Norman Invasion was the centre of Anglo-Saxon resis-

tance under Hereward the Wake. Ely also has a parish church, St Mary's, and the vicarage was the home of Oliver Cromwell for 11 years. Nine hundred-year-old Ely Cathedral's greatest glory is its unique octagon, designed by Alan de Walsingham after the earlier tower collapsed in 1322.

[i] Oliver Cromwell's House, 29 St Mary's Street

▶ Leave Ely on the **B1382** through Prickwillow, then take the **A1101** to Kennyhill, turning left on to an unclassified road to Lakenheath. Pick up the **B1112** as far as Hockwold cum Wilton, and finally another unclassified road to Weeting.

4 Weeting, Norfolk
Weeting is a good centre for exploring Breckland, a region of heathland that straddles the Suffolk and Norfolk border. Grime's Graves are found here and Thetford Forest Park is at Santon Downham. There are deer and red squirrels in the forest, and a rich variety of trees. Weeting Heath is the place to see the classic Breckland bird, the stone curlew.

FOR HISTORY BUFFS

Grime's Graves, named after the Anglo-Saxon god Grim, are situated on a patch of common land in Breckland. These grassy hollows are about 4,000 years old, and this is the largest known group of flint mines in Britain. You can climb down one on an iron ladder to see where the miners worked with wooden tools or deer antlers.

▶ Follow an unclassified road and the **A1065** to Brandon, then the **B1107** to Thetford.

5 Thetford, Norfolk
Formerly the capital of the region, Thetford is a cathedral city and contained as many as five monasteries. Some of the oldest fragments are the remains

A lone windmill stands sentinel in the Fens

of the 12th-century Cluniac priory, Castle Hill, the site of Iron Age earthworks, and a Norman castle mound. You should find time to visit Euston Hall, the 18th-century home of the Duke and Duchess of Grafton, which has fine paintings by Stubbs, Van Dyck and Lely. The 15th-century timber-framed Ancient House Museum has beautifully carved beam ceilings and exhibits on local history.

▶ *Leave Thetford on the A1075 heading north to Dereham.*

6 Dereham, Norfolk
St Withburga founded a nunnery here in the 7th century, and St Withburga's Well is in the churchyard of St Nicholas's Church. The town has some fine Georgian buildings, and Bishop Bonner's Cottage has attractive pargeting.

At Gressenhall, on the road north to Fakenham, is the Norfolk Rural Life Museum and Union Farm, which has rare breeds of sheep, cattle, pigs and poultry, and an interesting museum on farming.

▶ *Continue north on the B1110, then the B1146 to Fakenham.*

7 Fakenham, Norfolk
Fakenham is a delightful small market town which dates from Saxon times. Its parish church has a commanding 15th-century tower, and the two old coaching inns in the Market Place have traces of earlier architecture behind their Georgian façades. The fascinating Gas Museum, which is open on occasional days throughout the summer, explains how gas was made and contains the only complete gasworks in England.

Just a mile away is the Pensthorpe Waterfowl Park, which houses a large selection of birds, and aims to protect waterfowl and wetland habitats.

ℹ️ *Red Lion House, Market Place*

▶ *Cross the A148 and follow an unclassified road to Houghton St Giles.*

8 Houghton St Giles, Norfolk
The attractive village of Houghton St Giles has old links with Walsingham, including a

❾ Wells-next-the-Sea, Norfolk

The Wells and Walsingham Light Railway runs through 4 miles (6km) of countryside to the famous pilgrimage villages of Walsingham, and is the longest 10¼-inch (26cm) narrow-gauge steam railway in the world.

The town of Wells still has many of its 18th- and 19th-century houses, set in a network of alleys and yards near the small quay, which first started trading in wool over 600 years ago.

[i] *Staithe Street*

BACK TO NATURE

East of Wells-next-the-Sea, much of the coastline is owned by the National Trust, and there are several miles of nature reserves.

The sand and shingle spit of Blakeney Point can be reached by foot from Cley, or by boat from Blakeney or Morston Quay. Common and sandwich terns nest on the spit, together with waders such as ringed plover and oystercatcher, and several species of duck.

The Norfolk Naturalists' Trust reserve at Cley has hides overlooking pools and reedbeds. Bitterns, spoonbills, bearded tits and grey herons are regularly seen and a wide range of waders can be found during migration times.

▶ *Follow the A149 west for 2 miles (3km) to Holkham.*

❿ Holkham, Norfolk

In a beautiful deer park with a lake landscaped by Capability Brown, is the 18th-century mansion of Holkham Hall, just south of the village of Holkham. Its art collection includes work by Rubens, Van Dyck and Gainsborough and there is an amazing marble hall. In the Bygones Collection, over 4,000 items have been assembled from kitchens, dairies and cars.

▶ *Continue further along the A149, then left on to the B1155 to Burnham Market.*

⓫ Burnham Market, Norfolk

Burnham Market is the main village in a group of seven Burnhams, clustered closely together, and has a handsome, wide village green surrounded by elegant 18th-century houses. The Burnhams were made famous by Horatio Nelson, who probably learned to sail on the muddy creeks of the coast before being sent away to sea at the age of 12. He was born in 1758 at Burnham Thorpe, where his father was the rector, and the lectern in the church is made from timbers from his ship, the *Victory*.

▶ *Return to the A149 for 12 miles (19km) to Hunstanton.*

⓬ Hunstanton, Norfolk

Hunstanton developed as a seaside resort in the 19th century, and is famous for its red-and-white striped chalk cliffs and excellent beaches. At the Sea Life Centre fish, seals

Bishop Bonner's Cottage at Dereham

---

small chapel on the old Walsingham Way, known as the Slipper Chapel because pilgrims would remove their shoes before completing their journey barefoot to Little Walsingham, which has been a Christian shrine since 1061. The Anglican Shrine and the Roman Catholic Shrine are at either end of the Holy Mile, and a ruined abbey stands in pleasant gardens. Great Walsingham, just a few minutes along the unclassified road from Little Walsingham, is noted for its textile centre, where you can watch the screen-printing process.

[i] *Shire Hall Museum, Common Place, Little Walsingham*

▶ *Return to the unclassified road from Great Walsingham and follow to Wells-next-the-Sea.*

FOR CHILDREN

Hunstanton is an ideal place for children, with its sandy beach, rock pools and endless entertainment; and the Oasis all-weather leisure centre offers swirl pools, a toddlers' pool and a variety of indoor sports.

SPECIAL TO...

Hunstanton cliffs were laid down on the bed of the sea between 135 and 70 million years ago, in the Cretaceous period. Different colours mark the layers of rock. The carstone is reddish or brown, and is often used locally as a building stone; and most of the chalk is white. It is in the chalk that fossils are found: bivalves similar to those found on the beach today, as well as brachiopods, belemnites and ammonites.

Queen Victoria for the Prince of Wales in 1862. The extensive grounds contain the parish Church of St Mary Magdalene, a museum, nature trails and an adventure playground.

A former royal residence can be seen at Castle Rising, where the splendid Norman castle was built in the 12th century for the Earls of Sussex but subsequently belonged to the Earls of Norfolk. Set within huge earthworks, the shell of the Great Hall is still impressive.

▶ *Take the* **B1439** *back to rejoin the* **A149**, *then an unclassified road back to King's Lynn.*

The seaside resort of Hunstanton
Opposite: fine house in Lavenham

and crabs are all around as you walk through varied marine settings. England's only lavender farm, Norfolk Lavender, is just south of town, at Heacham. A national collection of lavender plants is assembled here, and there is a herb garden with over 50 varieties of culinary and decorative plants.

ⓘ *The Green*

▶ *Head south on the* **A149**, *then the* **B1440** *from Dersingham to Sandringham, and further south to Castle Rising.*

RECOMMENDED WALKS

Both the Norfolk Coastal Path and the Peddar's Way can be walked from Hunstanton, the one along the coast and the other through the heart of rural west Norfolk. Wherever you are on this tour of west Norfolk you will find a selection of gentle walks along rivers, across heathland, in the forests or along the coast.

�13 **Sandringham,** Norfolk
The royal estate of Sandringham covers 20,000 acres (8,094 hectares) and was bought by

SCENIC ROUTES

Driving anywhere near Ely, the tower of the cathedral will draw you towards it like a magnet.
Near Thetford, dark forests dominate the scene, but there are still a few patches of open heathland.

East Anglia's
Churches & Colleges

Thatch, stone and brick are major features of the villages in this rural area, but dominating the countryside are the churches and their spires. This gentle landscape, covered with colourful fields of rape in spring and wheat in summer, provided the inspiration for Constable's paintings and Brooke's poetry.

2 DAYS • 143 MILES • 229KM

ITINERARY		
IPSWICH	▶	**East Bergholt** (12m-19km)
EAST BERGHOLT	▶	**Sudbury** (15m-24km)
SUDBURY	▶	**Castle Hedingham** (7m-11km)
CASTLE HEDINGHAM	▶	**Finchingfield** (9m-14km)
FINCHINGFIELD	▶	**Thaxted** (7m-11km)
THAXTED	▶	**Saffron Walden** (7m-11km)
SAFFRON WALDEN	▶	**Duxford** (7m-11km)
DUXFORD	▶	**Grantchester** (8m-13km)
GRANTCHESTER	▶	**Cambridge** (3m-5km)
CAMBRIDGE	▶	**Lode** (6m-10km)
LODE	▶	**Newmarket** (9m-14km)
NEWMARKET	▶	**Clare** (19m-31km)
CLARE	▶	**Long Melford** (6m-10km)
LONG MELFORD	▶	**Lavenham** (5m-8km)
LAVENHAM	▶	**Hadleigh** (14m-23km)
HADLEIGH	▶	**Ipswich** (9m-14km)

i *St Stephen's Church, St Stephen's Lane, Ipswich*

▶ *Take the A137 from Ipswich, then right on to the B1070 shortly after Brantham and finally an unclassified road via Flatford to East Bergholt.*

❶ East Bergholt, Suffolk
The artist John Constable was born here in 1776 and said of the area: 'These scenes made me a painter'. Clustered round the 15th-century Church of St Mary, with its unfinished tower and remarkable bell house, are Elizabethan cottages set in beautiful gardens. Flatford Mill is now used as a Field Study Centre. Willy Lott's Cottage, an early 18th-century mill-house which appears in Constable's *The Hay Wain*, still stands beside the mill stream.

Thaxted's 15th-century timbered guild house

SPECIAL TO...

Dedham, near East Bergholt, is proud of its connections with the landscape artist John Constable, who went to school here. The beautiful scenery of Dedham Vale is at the heart of the area now known as Constable Country. There is an Art and Craft Centre on three floors of a converted congregational church, and prints, paintings and various crafts are on display and for sale. There is also a toy museum.

RECOMMENDED WALKS

From Flatford Mill there are several beautiful walks in Constable Country. Try the walk to Dedham Mill, a well-known scene to Constable enthusiasts, and only requiring 2 miles (3km) of easy walking.

▶ *Leave on an unclassified road, and cross the A12 on to the B1068 and A134 to Sudbury.*

❷ Sudbury, Suffolk
Charles Dickens used this ancient cloth and market town on the River Stour as the model for 'Eatanswill' in *The Pickwick Papers*. There is a bronze statue to Thomas Gainsborough, the artist, who was born here in 1727, in an elegant Georgian town house now containing many of his paintings. The town was formerly a river port, and one of the old warehouses has been turned into the Quay Theatre. St Peter's Church has fine painted screen panels and a splendid piece of 15th-century embroidery on velvet, the 'Alderman's Pall'.

i *Sudbury Town Hall, Market Hill*

▶ *Leave Sudbury on the A131, turning right on to the B1058 to Castle Hedingham.*

❸ Castle Hedingham, Essex
The De Vere family, Earls of Oxford, built Hedingham Castle on the hilltop in about 1140, and the banqueting hall with its minstrel gallery still survives. The keep overlooks medieval houses, which cluster round the Norman Church of St Nicholas. There are many reminders of the town's prosperous days in the 15th-century Moot Hall and

the elegant Georgian houses of the wealthy wool merchants. Just outside the village is the Colne Valley Railway, where there are restored steam engines and carriages.

▶ *Join the A604 south for a short distance, then take unclassified roads on the right via Wethersfield, then right on to the B1053 to Finchingfield.*

❹ Finchingfield, Essex
Finchingfield's charm has survived in spite of its great popularity. One of its many fine buildings is the gabled and barge-boarded Hill House, set opposite a row of 16th-century cottages and Georgian houses. The Church of St John the Baptist has a Norman tower and Georgian-style bell-cote.

▶ *Continue on the B1053 to Great Sampford, then turn left on to the B1051 to Thaxted.*

❺ Thaxted, Essex
Thaxted's 14th-century, cathedral-like flint church is one of the largest in Essex, with a thin, graceful spire rising 181 feet (55m). Another tall building, the

tower windmill, was built in 1804, and now houses a small rural museum. The 15th-century Guildhall is built of local wood and plaster, on a foundation of flint. Composer Gustav Holst once lived in Thaxted, and Sir John Betjeman wrote of it: 'There are few places in England to equal the beauty, compactness and juxtaposition of medieval and Georgian architecture'.

▶ *Head northwest on the **B184** to Saffron Walden.*

6 **Saffron Walden,** Essex
Saffron Walden's flint church rivals that of Thaxted in magnificence and size; 200 feet (61m) long and nearly as high. Its spire was added in 1831. Wool was a major industry here, but the town also prospered from growing saffron for medicine and dyes. There are delightful old narrow streets to explore, and the museum has exhibitions of furniture, ceramics and toys. Jacobean Audley End House, near by, is in grounds landscaped by Capability Brown. Elizabeth I stayed here with the poet Sir

Philip Sidney, in 1578, and the rooms have been laid out to give a 'lived in' feeling.

[i] *1 Market Place*

FOR CHILDREN

Linton Zoo, north of Saffron Walden on the B1052, was created by the Simmons family and opened in 1972. This is the Cambridgeshire Wildlife Breeding Centre, which focuses on conservation and education. Set in beautiful gardens, the centre has lions, pumas, snakes, owls, spiders and many others, as well as a children's play area.

▶ *Continue on the **B184** taking the **A1301** at **M11** junction and, in a short distance, turn left on to an unclassified road through Hinxton to Duxford.*

7 **Duxford,** Cambridgeshire
Duxford is a small village with a low, squat church and attractive thatched pub, the John Barley Corn. It is famous for the Imperial War Museum at

Duxford Airfield, a former Battle of Britain fighter station.

▶ *Continue along unclassified roads through Little Shelford to Great Shelford, then left on to the **A1301** and finally left on to unclassified roads again to Grantchester.*

8 **Grantchester,** Cambridgeshire
Grantchester was immortalised in a poem written by Rupert Brooke in 1912 about the Old Vicarage, where he lived. The village has a characteristic low church, with a small spire protruding.

▶ *Head north to Cambridge.*

9 **Cambridge,** Cambridgeshire
Cambridge became famous as a seat of learning when the University was established early in the 13th century, and its elegant colleges and chapels of mellow stone give this beautiful city a stately air. But this is an important market centre and a

Duxford Imperial War Museum

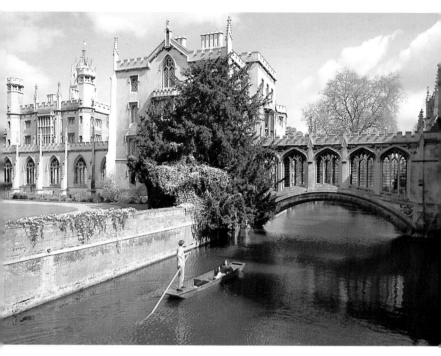

Punting along the River Cam under the Bridge of Sighs

leader in high technology industries, as well as a university city, and there are many fine buildings and riverside parklands. King's College Chapel and the Bridge of Sighs are musts for all visitors, and in summer you can punt along the River Cam that flows around the city. No visit would be complete without seeing the Fitzwilliam Museum, with its priceless collections of porcelain, antiquities, paintings and armour.

BACK TO NATURE

The Fowlmere RSPB Reserve lies just off the Royston to Cambridge road (A10) near the village of Fowlmere. It comprises an area of reed-bed with open water, and attracts breeding birds including sedge and reed warblers. In the winter, look for water rails, kingfishers and bearded tits.

$\boxed{i}$ *Wheeler Street*

▶ *Take the A1303 east, then turn north on to the B1102 to Lode.*

10 Lode, Cambridgeshire
Lode is famous for the Augustinian priory known as Anglesey Abbey, founded in the 12th century and converted into a house in about 1600. The estate was bought by Huttleston Broughton, who created 100 acres (40 hectares) of gardens. A vast collection of paintings, sculpture and *objets d'art* has been assembled inside amid sumptuous furnishings. Lode Watermill, across the lode, or canal, that skirts the gardens, has been restored and grinds corn on the first Sunday of each month.

▶ *From Lode follow the B1102 to Swaffham Bulbeck, then follow an unclassified road to the A1303 to Newmarket.*

11 Newmarket, Suffolk
Newmarket has been the headquarters of horse-racing in Britain since the 17th century, and the National Stud and many training stables are located on the surrounding heath. Guided tours of the Stud, where you can see some of racing's superstars, are possible by appointment. The National Horse Racing Museum takes you back to the origins of racing.

The famous Rowley Mile is named after a horse owned by Charles II, and a former coaching inn called the Rutland Arms, parts of which date back to his day, has kept some of its rooms in the style of the 1850s.

▶ *Follow the B1063 for 17 miles (27km) to Clare, then eastwards to Cavendish along the A1092.*

12 Clare, Suffolk
This ancient little market town has excellent examples of pargeting – fine plasterwork – such as those seen on the 15th-century Priest's House or Ancient House, now the local museum. The church, which has a most unusual design, is well

Newmarket: the headquarters of horse-racing in Britain

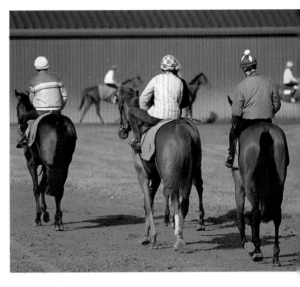

worth visiting. Norman Clare Castle was built in 1090 and stands high on a 100-foot (30m) mound.

At Clare Castle Country Park there is a butterfly garden, and you can take a pleasant walk along the old railway track. Three miles (5km) east is Cavendish, the ancestral village of the Dukes of Devonshire, and its attractions include a 16th-century farmhouse near the church, and philanthropist Sue Ryder's 16th-century rectory, which contains memorabilia and photographs explaining the origins and aims of her work.

▶ *Continue east on the **A1092**, then turn south on to the A134 to Long Melford.*

13 Long Melford, Suffolk
Long Melford is another of Suffolk's lovely villages, with fine wool merchants' houses. At the end of the mile-long main street is the Church of the Holy Trinity, one of the finest in the country, exhibiting a superb display of flushwork – ornate decoration in flint. The village green is overlooked by Elizabethan Melford Hall, a turreted Tudor mansion with tall chimneys.

One mile (1.6km) north of the village is Kentwell Hall (National Trust), a moated Elizabethan mansion with a brickpaved mosaic maze in the shape of a Tudor rose.

▶ *Follow unclassified roads northeast for 5 miles (8km) to Lavenham.*

14 Lavenham, Suffolk
Lavenham's remarkable church, the Church of St Peter and St Paul, has a flint tower 140 feet (43m) high, and the Guildhall, an early 16th-century timber-framed building, contains a display of local history. The Swan Inn is a famous hostelry which has been carefully preserved. Some of the black-

and-white buildings have been painted pink to add to the colour of this pretty village.

ℹ️ *Lady Street*

RECOMMENDED WALKS

The route from Lavenham to Long Melford, along a disused railway line, gives a gentle 3-mile (5km) walk between two of Suffolk's most appealing small towns.

FOR HISTORY BUFFS

Many of the local towns and villages were important for wool, but the most famous was probably Lavenham. In the time of Henry VIII it was one of the wealthiest towns in England, and the main source of this wealth was wool, yarn and various kinds of cloth. The town has not changed much since then: there are still half-timbered houses which lean over the narrow streets. Over 300 of the buildings are listed for architectural or archaeological interest.

▶ *Follow the **A1141**, turning right to pass through Kersey, then on to Hadleigh.*

15 Hadleigh, Suffolk
Before reaching Hadleigh, enjoy the rural charm of Kersey, with its old priory, ducks paddling in the ford and thatched cottages. In Hadleigh itself, the Guildhall and Deanery tower are listed buildings dating from the 15th century. Interesting marks on the side of the 1813 Corn Exchange show where the brickwork was used by schoolchildren for sharpening their slate pencils as they went to school.

ℹ️ *Toppesfield Hall*

▶ *Return to Ipswich on the A1071.*

SCENIC ROUTES

The Dick Turpin Heritage Route passes through Saffron Walden and Thaxted, as well as other attractive villages, historic sites and open countryside. On the approach to Thaxted on the B1051, the church and the windmill add variety to the rural charm of the rich farmland.

Cotswold
Wool & Stone

This is mainly a circuit of Cotswold countryside – a landscape of stone walls surrounding fertile fields and distinctive village architecture. The villages contain many fine churches, but the best known structure is the cross in the centre of Banbury. The family homes of two great men can be seen; one Englishman in Blenheim and one American in Sulgrave.

2 DAYS • 99 MILES • 159KM

i *The Old School, Gloucester Green, Oxford*

▶ *Leave Oxford on the **A44** and turn left along an unclassified road towards Cassington. Turn right to Bladon on the **A4095**, then left on the **A44** to Woodstock.*

❶ Woodstock, Oxfordshire

You can stop off in Bladon, to visit the churchyard where Sir Winston Churchill and his wife and parents are buried, before continuing along the road to Blenheim, where he was born. Blenheim Palace was given to the Marlborough family by Queen Anne as a reward for the 1st Duke of Marlborough's victory over the French at Blenheim in 1704. Just outside the park is the town of Woodstock, with its mellow stone buildings. Kings of England came here for the excellent hunting in the Forest of Wychwood, but modern visitors have gentler interests. A quiet hour can be spent in the Oxfordshire County Museum, in the town centre, where the history of the people and the changing landscape is conveyed in exhibitions ranging from the Stone Age to the present time.

BACK TO NATURE

The grounds of Blenheim Palace, at Woodstock, were landscaped by Capability Brown and comprise rolling, formal parkland and an attractive lake. This harbours breeding dragonflies and is home to Canada geese, mute swans, great crested grebes and kingfishers. In the winter months, look for roaming flocks of siskins, redpolls and long tailed tits in the birch trees.

i *Park Street*

▶ *From Woodstock take the **A44** turning left on to the **B4437** to Charlbury and then the **B4026** to Chipping Norton.*

❷ Chipping Norton, Oxfordshire

Gateway to the Cotswolds and historic market town, this was the market for the sheep farmers of the area, and the wide main street is a relic of those days (the name 'chipping' means market). There are many fine old stone buildings, including the church, market hall, pubs and big houses, but it is the fine wool church which dominates the town, one of over 40 in the Cotswolds. Paid for by the proceeds from sheep farming, it is mainly 14th- and 15th-century, but much of its stonework has been restored. Another of the town's landmarks is the chimney of Bliss Tweed Mill which is an important reminder of local history.

i *The Guildhall*

▶ *Take the **B4026**, then go north along the **A3400** for just over a mile (1.6km) and turn left along an unclassified road signed Little Rollright.*

❸ Rollright Stones, Oxfordshire

This Bronze Age circle, which dates from earlier than 1000 BC, was nearly as important as Stonehenge in the neolithic period. Nicknamed the 'King's Men', it measures a full 100 feet (30m) across. Over the road is the King Stone, a monolith, and near by, just along the road, is the group of stones called the Whispering Knights, at the site of a prehistoric burial chamber. The surrounding countryside is

Bliss Tweed Mill, now flats, near the old wool town of Chipping Norton

Broughton Castle is a fine example of a gracious Elizabethan Manor

patterned with stone walls of weathered limestone.

▶ *Return to the **A3400** and turn south before branching left on to the **A361**, then turn left in Bloxham along unclassified roads to Broughton.*

FOR CHILDREN

Just before reaching Bloxham, on the road from Rollright to Broughton, you will pass the Wigginton Heath Water Fowl Sanctuary. Conservation is the main aim, with flowers, goats, sheep, lambs and other animals, as well as a bewildering assortment of birds. Various ducks, geese, black swans, owls, doves and peacocks can all be seen at very close quarters. There is also a nature trail and an adventure playground.

4 **Broughton,** Oxfordshire

Broughton Castle is a fortified manor rather than a castle, turned into an Elizabethan house of style by the Fiennes family in about 1600. Surrounded by a great moat lake, it is set in gorgeous parkland, and has a stone church near by. The present owners, Lord and Lady Saye and Sele, are descendants of the family that has lived here for centuries. Celia Fiennes, the 17th-century traveller and diarist, was a member of this family. William de Wykeham, founder of Winchester School and New College, Oxford, acquired the manor and converted the manor house into a castle. The medieval Great Hall is the most impressive room, and suits of armour from the Civil War are on show.

▶ *Drive 3 miles (5km) east along the **B4035** to Banbury.*

5 **Banbury,** Oxfordshire

Banbury is a town of charm and character, with its interesting buildings and narrow medieval streets. Famous for the nursery rhyme 'Ride a cock horse to Banbury Cross', the town is also known for its spice cakes, which have been made here since the 16th century. The unusual church with its round tower replaced an older one demolished in the 18th century. There is still a weekly street market, which has been held regularly for over 800 years, and there used to be a livestock market, too, but nowadays the animals are taken to a permanent site on the edge of town, Europe's largest cattle market.

[i] *Banbury Museum, 8 Horsefair*

FOR HISTORY BUFFS

Banbury's wool industry was helped by the opening of the Oxford Canal in 1790, connecting Banbury with the Midland coalfields and markets in London. The narrow boats on the canals used to be pulled by horses which walked along the towpath, and a family would live permanently on the boat.

RECOMMENDED WALKS

Along the Oxford Canal, near Banbury, is the delightful 9-mile (14km) Banbury circuit, which takes in the villages of Wroxton with its duckpond, Horley, Hornton, Alkerton, an old Saxon village with ironstone houses, Shennington and Balscott.

▶ *Take the unclassified road through Helmdon, heading south to Brackley to join the A43, then shortly right on to the B4031 to Aynho.*

7 Aynho, Northamptonshire
This limestone village contains apricot trees from which, legend has it, fruit was paid as a toll to the Cartwrights, Lords of the Manor. They lived in the mansion in Aynhoe Park, and there are several memorials to them, including a Victorian marble cross in the church.

▶ *From Aynho go west along the B4031 to Deddington.*

8 Deddington, Oxfordshire
Dominating this village, which is built out of the honey-coloured local stone, is the church, with each of its eight pinnacles topped with gilded vanes. Adjacent Castle House was formerly the rectory, and parts of the building date from the 14th century. The area has many links with the days of the Civil War, and Charles I is believed to have slept at the 16th-century Castle Farm near by.

▶ *Drive southwards for 5 miles (8km) along the A4260 and then left on to an unclassified road to Steeple Aston.*

9 Steeple Aston,
Oxfordshire
Steeple Aston was winner of the Oxfordshire Best Kept Village Award in 1981 and 1983, and is still an eye-catching village. The village inn, Hopcroft's Holt, had associations with Claude Duval, a French highwayman who worked in these parts. Just beyond Steeple Aston is the Jacobean mansion of Rousham House, built by Sir Robert Dormer in 1635 and still owned by the same family. William Kent improved the house in the 18th century by adding the wings and stable block. In the magnificent garden, the complete Kent layout has survived. There is a fine herd of rare Long Horn cattle in the

park, and you should be sure not to miss the walled garden.

▶ *Another unclassified road leads south on to the B4030 in turn leading to the A4095 for the 9 miles (14km) to Bicester.*

10 Bicester, Oxfordshire
Little can be seen of the Roman town at Alchester, to the south of Bicester, but excavations show that people lived here from about the middle of the 1st century AD until the late Roman period. Bicester itself is a market town with many old streets. Its church contains elements of a 13th-century building, and there was once a 12th-century priory near by.

▶ *Take the A41 following the line of an old Roman road and then the B4011 towards Thame before turning sharp right to Boarstall.*

11 Boarstall, Buckinghamshire
This tiny hamlet is the location of Boarstall Tower, an amazing stone gatehouse which was originally part of a massive fortified house. It dates from the 14th century and is now looked after by the National Trust, who also own Boarstall Duck Decoy. This 18th-century decoy is in 13 acres (5 hectares) of natural old woodland. Attractions include a small exhibition hall, nature trail and bird hide.

▶ *Take unclassified roads via Horton-cum-Studley along the edge of Otmoor for the return to Oxford.*

SPECIAL TO...

Banbury's cross, in Horsefair, was built in 1859 to commemorate the marriage of Victoria, Princess Royal, and the Crown Prince of Prussia. Its design is based on the Eleanor Crosses, built in the 13th century to mark the resting stages of Queen Eleanor's funeral cortège *en route* to London for burial.

▶ *Head east along the A422. After 2 miles (3km) turn left on to the B4525, then to the unclassified road to Sulgrave.*

6 Sulgrave,
Northamptonshire
The old manor in this attractive stone village was the home of ancestors of George Washington from 1539 to 1659, having been bought by Lawrence Washington, wool merchant and twice Mayor of Northampton. Not to be missed is the family coat of arms with its stars and stripes carved above the entrance porch, and the most treasured possession inside is an original oil painting of George Washington.

SCENIC ROUTES

The A44 from Woodstock to Chipping Norton gives excellent views across rolling countryside. Bloxham and the village of South Newington show Cotswold settlements at their best, especially in the summer, and the skyline of Oxford, with its impressive array of dreaming spires, is unique.

The Rural
Heart of England

Across the Severn plain, through **2 DAYS • 128 MILES • 207KM** a gap in the Malvern Hills and into the Avon valley, this route eventually climbs up on to the hills of the Cotswolds, where stone-built villages have become part of the countryside.

ITINERARY

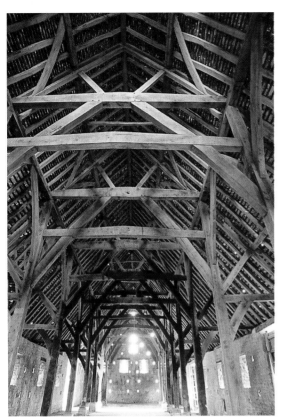

Bredon's medieval tithe barn

[i] 28 Southgate Street, Gloucester

BACK TO NATURE

The Wildfowl Trust reserve at Slimbridge, southwest of Gloucester off the A38, is known the world over for its impressive collection of wildfowl, at their most spectacular in late winter and early spring when the males are in full breeding plumage.

▶ Take the **A417** for 17 miles (27km) to Ledbury.

❶ Ledbury, Hereford and Worcester

The unspoilt market town of Ledbury, with its half-timbered buildings, has many literary links: Robert Browning and William Wordsworth used to visit, and John Masefield was born here. Elizabeth Barrett Browning spent her childhood at Hope End, just out of town, and her father lies buried in the north aisle of St Michael's Church. One of the most attractive buildings is the 16th-century Feathers Inn, and Ledbury Park is the house Prince Rupert used as his headquarters during the Civil War. Nineteenth-century Eastnor Castle, with its impressive interior is surrounded by a beautiful park.

[i] 3 The Homend

▶ Follow the **A449** through Wynds Gap and Malvern Wells to Great Malvern, 8 miles (13km).

❷ Great Malvern, Hereford and Worcester

Pure spring water from the Malvern Hills made this a popular spa town in Victorian days. A steep flight of steps by the Mount Pleasant Hotel leads up to St Anne's Well, the source of this water. The town is centred round its greatest treasure, the Priory Church of St Mary and St Michael, which contains exquisite 15th- and 16th-century stained glass and beautiful tiles. Malvern Museum portrays the town through the ages, and there is an elegant Victorian bandstand where bands play on Sunday afternoons in summer.

[i] 21 Church Street

▶ Take the **B4211** to Upton upon Severn, turning left on to the **A4104**, and in 1 mile (1.6km) on to the **A38** to Tewkesbury.

❸ Tewkesbury, Gloucestershire

Almost all Tewkesbury's buildings are old timber-framed structures, notably the Bell Inn, and the Royal Hop Pole Inn is mentioned in *The Pickwick Papers* by Charles Dickens. Tewkesbury Abbey is one of the finest Norman abbeys in the country and contains several medieval stained-glass windows.

[i] 64 Barton Street

▶ Return on the **A38** for a short distance, then take the **B4080** to Bredon.

❹ Bredon, Hereford and Worcester

Bredon, alongside the River Avon, at the foot of Bredon Hill, is a picturebook village. Its impressive Norman church has a graceful spire which soars 160 feet (48m) high, and the tithe barn dates from the 14th century. A mile (1.6km) east is the village of Kemerton, with its fine church. Overbury Park, just outside the village, leads to Bredon Hill, which rises to 961 feet (293m). It has a fine Gothic folly on its slopes and the remains of prehistoric and Roman earthworks on its summit.

▶ *Continue along an unclassified road through Kemerton and Beckford, then take the A46 to Evesham.*

5 Evesham, Hereford and Worcester

Evesham is a market town in the heart of the Vale of Evesham, noted for its fruit blossom in spring. A 15th-century half-timbered gateway in the market-place is one of the few remains of Evesham Abbey.

At the centre of town is the 110-foot (33m) high Bell Tower, which was built in 1539. There are two fine churches: 12th-century All Saints' Church and the Church of St Lawrence. A plaque near the river marks the burial spot of Simon de Montfort, the 'father of the English parliament', who led barons in revolt against Henry III and was killed at the Battle of Evesham in 1265.

[i] *The Almonry, Abbey Gate*

▶ *Take the B4088 and an unclassified road to Alcester.*

6 Alcester, Warwickshire

Pronounced 'Olster', this former Roman town contains many old streets and houses, notably Malt

Mill Lane, which is lined with ancient houses. Coughton Court, 2 miles (3km) to the north, is the family home of the Throckmortons, who were implicated in the Gunpowder Plot to blow up Parliament in 1605. The house contains the 'Throckmorton coat', which was made in 1811 to prove that it was possible to take the wool off a sheep and produce a coat from it in one day! Southwest of town is Ragley Hall, a Jacobean mansion whose great hall is decorated with exquisite rococo plaster-work.

▶ *Follow the B4089, then unclassified roads east to Wilmcote.*

7 Wilmcote, Warwickshire

This sprawling village is best known for the lovely timbered farmhouse which was the home of Mary Arden, Shakespeare's mother. It is now a museum of furniture and the farm buildings contain exhibitions of agricultural implements and country bygones, including man traps

The unpretentious simplicity of Mary Arden's home, Wilmcote

which were used to catch poachers.

▶ *Continue along the unclassified road, then the A3400 for 3 miles (5km) to Stratford-upon-Avon.*

8 Stratford-upon-Avon, Warwickshire

Stratford has retained its role as a market town despite being one of the world's most famous tourist centres. Shakespeare's Birthplace in Henley Street is now a museum and contains exhibits about the poet's life. Stratford is full of interesting places to visit, including the Royal Shakespeare Company Collection. One of the most ornate timbered houses is Harvard House, the former home of the mother of John Harvard, who founded Harvard University in the US. In a house in Greenhill Street, dating from Shakespeares' days, is the Teddy Bear Museum, which will appeal to all ages.

[i] *Bridgefoot*

SPECIAL TO...

With the exception of London, Shakespeare's Stratford is probably the best known town in England. A tour of selected locations can take you through his life, starting with his birth-place in Henley Street, then on to the 15th-century half-timbered Grammar School in Church Street, which he attended.

Most famous of all is Anne Hathaway's cottage, home of the woman he was to marry. New Place, on Chapel Street, was the site of his last home.

▶ *Leave Stratford, going west along the B439 for 4 miles (6km) before turning south along unclassified roads through Welford-on-Avon and Long Marston to the B4632. Turn right and soon left on to the B4081 to Chipping Campden.*

9 Chipping Campden, Gloucestershire

Wool made this town rich, and it retains a wealth of beautiful architecture such as the Jacobean Market Hall in the

Anne Hathaway's House, Shottery, where she lived before her marriage to William Shakespeare

High Street which was built in 1627, and the Woolstaplers' Hall. The Church of St James is one of the most splendid Cotswold churches. Hidcote Manor Garden, to the northeast has six gardens with winter borders, camellia corners, terraces and walks.

⌐i⌐ *2 Rosery Court,*
High Street

▶ *Take the B4081 and the A44 through Broadway, then the B4632 and a minor road to Buckland.*

10 Buckland, Gloucestershire
Buckland is a quiet village nestling at the foot of the Cotswolds, whose rectory is England's oldest and most complete medieval parsonage. Further along the B4632 is the

GWR Steam Railway Centre at Toddington, where you can make a 6-mile (9km) round trip.

Leave the B4632 to visit Hailes Abbey, where the old Cistercian ruins stand alongside the 12th-century parish church. In 1270, a small jar of blood, supposedly that of Christ, was given to the abbey, and brought it much fame as a centre of pilgrimage.

FOR CHILDREN

Broadway Tower Country Park, to the east of Buckland, is an ideal place to spend the day with the family. The late 18th-century mock castle has an observation room and telescope giving views over 12 counties. Other attractions include an educational display of local geology, an adventure playground, and a collection of rare animals.

▶ *Follow the unclassified road to Winchcombe, a distance of 8 miles (13km).*

11 Winchcombe,
Gloucestershire
This attractive town was once the capital of the Kingdom of Mercia. Its abbey, founded in 797, was destroyed during the Dissolution, but the site has been excavated. The Railway Museum has many relics of the steam age, and the town hall houses the Folk Museum and a Police Museum.

Sudeley Castle, reached through the village, was once the house of Catherine Parr, the last of Henry VIII's wives. The magnificent gardens have been developed and renovated.

Just east of town on the B4632, at the top of the hill at Cleeve Hill, are the remnants of a settlement and earthworks, and much good walking, including the Cotswold Way, a long distance footpath. Cleeve Cloud,

1031 feet (314m), is one of the highest points in the Cotswolds, and the views from its summit are quite spectacular.

FOR HISTORY BUFFS

From Winchcombe you can drive to within ¼ mile (1km) of the Bronze Age ancient long barrow at Belas Knap on its hilltop site, probably the finest example of a false-entrance longbarrow in the Cotswolds. When it was excavated 36 skeletons were found in 10 separate chambers.

ⓘ *Town Hall, High Street*

▶ *Continue along the B4632 to Cheltenham.*

🔟 Cheltenham,
Gloucestershire

Cheltenham started life as a typical Cotswold village, but the discovery of a mineral spring in 1718 turned it into a fashionable spa. The Promenade, a wide street with Regency houses, has been described as the most

Below: Hailes Abbey, Winchcombe
Right: Bridgnorth open-air market

beautiful thoroughfare in Britain. The famous Pittville Pump Room, with its colonnade and dome, is a masterpiece of 19th-century Greek revival. There are many other old buildings and museums worth visiting, such as the Holst Birthplace Museum which contains rooms with period furnishing. The town is famous for its two schools, the College for Boys and Cheltenham Ladies' College.

ⓘ *77 Promenade*

▶ *Take an unclassified road then the A417 south to Birdlip and follow the Stroud road until an unclassified road leads through Cranham and on to the A46 to Painswick.*

🔢 Painswick, Gloucestershire

Painswick is an old wool town with many buildings of note, but is dominated by 15th-century St Mary's Church and its collection of '99' yew trees. Tradition says that only 99 will grow at any one time – the Devil always kills off the 100th. Among the town's many old houses are Court House, with its tall chimneys, and 18th-century Painswick House. South of town a few old

cloth mills have survived on Painswick stream.

ⓘ *Painswick Library, Stroud Road*

▶ *Return to Gloucester on the B4073.*

SCENIC ROUTES

Cotswold villages and towns are all attractive but the view over Cranham from the unclassified road to Painswick is one of the most exciting. The Malvern Hills and the dramatic silhouette of the Herefordshire Beacon (the British Camp) are best seen along the A449 from Ledbury.

RECOMMENDED WALKS

Footpaths on this tour range from very easy gentle strolls to much longer and arduous walks. A climb to the top of the Worcestershire Beacons in the Malverns will give one of the finest views in England, with the green undulations of Hereford to the west and the flatter Severn valley to the east.

Old Volcanoes
& Bridges in
Shropshire

1/2 DAYS • 102 MILES • 164KM

The Welsh border counties are among the greenest parts of Britain. Gentle hills and steep-sided volcanic cones add variety to the scenery. The Severn Valley is the birthplace of the industrial revolution.

ITINERARY		
SHREWSBURY	▶	Acton Burnell (8m-13km)
ACTON BURNELL	▶	Church Stretton (9m-14km)
CHURCH STRETTON	▶	Craven Arms (8m-13km)
CRAVEN ARMS	▶	Ludlow (7m-11km)
LUDLOW	▶	Cleehill (6m-10km)
CLEEHILL	▶	Bewdley (15m-24km)
BEWDLEY	▶	Bridgnorth (14m-23km)
BRIDGNORTH	▶	Shipton (10m-16km)
SHIPTON	▶	Much Wenlock (6m-10km)
MUCH WENLOCK	▶	Ironbridge (4m-6km)
IRONBRIDGE	▶	Wroxeter (10m-16km)
WROXETER	▶	Shrewsbury (5m-8km)

⃞ *The Square, Shrewsbury*

▶ *Take the **A458** as far as the ring road where unclassified roads lead to Cantlop Bridge and Acton Burnell, 8 miles (13km).*

❶ Acton Burnell, Shropshire
On the edge of this picturesque village, with its timber-framed black-and-white cottages and grey-green stone buildings, is a cast-iron bridge, built in 1810 to a design by Thomas Telford. Acton Burnell Castle is a red sandstone ruin, which dates from the 13th century; it is said the first English Parliament met here in 1283. The Church of St Mary is almost entirely 13th-century, apart from its Victorian tower, and contains memorials to the Burnell family who held the manor in 1183. It also houses memorials to the Lees family, who owned the village in the 17th century and who were ancestors of General Robert E Lee, chief commander of the Southern forces in the American Civil war.

▶ *Follow unclassified roads via Frodesley then the **A49** to Church Stretton, 9 miles (14km).*

❷ Church Stretton, Shropshire
Church Stretton is in fact three settlements. All Stretton lies to the north of the main town, and Little Stretton stands 1½ miles (2.5km) south. The town's medieval remains are in the High Street, along with its 18th- and 19th-century buildings. The Church of St Laurence is partly 12th-century Norman with a 14th-century roof. In the south transept is a memorial to Sarah Smith, the Victorian novelist who wrote under the name of Hesba Stretton. The town was popular with Victorians who came to sample its natural spring water.

▶ *Continue south along the **B4370**, joining the **A49** to Craven Arms.*

FOR CHILDREN

Acton Scott Historic Working Farm, near Church Stretton, shows life on a Shropshire farm before the introduction of the internal combustion engine. This is not just a show place but a going concern, and visitors can even lend a helping hand. The farm is stocked with rare breeds – it is one of the few places you can see the Tamworth pig – and has a fish-pool, waymarked nature trail, café and paddocks. Strong boots and warm clothing are recommended.

BACK TO NATURE

The Long Mynd, near Church Stretton, is a rocky plateau covered in moorland. Bracken and bilberry grow on the slopes and boggy areas harbour sundews and butter-worts. The open moors are home to red grouse, with ring ouzels and wheatears favouring rocky outcrops. Bleak and dan-gerous in winter, it is splendid walking country in good weather.

❸ Craven Arms, Shropshire
This small village was originally the hamlet of Newton, but in the 19th century it developed and was named after a coaching inn. Today it is a centre for live-stock auctions, at the foot of Wenlock Edge, a steep outcrop of limestone. Stokesay Castle, ½ mile (1km) along the road, is the best preserved and the oldest example of a fortified manor house in England.

▶ *Keep on with the **A49** a further 7 miles (11km) to Ludlow.*

❹ Ludlow, Shropshire
Ludlow is a pearl in a sea of riches and has been described as 'the perfect historic town', with nearly 500 listed buildings. Two buildings worthy of a visit are

---

Ludlow Castle, which dates from Norman times, and the magnificent sandstone Church of St Laurence. Mainly 15th-century, it is the largest in the county and the ashes of the poet A E Housman lie in its churchyard. Near by are the 17th-century Feathers Hotel and the beautiful black-and-white Reader's House. Ludlow Museum, in Buttercross, tells the story of the town from Norman times, and a major arts festival takes place here in late June and early July.

FOR HISTORY BUFFS

Before Catharine of Aragon married Henry VIII she was his brother's bride. Prince Arthur, the eldest son of Henry VII, brought Catharine to Ludlow Castle and had the gardens designed in a series of walks for her. Arthur died at Ludlow and his younger brother Henry became king.

⃞ *Castle Street*

▶ *Take the **A4117** going east for 6 miles (10km) to Cleehill.*

Reader's House, Ludlow, has a three-storey Jacobean porch

Stokesay Castle is really a fortified manor house

⑤ Cleehill, Shropshire
East of Cleehill, on the A4117, is an AA Viewpoint which offers amazing views over Tenbury and the Teme Valley, towards the hills in the distance. The strange 'golf ball' on 1,750-foot (533m) Titterstone Clee Hill, north of the village, is part of a satellite tracking station. Further along the A4117, running east, is Cleobury Mortimer, with its remarkable twisted wooden church tower. Hugh de Mortimer built a fortress here in 1160 and its earthworks can still be seen near the church.

▶ Follow the **B4363** turning right on to the **B4194** through Wyre Forest to Bewdley.

⑥ Bewdley, Hereford and Worcester
This elegant Georgian town was a major port of England in the 17th and 18th centuries. For many years boats were man-handled up the River Severn by a hardy breed of boatmen called 'bow hauliers'. There are pleasant walks in the Wyre Forest, and the Severn Valley Railway

runs to Bridgnorth through fields and woods. Near by is West Midlands Safari Park, a leisure park with animal reserves and amusements.

BACK TO NATURE

West of Bewdley is Wyre Forest, all that remains of a vast royal hunting forest mentioned in the Domesday Book. It is an area of mixed heath, scrub and oak woodland, with plantations of Douglas fir and larch, where fallow deer roam and silver-washed fritillary butterflies glide.

ⓘ Load Street

▶ Take the **B4190** towards Kidderminster turning left on to unclassified roads towards Shatterford, then turning left on to the **A442** to Bridgnorth.

⑦ Bridgnorth, Shropshire
There are two parts to this historic market centre, connected by a winding main road, a cliff railway and a steep

flight of steps. The original settlement was in the High Town, where Bridgnorth Castle was built. The only remaining fragment is the leaning tower, which is set at a steeper angle than the Leaning Tower of Pisa. The most graceful building is Italianate St Mary Magdalene's Church, built in 1792 by Thomas Telford. For railway enthusiasts there is not only the Severn Valley Railway, but also the funicular, linking the upper and lower parts of the town. In Low Town is Bishop Percy's House, a fine half-timbered building of 1580.

ⓘ The Library, Listley Street

▶ Leave Bridgnorth on the **A458**, then after 3 miles (5km) turn left at Morville on to the **B4368** to Shipton.

⑧ Shipton, Shropshire
Set in the heart of Corve Dale, with views of Brown Clee Hill to the south, this small village sits

The town of Ironbridge, famous for its bridge, took a leading role in the Industrial Revolution

snugly in the midst of the green fields and valley. Shipton Hall is the focal point, a beautiful complex of stone buildings dating from 1587. There is an attractive walled garden, medieval dovecote and old parish church, as well as a fine 18th-century stable block.

▶ *Take the **B4378** to Much Wenlock*

9 Much Wenlock, Shropshire
This charming market town has many half-timbered buildings, notably the Manor House, the Guildhall and Raynald's

Mansion. Ruined Wenlock Priory was founded by St Milburga in the 7th century as a convent and destroyed by Danes in the 9th century. It was rebuilt by Lady Godiva and her husband, Leofric, in the 11th century, though it was soon destroyed again by the Normans. Benthall Hall, 4 miles (6km) northeast, is a 16th-century house with fine panelling, a carved oak staircase and mullioned windows.

ⓘ *The Museum, High Street*

▶ *Leave Much Wenlock on the **B4376**, turning left on to the **B4375**. In a short distance turn left on to an unclassified road to Ironbridge.*

10 Ironbridge, Shropshire
Ironbridge was in the forefront of the Industrial Revolution. Its splendid iron bridge over the River Severn, the first of its kind in the world, was built in 1778 by Abraham Darby to enable traffic to pass across the river without interrupting its naviga-tion. West of Ironbridge, the B4380 brings you to Buildwas, where the bridge over the Severn is a 1906 replacement of Telford's original one. The ruins of nearby 12th-century Buildwas Abbey, now roofless and without its aisle walls, are a striking contrast to the enormous cooling towers of the power station downstream. Stone from the ruin was incorporated in the local church.

i The Wharfage

▶ Continue for 2 miles (3km) on an unclassified road to take the **B4380** to Wroxeter.

11 Wroxeter, Shropshire
Near this quiet little village is the Roman town of *Viroconium*, which was the fourth largest town in Roman Britain. A walk round the site reveals the baths, a market hall and fragments of other buildings. The most impressive relic of the baths is the 20-foot (6m) wall, where a square entrance once had double doors leading to the *frigidarium* or 'cooling off' room. A museum displays pottery, painted plaster and coins from the site.

Two miles (3km) northwest on the B4380 is Atcham, where Attingham Park features magnificent gardens, woodlands and a deer park. The gardens are open throughout the year, and the house contains a fine collection of early 19th-century English and Italian furniture. Parts of the red sandstone 13th-century Church of St Eata were built with stones from the ruins of *Viroconium*.

▶ Continue along the **B4380** to return to Shrewsbury, 5 miles (8km).

SCENIC ROUTES

In the Shipton area the scenery is gentle and the B4378 to Much Wenlock runs through Corve Dale, with fine views of the River Corve. From Acton Burnell to Church Stretton, along the A49 and the unclassified road, the views are spectacular, with Long Mynd to the west and Caer Caradoc Hill, where it is thought the Romans defeated the British leader Caractacus in AD 50, to the east.

RECOMMENDED WALKS

The Shropshire Way is a long-distance walk from Whitchurch through Shrewsbury to Clun and the Clee Hills. There are several walks around Ludlow, notably across the Teme and on to Whitcliffe Common, which was the town's common land in the Middle Ages, and the Forestry Commission have several attractive, clearly marked walks, such as from the Wyre Forest centre near Bewdley.

The ruins of Wenlock Priory

SPECIAL TO...

Six miles (9km) of the Severn Valley changed the world as a result of industrial developments in the late 18th and 19th centuries. Here, the past is portrayed in the museums of Ironbridge, Coalbrookdale, Jackfield and Coalport.
The Ironbridge Gorge Museum was one of the first World Heritage Sites in Britain, and one ticket admits you to the bridge, the Darby furnace, Blists Hill, Coalport China Museum, the tile museum, Rosehill House and elsewhere. The ticket is valid indefinitely.

THE NORTH

The North of England is noted for the old industrial towns of Lancashire and Yorkshire, where communities developed in the wake of the coal mining, engineering, woollen and cotton manufacturing industries. They have become modern thriving towns, while retaining much of historical interest, including relics of the industrial revolution. Surrounding these urban areas are some of the finest expanses of British countryside, especially in the Lake District, which has spellbound the adventurous traveller since the earliest days of tourism, and the Pennines, known as 'the backbone of England'.

Visitors from all over the world are attracted by the scenic beauties of the Lake District, with its mountains, still lakes and villages which seem to have grown out of this rocky landscape. Stone walls can be seen stretching skywards over all but the highest hills, in an area where beauty inspired Wordsworth, bringing walkers and climbers in their droves.

Dry stone walls at Grassington

The Lake District villages are generally built of lava or slate, except in Eskdale, to the west, where pink granite is found, but those in the Pennines are quite different: dark and somewhat forbidding in areas of millstone grit, or light and cheery where carboniferous limestone is the local rock. Old quarries and mines are dotted around the hills, and the higher parts of the Pennines become moorland, often bleak and isolated.

Down in the valleys, conditions are kinder to man and animals, and on the lowlands which surround these hill masses there is much rich farming, generally of cattle and sheep, which appreciate the lush grasslands. The larger lowlands, such as the Vale of York, the Lancashire and Cheshire Plain and lowlands of Solway, are where most of the large towns have grown up.

Carlisle

The regional capital of Cumbria is a well-placed city, with the Lake District to the south and Hadrian's Wall to the north. Carlisle's castle has been a border fortress since Norman times, and its detailed history is portrayed in an exhibition in the keep. A military museum, dedicated to the Border regiments, is also housed here. The cathedral is one of England's smallest, and has remarkable carved choir stalls. Near by is the Carlisle Cross, where servants were once hired, and where Bonnie Prince Charlie stood to claim the throne of England in 1745.

Morecambe

This Victorian seaside resort overlooks Morecambe Bay, with its miles of sand, and the Lake District hills are clearly visible to the north. Traditionally a holiday centre for visitors from northern England, Morecambe retains its popularity, and the late weeks of the summer season have the added attraction of 'illuminations'. Another attraction Morecambe has to offer is the new seafront promenade where sculptures are displayed.

Ripon

Ripon is a busy little town, dominated by its cathedral, one of the oldest in England. An ancient Saxon crypt, thought to date from AD 672, lies beneath the cathedral, and inside the cathedral fine features include a 16th-century Gothic nave. Another ancient building is the Wakeman's House, built in the 14th century for the man who would 'set the watch' by blowing a horn at 9pm every evening – a practice which continues today. An inscription on the 19th-century Town Hall reminds residents that 'Except ye Lord keep ye cittie, ye Wakeman waketh in vain'. The Prison and Police Museum is well worth a visit.

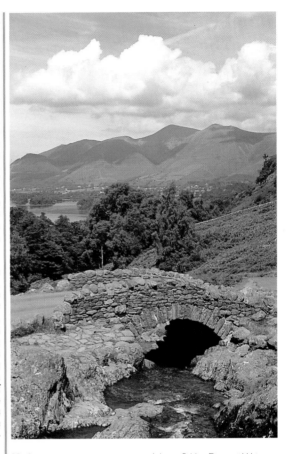

Ashness Bridge, Derwent Water

York

It was the Vikings who established the settlement of Jorvik, which was developed by the Normans as the capital of the north. History lives in every street of this glorious city, which celebrates its 10th-century origins in the time-travelling Jorvik Viking Centre and re-creates whole streets from the past in the York Castle Museum. But the greatest treasure is York Minster, the largest medieval cathedral in northern Europe, whose grandeur and beauty are unsurpassable. You will need a long stay to see everything of interest in York: medieval houses overhanging the narrow Shambles; the extensive city walls; and the National Railway Museum, a favourite with children and railway buffs, are only a few of its wealth of attractions.

Macclesfield

This old textile town made its name from the manufacture of silk, and there are still some of the 18th- and 19th-century mills on the steep streets overlooking the Bollin Valley. The story of silk can be seen in the award-winning Silk Museum, and you can visit the Paradise Mill, a working mill until 1981. Macclesfield's other outstanding attraction is the church, originally founded in the 13th century, which sits high above the town and can be reached by climbing 108 steps.

The Heart of
Lakeland

Leave the soft red sandstones of Carlisle and the Eden Valley to weave through hills of volcanic rocks and lakes carved out during the last Ice Age, before heading into the Pennines, with their different, gentler beauty.

2 DAYS • 175 MILES • 281KM

ITINERARY

CARLISLE	▶	Caldbeck (13m-21km)
CALDBECK	▶	Bassenthwaite (9m-14km)
BASSENTHWAITE	▶	Buttermere (20m-32km)
BUTTERMERE	▶	Keswick (13m-21km)
KESWICK	▶	Grasmere (15m-24km)
GRASMERE	▶	Ambleside (4m-6km)
AMBLESIDE	▶	Coniston (7m-11km)
CONISTON	▶	Bowness (10m-16km)
BOWNESS	▶	Patterdale (13m-21km)
PATTERDALE	▶	Penrith (14m-23km)
PENRITH	▶	Haltwhistle (34m-55km)
HALTWHISTLE	▶	Carlisle (23m-37km)

i *Old Town Hall, Green Market, Carlisle*

▶ *Take the B5299 south from Carlisle to Caldbeck.*

❶ Caldbeck, Cumbria

This stone-built village is set in undulating countryside with the Lake District hills to the south. In the churchyard is the grave of John Peel, who was buried here in 1854. The famous huntsman inspired his friend, John Woodcock Graves, to write the song '*D'ye ken John Peel*'. There is a plaque outside the house where Graves composed the song.

▶ *Continue on the B5299 before branching left on to unclassified roads through Uldale to Bassenthwaite.*

❷ Bassenthwaite, Cumbria

Bassenthwaite is situated off the A591. 'Thwaite' is a Norse word for a clearing in the forest, and is found in many village names in the area. Bassenthwaite Church, 3 miles (5km) south, was founded in the 12th or 13th century and retains its Norman chancel arch and many Early English features. Nearby Lake Bassenthwaite is a large ice-cut lake, and towering above its western shore is Skiddaw, one of only three Lake District hills higher than 3,000 feet (931m).

▶ *Leave Bassenthwaite on unclassified roads towards the B5291 round the northern shores of the lake, then take the A66 south to Braithwaite. Continue on the B5292 and over Whinlatter Pass to Low Lorton then left on to the B5289 to Buttermere.*

❸ Buttermere, Cumbria

The tiny village of Buttermere stands in the heart of spectacular landscape. A stiff climb to Whinlatter Pass, beyond the Forestry Commission's Visitor Centre, takes you on to wild moorland. The surrounding hills, Red Pike and High Stile, tower over the flat green valley floor, with impressive waterfalls such as Scale Force. The B5289 takes you through Borrowdale, a valley, which is reached by crossing 1,174-foot (358m) Honister Pass. Dark rocks tower above the skyline and quarries scar the landscape where Borrowdale rock, formed by volcanic activity about 500 million years ago, is extracted. This famous rock is used in buildings as far away as Dallas and Hong Kong, and you can buy small souvenirs from many of the local shops. The southern end of the valley is dominated by the summits of 2,560-foot (780m) Glaramara and 2,986-foot (910m) Great End.

▶ *Take the B5289 to Keswick.*

Crummock Water, Buttermere

❹ Keswick, Cumbria

The capital of the northern Lake District now caters for walkers, climbers and holiday-makers, but one of its oldest industries is the manufacture of coloured pencils, which originally used local graphite. The Cumberland Pencil Factory has a museum and among its exhibits is the world's largest pencil.

On a hill to the east of Keswick is Castlerigg Stone Circle, a prehistoric monument in a setting of magical beauty. Cumbrian folklore claims that the famous great stones were once men who were turned into boulders by witches.

i *The Moot Hall, Market Square*

▶ *Take the A66 for 4 miles (6km), then turn right on to the B5322 through St John's in the Vale and then the A591 south to Grasmere.*

❺ Grasmere, Cumbria

Grasmere's hills and lakes are a real tourist magnet. William Wordsworth wrote much of his greatest verse here, and his friends Coleridge, de Quincey and Southey were inspired by the location. Dove Cottage, where Wordsworth lived with his sister Dorothy, is open to the public and contains relics of his life and times. A few miles further along the A591 is Rydal Mount, where Wordsworth lived from 1813 until his death in 1850. It houses many of the family's belongings and has a beautiful view of tranquil Rydal Water.

ⓘ *Redbank Road*

SPECIAL TO...

For over a hundred years, Grasmere gingerbread has been made in the village. The recipe is such a closely guarded secret it has to be kept in the vaults of a local bank!
The rush-bearing ceremony, held every year, involves the carrying of elaborately decorated bundles of rushes to the church, after which the bearers are rewarded with a piece of delicious gingerbread.

▶ *Continue to Ambleside.*

⑥ Ambleside, Cumbria
Ambleside is a major Lake District centre at the northern end of Lake Windermere. Its

Mysterious Castlerigg Stone Circle

many stone houses include Bridge House, the smallest in the Lake District. Built on a tiny bridge over the Stock Ghyll, it is now owned by the National Trust and is open to the public. In the town library are the relics excavated from the Roman site of Galava Fort, at Borrans Park, and the woodland gardens of Stagshaw, just south of the town, have superb views of the lake.

ⓘ *Central Buildings, Market Cross*

▶ *Leave on the A593 to Coniston.*

⑦ Coniston, Cumbria
Coniston Water is famous as the place where Donald Campbell set a new world record and later died in 1967. The Steam Yacht *Gondola*, an 1859 steam launch, has been restored, and now takes passengers on regular scheduled trips around the lake.

A little further on, at Hawkshead, is the Beatrix Potter Gallery; at Hill Top, in Near Sawrey, Potter wrote some of her world-famous children's stories. The house is open to the public.

ⓘ *Ruskin Avenue*

▶ *Take the B5285 to the Windermere ferry.*

⑧ Bowness and Windermere, Cumbria
The ferry across Lake Windermere to Bowness was restored in 1990 and leads to this small town with its narrow streets and fine 15th-century church.

Windermere, just north of Bowness, is a focal point in the Lake District for sailing and boating. The Steamboat Museum, at Rayrigg Road, has a collection of Victorian and Edwardian boats, many of which still float and are in working order. The lake has 14 islands, including Belle Isle, a privately owned landscaped estate with a round 18th-century mansion house.

ⓘ *Glebe Road, Bowness; Victoria Street, Windermere*

RECOMMENDED WALKS

For a gentle walk, follow the footpath opposite the railway station in Windermere to the top of Orrest Head, 784 feet (239m), where there are fine views of the lake and Belle Isle.

Dove Cottage, Grasmere

RECOMMENDED WALK

A popular walk leads up Helvellyn from Patterdale, via Striding Edge, to the summit and returns by way of Swirral Edge. On a clear day the whole circle of Lake District summits can be seen.

FOR CHILDREN

The Lake District National Park Visitor Centre is on the eastern shore of Lake Windermere at Brockhole, northwest of Windermere. As well as providing information about the park, it offers a wide variety of attractions, including special family events during school holidays, lake trips in summer, garden tours from May to September, Teddy Bears' Picnics in spring and summer and a children's Squirrel Nutkin Trail.

▶ Take the **A592** north to Patterdale.

9 **Patterdale,** Cumbria
Patterdale was named after St Patrick, who is said to have walked here after being shipwrecked on Duddon Sands in AD 540. St Patrick's Church, built in 1853, is notable for its tapestries by embroidress Ann Macbeth, who lived here until her death in 1948. This attractive village is at the head of Ullswater, a popular boating lake. A steamer plies from the pier at Glenridding to the opposite end of the lake, and the scenery is dominated by 3,117-foot (950m) Helvellyn. At the foot of the sheer eastern slopes is Red Tarn, a corrie lake in a hollow scooped out of solid rock during the Ice Age. Two miles (3km) from Glenridding is Aira Force, and it was here that Wordsworth was inspired to write of his 'host of golden daffodils'.

ⓘ *Main Car Park, Glenridding*

▶ *Take the **A592** alongside Ullswater to Penrith.*

10 **Penrith,** Cumbria
Penrith was the capital of Old Cumbria, and there are remains of buildings suggesting its former importance. The 12th-century ruins of Brougham Castle are just outside the town, and remnants of a Roman fort built by Agricola are near by. Beautiful Lowther Leisure and Wildlife Park is a few miles south and is set in 100 acres (40 hectares) of parkland. The Gloucester Arms, dating from 1477, is one of the oldest inns in England, and the Duke of Gloucester, later Richard III, is said to have lived here. The wild, open spaces round Penrith may be bleak, even in summer, and crossing the Pennines can prove difficult in winter.

ⓘ *Robinson's School, Middlegate*

▶ *Follow the **A686** through Langwathby towards Alston. Turn left on to the **A689** then right along an unclassified road to Haltwhistle.*

11 **Haltwhistle,** Northumbria
This small, grey market town is a good starting point for Hadrian's Wall, built in the 2nd century AD to ward off Scottish tribes. Holy Cross Church, founded in 1178, is a fine example of Early English architecture. There is no tower, and the sanctuary preserves three carved coffin lids which are thought to date from the 14th century. The South Tynedale Railway, England's highest narrow-gauge railway, runs from Alston for a few miles towards Haltwhistle. Further along the A69, at Greenhead, the Roman wall, turret, fort and museum recall life 2,000 years ago.

ⓘ *Railway Station, Station Road*

▶ *From Greenhead take the **B6318** and unclassified roads to rejoin the **A69**. Continue through Brampton to Carlisle.*

FOR HISTORY BUFFS

Housesteads, to the east of Haltwhistle, just off the B6318, is the best preserved Roman fort on Hadrian's Wall. Excavations have revealed granaries, a commandant's house, military headquarters, a hospital, baths, latrines and barracks. In the opposite direction, on the way back to Carlisle is the ruined fort of Camboglanna, occupying a ridge-top site near Birdoswald. It was built to guard the Roman bridge carrying Hadrian's Wall over the river at Willowford.

Across the
Backbone of England

The green valleys and wild, often wind-swept moorland of Yorkshire provide a rich variety of scenery, with ever-changing views. Curiously weathered rocks add an eerie atmosphere to the landscape of hills and vales, and castles and monastic ruins recall the prosperity of the Middle Ages on this tour.

2 DAYS • 153 MILES • 246KM

ⓘ *Minster Road, Ripon*

▶ *Continue north to Leyburn.*

FOR CHILDREN

Four miles (6km) southeast of Ripon is Newby Hall and gardens. The grounds cover about 25 acres (10 hectares) and include thrilling adventure gardens for children, a memorable ride on a miniature train and woodland discovery walks.

▶ *Take the A6108 to Masham.*

❶ Masham, North Yorkshire
Masham's importance as a market town is illustrated by the huge market square, dominated by its Market Cross. Masham Market is held every Wednesday and Saturday. The town is full of interesting features: a four-arched bridge over the Ure dates from 1754, and St Mary's Church is older, its 15th-century spire standing on top of a Norman tower. The town is the home of Theakston's brewery, famous for its 'Old Peculier' ale.

Five miles (8km) from town is Jervaulx Abbey, in an attractive riverside setting. This Cistercian abbey was founded in 1156 and later destroyed in the 15th century, though enough of it remains to show how impressive it once was.

▶ *Follow the A6108 for 8 miles (13km) to Middleham.*

❷ Middleham, North Yorkshire
Grandiose building traditions of the past can be seen in the ruins of 12th-century Middleham Castle, a former seat of the Neville family, where some of the walls are 12 feet (3.5m) thick. This was the childhood home of Richard III and its massive keep is one of the largest ever built. The view from the top is magnificent, looking out across Wensleydale over wild but beautiful moorlands. Now an important horse breeding and training centre, Middleham is a good base for exploring Wensleydale.

❸ Leyburn, North Yorkshire
Leyburn is a major commercial centre for the area. Its appearance is that of a prosperous late Georgian market town, and even though most shop fronts have become largely modern, some 18th-century houses survive, notably around Grove Square; the Bolton Arms and Leyburn Hall are probably the best examples. This is another good Wensleydale centre, and there are fine views from The Shawl, a 2-mile (3km) limestone scar not far from the town centre.

ⓘ *Central Chambers, Railway Street*

▶ *Keep on the A6108 to Richmond.*

❹ Richmond, North Yorkshire
There is much to see in this capital and gateway to Swaledale, thought to be the finest of all Yorkshire Dales. From every angle Richmond Castle dominates the town. This fine Norman fortress, built on to solid rock, was started in 1071 overlooking the Swale, Britain's fastest river, but was never finished. The large, cobbled market-place is surrounded by such architectural gems as the Georgian Theatre Royal, built in 1788, which was restored and reopened in 1962. You can see the home of the original 'sweet lass of Richmond Hill', of whom the famous song was written in 1785, and the award-winning Green Howards Museum covers the history of the regiment, including a unique collection dating from 1688 of war relics, weapons, medals and uniforms. Other interesting sights include Greyfriars Tower, the one surviving feature of an old abbey, and the Holy Trinity Church.

ⓘ *Friary Gardens, Victoria Road*

FOR HISTORY BUFFS

Lead mining helped the growth of Richmond and many of the surrounding villages in the 17th and 18th centuries. There are numerous footpaths leading to the old mine workings, where you can see the crushing floors and other remnants, and perhaps find tiny fragments of lead glistening in the sunlight.

▶ *Take the B6274 to the junction with the A66 and continue to Greta Bridge. After crossing the River Greta turn right on to unclassified roads to Barnard Castle.*

❺ Barnard Castle, Durham
Medieval Barnard Castle, after which the town is named is now

Middleham's impressive castle ruins

Bainbridge was the centre of the once-great Forest of Wensleydale

a ruin, but in its great days it stood guard over a crossing point of the River Tees. The town boasts one of the finest museums in Britain, Bowes Museum, in a splendid French château-style mansion which was built in 1869 by John Bowes, son of the Earl of Strathmore. It contains an outstanding collection of paintings, porcelain, silver, furniture and ceramics.

A few miles south, off the B6277, are the ruins of Egglestone Abbey, in a delightful setting on the bank of the Tees, and southwest, along the A67, is the village of Bowes, where the local boarding schools gave author Charles Dickens the idea for Dotheboys Hall in his novel *Nicholas Nickleby*. William

Shaw, the unfortunate model for sadistic schoolmaster Wackford Squeers, is buried in the churchyard. The Church of St Giles contains a Roman dedication stone, one of many relics of the Roman invasion in the area. Bowes Castle, like the church, used Roman stone for its building.

i Woodleigh, Flatts Road

▶ Take the **A67** to Bowes and follow the **A66** west along the line of an old Roman route to Brough.

6 Brough, Cumbria
Standing on the site of Roman *Verterae*, Brough Castle, now in ruins, was built by William II and later restored by Lady Anne Clifford in the 17th century. During the 19th century this old

settlement was a coaching town, and used to hold an annual horse fair, now at Appleby. The area has many miles of good walking.

▶ Take the **A685** to Kirkby Stephen, then the **A683** to Sedbergh.

7 Sedbergh, Cumbria
Sedbergh is an old weaving town, and the Weavers' Yard still exists behind the King's Arms. The town is now more important as a tourist centre, and the rich natural history and beautiful scenery of the area have given rise to the creation of a National Park Centre. The Public School has gained a national reputation for its academic standards and sporting traditions. The A684 east takes you through Garsdale, whose only community is a line of houses called The Street.

narrow valley, once the venue for brass band competitions.

i *Dales Countryside Museum, Station Yard*

▶ *Take the A684 for a further 4 miles (6km) to Bainbridge.*

9 Bainbridge, North Yorkshire

This little Dales village, with its lovely stone buildings set round the green, was the former centre of the once great Forest of Wensleydale. Low Mill, on the east side of the green, has been restored and is occasionally open to the public. Brough Hill, a natural grassy hillock to the east is the setting for a Roman fort, and gives fine views of Wensleydale and the village.

A little further along is Askrigg, another charming village, built of local stone and set among hills, valleys and waterfalls. Most of the buildings are 18th- and 19th-century, built as a result of increasing prosperity in the clock-making, lead-mining and textile industries. Waterfalls are numerous, but especially dramatic is Aysgarth Force.

▶ *From Bainbridge cross the River Ure and turn right, continuing on unclassified roads, then at Aysgarth take the B6160 to Buckden.*

10 Buckden, North Yorkshire
Buckden, in Wharfedale, is a very popular holiday and walking area. Kettlewell, further down the valley, was formerly part of the estate of the Percy family, ancestors of the Dukes of Northumberland.

This stretch of road passes the imposing limestone outcrop of Kilnsey Crag, one of Yorkshire's most distinctive landmarks, alongside the all-weather attraction of Kilnsey Park, which has been established as a Visitor Centre.

▶ *Follow the B6160 south and turn left at Threshfield on to the B6265 into Grassington.*

SPECIAL TO...

This area of the Dales was chosen as the location for the successful BBC TV series *All Creatures Great and Small*, the story of a country vet's practice based on the autobiographical books by James Herriot. Cringley Hall, in the centre of the village of Askrigg is 'Skeldale House' and Askrigg itself is 'Darrowby', where the vets have their surgery. For thousands of visitors 'Herriot Country' is every bit as important as 'Brontë Country'.

11 Grassington, North Yorkshire
This is Wharfedale's principal village and another National Park Centre, for the North York Moors. Its small passageways, cobbled market-place, medieval bridge and interesting old buildings all add to the appeal. There are Bronze and Iron Age settlements at Lea Green, north of the village, and further east, along the B6265, are the underground caverns of Stump Cross. The main cave has been developed into an impressive floodlit show cave, with wonderful stalagmite and stalactite formations.

i *Grassington National Park Centre, Hebden Road*

▶ *Continue along the B6265 to Pateley Bridge.*

12 Pateley Bridge, North Yorkshire
This pleasant town has been the focus of everyday life in Nidderdale since ancient times. The picturesque ruins of Old St Mary's Church stand above the village on the hillside, and the Nidderdale Museum has fascinating exhibits including the Victorian Room and a replica cobbler's shop. A mile (1.6km) from town is the former Foster Beck Hemp Mill, now a restaurant, which features a huge 17th-century water wheel, the second largest in the country.

i *72 Main Street*

▶ *Continue east along the A684 to Hawes.*

8 Hawes, North Yorkshire
Hawes is a centre for sheep-marketing and a focal point of Upper Wensleydale life. Just off the main street are quaint alleyways and old cottages which have not changed much for 200 years. The National Park Centre is located at the Dales Countryside Museum, which is housed in an engine shed of the old railway.

Hardraw Force, the highest waterfall in England, is also considered to be the most spectacular, and is accessible only by foot through the grounds of the Green Dragon Inn. The water drops 90 feet (27m) over the limestone Hardraw Scar, into a

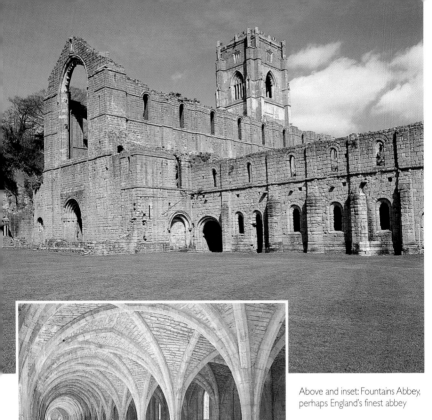

Above and inset: Fountains Abbey, perhaps England's finest abbey

East of town, along the B6165 (turn off at Wilsill) and unclassified roads are Brimham Rocks. These curious rock formations have been sculpted out of the millstone grit by wind and rain over thousands of years, and there are wide views from the surrounding moorlands.

i *18 High Street*

▶ *Leave by the **B6265** turning right after 1 mile (1.6km) on to the **B6165**. At Wilsill turn left and follow unclassified roads past Brimham Rocks to Fountains Abbey.*

B Fountains Abbey, North Yorkshire

Founded by Cistercian monks in 1132, Fountains is the largest and perhaps the finest abbey in England. Particularly notable are the tower, nave and lay brothers'

quarters. It was acquired by William Aislabie in 1768 and became the focal point of his magnificent landscaped gardens at nearby Studley Royal Park, which contains typical ornaments of the period, such as a lake, a temple and statues. The park's original house burned

down in 1945, but there are still estate cottages, huddled round a 19th-century church designed by William Burges. Deer and other livestock can be seen grazing in the park.

▶ *Return to the **B6265** for the journey back to Ripon.*

BACK TO NATURE

In the gritstone area of the Yorkshire Dales, above Nidderdale and Swaledale, purple heathers dominate the scene, but in the limestone country round Wharfedale you will find more variety, with the tiny coloured flowers which thrive in the calcite-rich soils. Plants such as yellow pimpernel, giant bell-flower, lily of the valley and ramson grow well in the light shade cast by ash, which grows on the limestone scars, while the unmown roadside verges and hay meadows are favoured by knapweed, sneezewort, early purple orchids and cowslips.

RECOMMENDED WALKS

The various National Park Centres provide a programme of guided walks at Bank Holidays and during July and August. These start at 2pm and usually last 2½ to 3 hours. Local people with a special interest in some aspect of the Dales act as guides. Information about these walks is given in *The Visitor*, a free publication.

Over Hills
& Plains

Lush green valleys, wild grouse moorland and one of the liveliest seaside resorts in the country are included in this tour, which starts at Morecambe, on the edge of the Irish Sea, and climbs to the Pennines, before returning to the coast.

1/2 DAYS • 152 MILES • 245KM

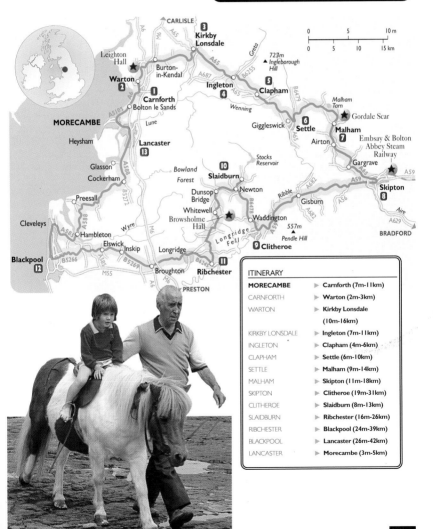

ITINERARY

MORECAMBE	▷ Carnforth (7m-11km)
CARNFORTH	▷ Warton (2m-3km)
WARTON	▷ Kirkby Lonsdale (10m-16km)
KIRKBY LONSDALE	▷ Ingleton (7m-11km)
INGLETON	▷ Clapham (4m-6km)
CLAPHAM	▷ Settle (6m-10km)
SETTLE	▷ Malham (9m-14km)
MALHAM	▷ Skipton (11m-18km)
SKIPTON	▷ Clitheroe (19m-31km)
CLITHEROE	▷ Slaidburn (8m-13km)
SLAIDBURN	▷ Ribchester (16m-26km)
RIBCHESTER	▷ Blackpool (24m-39km)
BLACKPOOL	▷ Lancaster (26m-42km)
LANCASTER	▷ Morecambe (3m-5km)

[i] *Old Station Buildings, Morecambe*

▶ *From Morecambe take the A5105, then the A6 for 7 miles (11km) to Carnforth.*

❶ Carnforth, Lancashire

Carnforth is a small Victorian market town on the west coast railway line to Scotland. The Lancaster Canal threads through the town providing fascinating towpath walks that quickly take you into the surrounding countryside. Here, close to the A6 and the town centre, the marina is popular with canal enthusiasts and those just seeking peace and quiet. Craft can be hired here by the day or the week.

▶ *Turn left out of Steamtown and follow the unclassified road 2 miles (3km) to Warton.*

The Devil's Bridge at Kirkby Lonsdale is one of the most ancient bridges in the country

---

BACK TO NATURE

The RSPB reserve at Leighton Moss, 3 miles (5km) northwest of Carnforth, is famous for its reed-beds and wetland wildlife. Otters are regularly seen, and bitterns and bearded tits can be spotted by persistent observers. Arnside Knott, further north, is a limestone outcrop which shows fine examples of limestone pavements. Interesting flowers grow in the cracks and crevices, including several species of ferns and dark red helleborines.

---

❷ Warton, Lancashire

The peaceful village of Warton has an unusual claim to fame. George Washington had ancestors living here, and legend has it that the famous 'Stars and Stripes' come from the family's coat of arms, which can be found in the 14th-century church.

Near Warton is 18th-century Leighton Hall, built on the site of an earlier medieval house. In 1826 the estate was bought by Richard Gillow, a distinguished maker of fine furniture, and the house is a treasure chest of priceless pieces.

▶ *Continue on unclassified roads, across the A6 just south of Burton-in-Kendal then join the B6254 at Whittington and follow to Kirkby Lonsdale.*

❸ Kirkby Lonsdale, Cumbria

Kirkby Lonsdale is a fascinating town to explore. Look out for the three-arched Devil's Bridge spanning the River Lune. Possibly 13th-century, it is one of the finest ancient bridges in the country. John Ruskin, the 19th-century writer and painter, loved this area of the Lune valley. The 'Ruskin Walks', which start near the churchyard, are well signposted. Cowan Bridge, just down the road, has further literary links, for it was here that novelists Charlotte and

Emily Brontë endured a harsh boarding school education from 1823 to 1825. Now only a few cottages mark the site of the Clergy Daughters' School, immortalised by Charlotte as Lowood in her novel *Jane Eyre*.

ℹ️ *24 Main Street*

▶ *Continue on the **A65** for 6 miles (10km), then turn left on to the **B6255** into Ingleton.*

4 Ingleton, North Yorkshire

Ingleton thrives as a centre for visitors to the Yorkshire Dales. The limestone hills to the north are honeycombed with caves, many accessible only to experienced potholers, but White Scar Cave is open to everyone. It is below the heights of 2,373 feet (723m) Ingleborough which, with Whernside at 2,419 feet (737m) and Pen-y-ghent at 2,273 feet (693m), forms the most formidable trio of peaks in the Dales.

ℹ️ *Community Centre Car Park, High Street*

▶ *Take the unclassified road along the foot of Ingleborough for 4 miles (6km) to Clapham.*

5 Clapham, North Yorkshire

Tiny Clapham is the unlikely Fleet Street of the Dales, for it is here that *The Dalesman* magazine is published. The village has a Yorkshire Dales National Park Information Centre, and like Ingleton is a noted potholing centre. To the north of the village is Ingleborough Cave, and the famous Gaping Gill pothole, 378 feet (123m) deep, with a central chamber large enough to hold a small cathedral.

▶ *From Clapham take the **B6480** to the **A65** and follow before branching off left to Settle.*

6 Settle, North Yorkshire

Settle is an attractive town, with its picturesque narrow streets, secluded courtyards and Georgian houses. By far the most outstanding building is The Folly (1675), an extravaganza of windows and fine masonry. The 71-mile (114km) railway line from Settle to Carlisle runs through the Ribblesdale valley and is one of the most scenic routes in the country. Just outside the town is Giggleswick Scar, a rock wall caused by massive earth move-

St Mary's Church, Ingleton

ments millions of years ago. In 1838, the chance discovery of Victoria Cave led to the retrieval of many bones of prehistoric animals long extinct in the British Isles.

ℹ️ *Town Hall, Cheapside*

▶ *Take the **B6479** north from Settle, turning off right at Langcliffe on to unclassified roads to Malham Tarn and Malham.*

7 Malham, North Yorkshire

Malham is a focal point for geographers and geologists, and the Yorkshire Dales National Park Interpretation Centre is based here. Stroll up the Pennine Way to Malham Cove, a 250-foot (76m) limestone amphitheatre. It used to be a spectacular waterfall, but the river now crawls out at the foot of the cliff. To the east is Gordale Scar, an almost vertical gorge thought to be a collapsed cavern and boasting a dramatic waterfall.

▶ *Follow the road from Malham to Gargrave, then take the **A65** to Skipton.*

The geological curiosity of Malham Cove lends an other-worldly air to this spectacular area

today it still stands boldly on its limestone knoll overlooking the town. The town itself was once filled with the sound of looms – first wool, then cotton brought prosperity in the last century. Pendle Hill, associated with the trial of several Lancashire women accused of being witches, rises to 1,828 feet (557m) on the east side of Clitheroe.

☐ *12–14 Market Place*

SPECIAL TO...

Clitheroe Castle contains a fine collection of carboniferous fossils from the local rocks. Similar fossils can be found in the limestone areas around Malham or Ingleton. Brachiopods look like some of the modern shells you can find on beaches today and there are pieces of coral from a warm ocean floor of 300 million years ago, and crinoids, which look like screws made out of stone.

FOR HISTORY BUFFS

A few miles northwest of Clitheroe, just beyond Bashall Eaves, is Browsholme Hall. Pronounced 'Broozum', it is a modified Tudor mansion set in beautiful gardens that were landscaped in honour of the Prince Regent and Mrs Fitzherbert. It contains fascinating collections of tapestry work, armour, furniture and pictures.

▶ *Follow the B6478 north for 8 miles (13km) to Slaidburn.*

⑩ Slaidburn, Lancashire
The little village of Slaidburn, on the River Hodder, was for centuries the administrative 'capital' of the Forest of Bowland. This wild region of grouse moor and high fells was one of the ancient royal forests of Saxon England. At the centre of the village is an inn called Hark to Bounty. Legend says

RECOMMENDED WALKS

Malham village is close to the highly dramatic Malham Cove and Gordale Scar. Walk up the steep path to the top of the cove, and continue along the route of the old river, now dried up. You will soon reach the point at which the stream disappears underground through a series of holes. Retrace your steps or turn right and follow the signs to Gordale, where you can scramble down a waterfall and walk through a gorge on the way back to the village.

⑧ Skipton, North Yorkshire
This pleasant market town is dominated by Skipton Castle, one of the most complete medieval castles in England. It was originally built in Norman times and was partly rebuilt in the 1650s after being damaged in the Civil War. Opposite the castle entrance is the Craven Museum, with exhibits on geology and local folk history. Near by, at Embsay, is the Embsay and Bolton Abbey Steam Railway which runs 20 locomotives.

☐ *Craven Court*

▶ *Take the A59 to Clitheroe.*

⑨ Clitheroe, Lancashire
After the Civil War the small keep of Clitheroe Castle was presented to General Monk, and

Bounty was a foxhound belonging to a local vicar, and that its barking was easily distinguishable from the rest of the pack. Gisburn Forest, northeast of the village, is an extensive coniferous plantation sloping down to Stocks Reservoir, which takes its name from the village drowned to create it during the 1930s.

▶ *Take the B6478 back to Newton, then branch off on to unclassified roads through Dunsop Bridge, Whitewell and over Longridge Fell to Ribchester.*

⓫ Ribchester, Lancashire
The country round Ribchester was guarded by a Roman fort called *Bremetennacum*, built around AD 70. In the 18th century a schoolboy found a Roman ceremonial helmet, and since then the extensive remains have been excavated and you can see many of the finds, including pottery, coins, a bathhouse and granaries, in the Ribchester Roman Museum. Two Roman columns support the oak gallery in 13th-century St Wilfred's Church, and the pillars at the entrance of the White Bull Inn are said to come from a Roman temple.

▶ *Take the B6245 to Longridge and then the B5269 west via Broughton and Elswick to join the B5266 to Blackpool.*

⓬ Blackpool, Lancashire
Blackpool stretches in a long, multicoloured ribbon by the sea, punctuated with three piers and dominated by its 519-foot (158m) tower. Built between 1891 and 1894, Blackpool Tower was for many years the highest building in Britain, and it gives a breathtaking view of the surrounding coast. The heart of Blackpool, the Golden Mile, is more like a quarter of a mile. It is possible to walk the whole length of the seafront between Fleetwood in the north and Squires Gate in the south, but it is more fun to go on one of the

trams which still run along the promenade. During autumn evenings, the whole front is ablaze with more than 375,000 bulbs, laser beams, animated displays and tableaux.

ⓘ *1 Clifton Street and Blackpool Pleasure Beach*

▶ *Follow the trams to Cleveleys, before turning inland on the B5412 then right on to the A585. Turn left on to the A588 to Lancaster via Pilling and Cockerham marshes.*

Blackpool's famous roller-coaster

FOR CHILDREN

The Pleasure Beach amusement park, with the first 360-degree 'loop the loop' roller-coaster in Britain, and Sandcastle, the world's greatest 'inside seaside' with tropical fun pools and a 300-foot (91m) water slide are popular with children, as are the Blackpool Sea Life Centre and Magic of Coronation Street.

⓭ Lancaster, Lancashire
This county town was England's chief port for the American trade throughout the 18th century. The elegant Customs House, designed by Robert Gillow now houses the Lancaster Maritime Museum. The massive Norman

keep of Lancaster Castle now serves to keep people in rather than out: it is the county gaol. It contains a well tower where prisoners languished while awaiting trail – including 10 Lancashire witches convicted and hanged in 1612. On show are grim relics such as the clamp and iron used to fasten a criminal's arm while the initial 'M' (for malefactor) was burned on to his hand. The City Museum in Market Square is also the Museum of the King's Own Royal Lancashire Regiment, and the Judges' Lodgings on Castle Hill contain a Museum of Childhood.

ⓘ *29 Castle Hill*

▶ *Cross the River Lune on the A589, and a short drive takes you back to Morecambe.*

SCENIC ROUTES

Spectacular views can be found as you pass through the mountainous spine of England, the Pennines, on the road from Malham to Skipton before it joins the A65. The dramatic form of Ingleborough dominates the landscape, especially from Kirkby Lonsdale and along the A65.

Derbyshire's
White Peak

This tour of the Peak District explores the gentler southern side, the White Peak, with its high close-cropped sheep pasture, limestone dry walling and pretty wooded valleys, but our route also offers a small glimpse of the Dark Peak – bleaker moorland and angular outcrops of blackened millstone grit.

1/2 DAYS • 85 MILES • 138KM

ITINERARY		
MACCLESFIELD	▶	**Castleton** (19m-31km)
CASTLETON	▶	**Eyam** (10m-16km)
EYAM	▶	**Chatsworth** (6m-10km)
CHATSWORTH	▶	**Matlock** (8m-13km)
MATLOCK	▶	**Bakewell** (14m-23km)
BAKEWELL	▶	**Tideswell** (8m-13km)
TIDESWELL	▶	**Buxton** (8m-13km)
BUXTON	▶	**Macclesfield** (12m-19km)

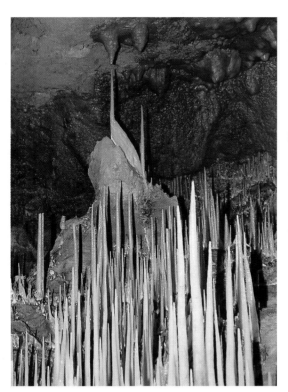

Stalactites in Treak Cliff Cave,
near Castleton
Left: Saxon cross, Eyam

i   *Town Hall, Macclesfield*

BACK TO NATURE

Situated near Macclesfield,
Goyt Valley is an area of bog,
moorland, forest and open
water. The two reservoirs –
Errwood and Fernilee – have
wintering wildfowl and species
such as red grouse, curlew,
lapwing and redshank breed on
the open moorland.

▶ *Leave Macclesfield by the
B5470 to Rainow, then in 4
miles (6km) cross the A5004,
taking the B5470 to Chapel-
en-le-Frith. Take the unclassified road signed Rushup and
Edale, then turn right and
shortly left signed Castleton
Caverns for Castleton.*

❶ Castleton, Derbyshire
Dominating this pretty Peak
village is Peveril Castle, built by
William Peveril, illegitimate son
of the Conqueror, and immortalised in Sir Walter Scott's 1825
novel *Peveril of the Peak*.
Although roofless, Henry II's
huge keep still stands. Castleton
has a 200-year history of visitors,
who come mainly to see the
spectacular caverns in the limestone hills. Follow the stream to
Peak Cavern, which has Britain's
largest natural cave entrance.
You can still see evidence here
of the rope makers who lived
and worked in the cavern: their
speciality was hangman's nooses.
There are other local caverns,
carved out by miners looking for
lead and the lovely Blue John
Fluorspar. Treak Cliff,
Speedwell (explore it by boat)
and Blue John Caverns are all
open to visitors.
   A trip behind Mam Tor, 'the
shivering mountain', leads to
nearby Edale, which lies snugly

in the Noe Valley and is the
starting point of the Pennine
Way footpath.

▶ *Go east on the A625, then
turn right on to the B6049.
Soon turn left on unclassified
roads to Great Hucklow,
through Foolow to Eyam.*

❷ Eyam, Derbyshire
In 1665, the year of the Great
Plague in London, a chest of
clothes was sent from the capital
to the village of Eyam, high up
among the moors. Soon four out
of every five villagers were dead.
But what made Eyam special
was the extraordinary sacrifice
that these villagers made. Led
by the rector, William
Mompesson, they resolved to
isolate themselves and prevent
the disease from wiping out
neighbouring communities. The
churchyard's graves reflect this
sad story and every August a
service is held in a nearby dell,
known as Cucklet Church,
where Mompesson held his
open-air services. Near his wife's
grave is a unique sundial, telling
the time throughout the world.

▶ *Turn right on to the B6521,
then left on to the A623. At
Baslow turn right on to the
A619, then shortly left on to
the B6012. In 5 miles (8km)
turn left again at Edensor for
Chatsworth.*

❸ Chatsworth, Derbyshire
Chatsworth is one of the grand-
est country houses in England,
popularly known as the 'Palace
of the Peak'. The Elizabethan
house, built in 1555 by Bess of
Hardwick, was virtually replaced
with the 1st Duke of
Devonshire's baroque mansion
of the late 17th century, finished
by the 6th Duke in the 1820s.
Although Capability Brown
landscaped the grounds, their
crowning feature is Joseph
Paxton's stunning Emperor
Fountain, at 260 feet (80m) the
tallest in Britain. When you
rejoin the main road, take a look
at the golden stone village of
Edensor. Before 1839 the village

lay in full view of the big house, so the 6th Duke had Paxton demolish it and rebuild it out of sight!

▶ *Leave Chatsworth and turn left on to the **B6012**. At Rowsley turn left on to the **A6** for Matlock.*

❹ Matlock and Matlock Bath, Derbyshire

Matlock is the administrative centre of Derbyshire, a busy town built around an ancient stone bridge across the river. Next door is Matlock Bath, a 19th-century spa town, where the water still bubbles up at a constant 20°C, although the Pavilion where Victorians used to take it is now an entertainment centre. Commanding the heights above Matlock Bath are the Victoria Prospect Tower and the strange folly of Riber Castle. Behind its imposing front is a wildlife park for rare breeds and endangered species.

A mile (1.6km) from Matlock is Cromford, an important benchmark in the development of England as an industrial nation. Here, in 1771, Richard Arkwright built the world's first mechanised textile factory. It survives today, with the new village he built for his workers.

ⓘ *The Pavilion, Matlock Bath*

FOR CHILDREN

A spectacular cable-car journey takes you from the river at Matlock Bath to the 1,000-foot (305m) Heights of Abraham. At the top, you can climb the Victoria Prospect Tower, and below ground there are two huge caverns to explore, the Great Rutland and the Great Masson.

▶ *Leave Matlock Bath on the **A6** and at Cromford turn right on to the **A5012** signed Buxton. Turn right on to the **B5056** then the **A6** to Bakewell.*

Bakewell is famous for its puddings

SPECIAL TO...

The National Tramway Museum at Crich, just south of Cromford, is unique. Over 40 trams from all over the world, built between 1873 and 1953, are kept here in pristine condition by volunteers, and on any one day several trams run. For the price of admission you can hop on and off as much as you like anywhere along the 1 mile (1.6km) route. Open from April to October.

❺ Bakewell, Derbyshire

The fine five-arch stone bridge built in 1300 to span the River Wye, is the principal feature of this market town. The Romans came here first for the warm springs; the Saxons named it Bad Quell or 'bath well'. Most of the buildings are 17th- and 18th-century, but the Old House Museum, with its wattle and daub walls, is at least a hundred years older. The town boasts more than 50 shops, including the Old Original Bakewell Pudding Shop. Bakewell Pudding – don't dare call it 'tart' here – is supposed to have originated in the kitchens of the Rutland Arms Hotel, when a cook poured egg on to the jam instead of the pastry.

ⓘ *Old Market Hall, Bridge Street*

FOR HISTORY BUFFS

Haddon Hall, near Bakewell, is reputed to be England's most complete and authentic medieval manor house, and is certainly one of Derbyshire's finest buildings. Unlike many large country houses, it remains very much as it was 300 years ago.

▶ *Go north on the **A6** from Bakewell. At Ashford-in-the-water turn right on to the **B6465** and, in 4 miles (6km), left on to the **A623**, then turn left into Tideswell.*

❻ Tideswell, Derbyshire

Tideswell grew with the medieval wool trade – being granted market status as early as the 13th century. Over the intervening years it has become a sleepy backwater away from the main roads, and little remains to indicate the town's heyday, with one glorious exception. The 14th-century Church of St John the Baptist, with its soaring tower, is known as the 'Cathedral of the Peak'. Tideswell is a venue for well-dressing, the tradition of decorating wells with flowers, which takes place at the end of June or very early in July.

▶ *From Tideswell go south on the B6049, then join the A6 heading west to Buxton.*

7 Buxton, Derbyshire
At 1,007 feet (307m), Buxton is one of the highest towns in England. People have sought the town out since Roman times for its springs of mineral water. Not only is it good for rheumatics, but it tastes nice too. Bring a bottle and help yourself, free,

from St Anne's Well; you can even swim in warm spa water in the Pavilion's indoor pool. It was in the 18th century that the town took off as a spa resort, thanks to the 5th Duke of Devonshire, who built the beautiful Doric-style Crescent and the huge domed riding school and stables, now the Royal Devonshire Hospital. The town has two golf-courses, an elegantly restored Opera House and the lovely Pavilion Gardens. Walks are plentiful; one that offers a panoramic view of the town is the round trip up to Solomon's Temple, a folly on Grinlow.

ℹ *The Crescent*

▶ *Leave Buxton on the A53, going right on to the A54. Turn right again on to the A537 signed Macclesfield and in 5 miles (8km) turn left*

Buxton is a sophisticated and elegant Georgian spa town

on to unclassified roads past Tegg's Nose Country Park into Macclesfield.

SCENIC ROUTES

The route between Macclesfield and Castleton offers a picturesque introduction to the Dark Peak. The road undulates up hill and down dale between dry-stone walls, through gritstone villages whose cottages have been blackened by centuries of industrial smoke. On a clear day there are lovely views across the Cheshire Plain. On your left as you approach Rainow on the B5470 is White Nancy, a curious monument at the end of prominent Kerridge Hill.

From Vale
to Moor

2 DAYS • 124 MILES • 201KM

This area of the North Riding extends from the gentle farm lands of the Vale of York to the wild beauty of the North York Moors, taking in delightful villages and evocative ruins.

Castle Howard is one of the architect Vanbrugh's finest works

ℹ️ *York Railway Station*

▶ *Take the A64 and turn left on to an unclassified road before Whitewell-on-the-Hill, passing Castle Howard, through Coneysthorpe to Malton.*

❶ Malton, North Yorkshire
Malton is divided in two by the site of a Roman station. New Malton is the busy market town, and Old Malton, a mile (1.6km) northeast, is a small village. Malton Museum, in the town, contains extensive Romano-British remains from the fort of *Derventio* and other settlements. Northwards is Eden Camp Modern History Museum, a former prisoner-of-war camp, where displays include women at war and the rise and fall of the Nazi Party.

Six miles (10km) southwest of Malton, on a signed road, is Castle Howard, a magnificent 18th-century house designed by Sir John Vanbrugh. It has been the home of the Howard family for nearly 300 years and notable features include the central dome, the Temple of the Four Winds and Hawksmoor's mausoleum.

ℹ️ *58 Market Place*

FOR CHILDREN

Kirby Misperton, near Malton, is the home of Flamingo Land. Over 1,000 animals include camels and polar bears, many of which have been bred here. Special attractions are organised, such as the parrot and dolphin shows.

▶ *Follow the road to Old Malton, cross the A64 on to the A169, turning almost immediately left on to an unclassified road through Kirby Misperton, rejoining the A169 north to Pickering.*

❷ Pickering, North Yorkshire
This ancient town is the starting point for the North Yorkshire Moors Railway, which runs between Pickering and Grosmont. Parts of the Church of St Peter and St Paul date from the 11th century and it contains splendid medieval wall paintings, notably *St George and the Dragon*. The ruins of Pickering Castle include a motte-and-bailey which was founded by William the Conqueror, and the Beck Isle Museum of Rural Life, in a fine Georgian building, is packed with bygones of the Victorian era.

ℹ️ *Eastgate Car Park*

▶ *Continue along the A169 for about 12 miles (19km), then turn left on to an unclassified road to Goathland.*

❸ Goathland, North Yorkshire
Goathland is one of the most picturesque villages in the North York Moors. This is a marvellous centre for walking and the area is renowned for spectacular waterfalls, including Nelly Ayre Foss, Mallyan Spout and Thomason Foss.

SPECIAL TO...

Goathland is the home of the Goathland Plough Stots, a sword dance team whose displays originated with Viking raiders over 1,000 years ago. It takes place on Plough Monday, the first Monday after 6 January, when a service is held to bless the Plough Stots ('stot' means bullock).

▶ *Return to the A169 for a short distance, then turn left on to unclassified roads to Grosmont.*

❹ Grosmont, North Yorkshire
Grosmont is the northern terminus of the North Yorkshire Moors Railway, and its popular-

All aboard the North Yorkshire Moors Railway

ity owes much to the railway. A trip on the Moorsrail will take you back to a gentler and slower age, and the locomotive sheds are worth a visit to see engines being prepared and restored.

▶ *Continue west along unclassified roads to Danby.*

FOR HISTORY BUFFS

A remarkably well-preserved stretch of an old Roman road, Wade's Causeway, passes near Grosmont. It was built 2,000 years ago as part of a Roman route from Malton to the coast near Goldsborough, and lay hidden until it was rediscovered in 1914.

---

5 Danby, North Yorkshire
The Moors Centre is located in Danby in a former shooting lodge, with exhibitions and impressive gardens. Southeast of the village are the ruins of 14th-century Danby Castle, where Catherine Parr, Henry VIII's sixth wife, once lived. The route now goes on to the moors past two old crosses, Fat Betty and

the Ralph Cross, which is used as the symbol for the North York Moors National Park.

ℹ️ *The Moors Centre, Danby Lodge, Lodge Lane*

▶ *Follow unclassified roads south to Rosedale Abbey.*

6 Rosedale Abbey, North Yorkshire
Rosedale's 12th-century Cistercian abbey no longer exists: only a few stones remain in the village. Ruins of railways and kilns at Chimney Bank Top are reminders of the old 19th-century ironstone industry. The famous chimney, once visible for miles, was demolished in 1972 when it was declared unsafe.

▶ *Continue to Hutton-le-Hole.*

7 Hutton-le-Hole, North Yorkshire
Hutton-le-Hole's Ryedale Folk Museum, in an ancient cruck-type building, features a marvellous collection of farm equipment, and reconstructed buildings. There are two 3½-mile (6km) walks signposted from the centre of the village into the countryside.

ℹ️ *Ryedale Folk Museum*

▶ *Continue on unclassified roads, crossing the River Dove and through Gillamoor to Kirkbymoorside.*

8 Kirkbymoorside, North Yorkshire
Situated at the edge of the moor, this small, peaceful town is just off the main road, with quiet streets and squares. The church dates from the 12th century and retains some fine Norman masonry and fragments of a Saxon cross.

▶ *Take the A170 for 6 miles (10km) to Helmsley.*

9 Helmsley, North Yorkshire
Roads from Cleveland, Thirsk and York converge upon the town square, making Helmsley a

busy trade centre. Helmsley Castle, dates from 1186 and was once inhabited by the Duke of Buckingham, court favourite of James I and Charles I.

Two miles (3km) west of Helmsley is Rievaulx, one of the largest Cistercian abbeys in England. The 12th-century ruins are surrounded by wooded hills, and above the abbey wall is Rievaulx Terrace, a beautiful landscaped garden with mock-Greek temples completed in 1758.

ℹ️ *Town Hall, Market Place*

RECOMMENDED WALKS

Highly recommended is the 3½ miles (6km) from Helmsley to Rievaulx, which runs along the richly wooded valley of the River Rye.

▶ *Follow unclassified roads from Rievaulx through Scawton to rejoin the A170, then turn left to White Horse Bank and Kilburn.*

10 Kilburn, North Yorkshire
Kilburn White Horse is the only turf-cut figure in the north of England. Almost 314 feet (96m) long by 228 feet (70m) high, it can be seen from the central tower of York Minster, 19 miles (30km) away. The village is well known for its woodcarvings, the work of Robert Thompson, who died in 1955. His trademark, a mouse, is still carved into the items produced by craftsmen at his works.

▶ *Continue on unclassified roads for 2 miles (3km) to Coxwold.*

11 Coxwold, North Yorkshire
Coxwold's most outstanding building is the 15th-century octagonal-towered church. In the churchyard is the gravestone of the 18th-century author Laurence Sterne, who named his house Shandy Hall, after the hero of his novel *The Life and*

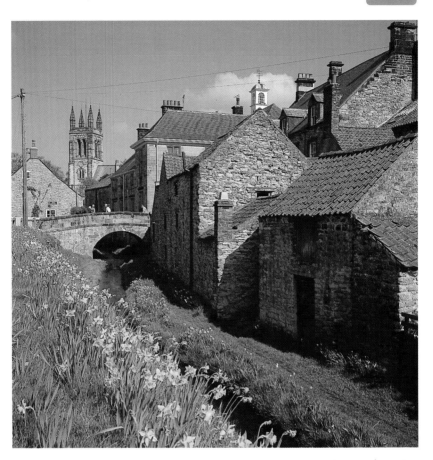

Opinions of Tristram Shandy; today it is a museum devoted to his life and works. Just beyond the village is Newburgh Priory, a 17th- and 18th-century house with a lake and gardens.

▶ *Return to Coxwold, then take an unclassified road to Wass.*

12 Wass, North Yorkshire
Wass was partly built from the ruins of nearby Byland Abbey, the largest Cistercian church in the country, with a 26-foot (8m) diameter window dating from the 13th century.

Two miles (3km) east of Wass is Ampleforth, which was chosen as the site of a school by English monks escaping from the French Revolution. Ampleforth College is now England's premier Roman Catholic public school.

Nearby Studford Ring is thought to date from the Bronze Age and is probably the finest earthwork enclosure in the area.

▶ *Continue east on unclassified roads to Oswaldkirk. Turn right on to the B1363 and continue south to Sutton-on-the-Forest.*

13 Sutton-on-the-Forest, North Yorkshire
Set in the undulating Howardian Hills, this is an unusual brick-built village with a stone church. Sutton Park, an early Georgian house, contains antique furniture by Chippendale and Sheraton and a collection of porcelain.

▶ *Return to York via the B1363, 8 miles (13km).*

Helmsley nestles beneath the southern rim of the moors

RECOMMENDED WALKS

The 100-mile (160km) Cleveland Way curves round the edge of the Moors, and certain stretches along it make ideal short walks.

BACK TO NATURE

The North York Moors are managed primarily to encourage the numbers of red grouse, but birds such as golden plovers, dunlins, curlews and lapwings also take advantage of the varied habitat.

135

SCOTLAND

Cross the border from England to Scotland, and you will find that the landscape, architecture and historical emphasis all change. This is part of the United Kingdom which retains its own educational and legal systems, banknotes and established church. Scotland joined the Union in 1707, but many of its castles and historic houses, heroes and battlefields are from the time when England was 'the auld enemy'. Football and rugby internationals retain something of that ancestral rivalry.

The ruined Border abbeys are evidence of the old raiding days. Along the Galloway coast, revenue duties on brandy, wine, silks and other goods were so resented that generations of Solway men made their living by smuggling. This was no casual trade. Several smuggling companies were proper businesses, with shareholders and accurate, if secret, books of accounts. Further north, in the Highland and Grampian glens, it was whisky taxes that were bitterly disliked. Pure mountain water, often flavoured by the peaty ground through which it flowed, was the basis of hundreds of illicit whisky stills. Some respectable modern distilleries happily admit to a raffish past.

Scotland has its own character and its own history. At the turn of the 13th and 14th centuries the story was one of avoiding an English conquest, and Scotland's independence was re-asserted during the reign of Robert I – Robert the Bruce. His descendants founded the dynasty of the Stuart kings and queens, and the story of the Highlands in the first half of the 18th century is largely bound up with the efforts of the Stuarts to regain the British throne. All their attempts were failures, but the history of the Jacobites is still well remembered.

The tours take you to Jacobite country, to the land of the Solway smugglers, to ground fought over in the Border wars, and to lonely northwestern districts, where the people were forced off their holdings by 19th-century landlords wanting the larger rents offered first by incoming sheep-farmers and then by wealthy deer-stalkers. In places you will wonder why the land seems so empty: it was not always so.

Neidpath Castle was battered by Cromwell during the Civil War

Gentle hills slope away from the banks of Loch Lomond

Inverness

Inverness is the capital of the Highlands. Industry is confined to one area, and the town can boast some fine old buildings among clumsy modern developments. Inverness makes a feature of its riverside walks, overlooked by a 19th-century castle, and footbridges cross to the Ness Islands. There are cruises on the Caledonian Canal, a good local museum, and the curious claim – which you can judge on Tomnahurich Hill – that the town has the most beautiful burial ground in the country!

Aberdeen

Aberdeen is the grey Granite City, the capital of North Sea oil, but the granite of its buildings comes to life and sparkles in the sun. There are excellent museums and galleries, such as Provost Skene's House, golf-courses and a long beach, while its parks rival any in Britain. Aberdeen is a regular top prizewinner in the Britain in bloom competition: look for the 100,000 roses planted along one city dual-carriageway.

Edinburgh

Even if no longer a seat of government, Edinburgh is obviously a capital city. The New Town is one of the most graceful examples of Georgian planning, and few shopping streets have such an imposing backdrop as Princes Street, dominated by the castle rock. Edinburgh houses Scotland's national galleries and some splendid museums, as well as being, every August and September, a world-famous festival city.

Within the city limits, look for Dean Village, a remarkable survival of lovely buildings by the Water of Leith, and for Cramond, once an oyster-fishermen's village, where the Almond Water flows into the Forth.

Dumfries

Dumfries is the Queen of the South, the principal town in the region which stretches from the English border to the Mull of Galloway. Its museums are varied and impressive, one featuring an old windmill adapted to house a camera obscura. Robert Burns is remembered affectionately in Dumfries, his home in later years. His house is one of the town museums and his favourite pub, the Globe Inn, retains many Burns mementoes.

Dumbarton

Dumbarton was once the capital of the Celtic kingdom of Strathclyde. Later, it became an innovative shipbuilding centre and, almost in passing, a pioneer of the helicopter and the hovercraft. It is still an exhilarating experience to climb to the viewpoint summit of Dumbarton Rock, the old Celtic stronghold and later a fortress of the Crown. Although the shipyards have been abandoned, the Denny Experiment Tank, where scale-models of hulls were tested to see how they performed in miniature storms still survives.

137

History &
Mystery

History and magnificent scenery are ever present on this tour. Just outside town lies Culloden, where Bonnie Prince Charlie's defeat in 1746 ruined the last hope of a Stuart restoration to the British throne. There are glorious sea, loch, island and mountain views, and who knows what may be lurking in Loch Ness?

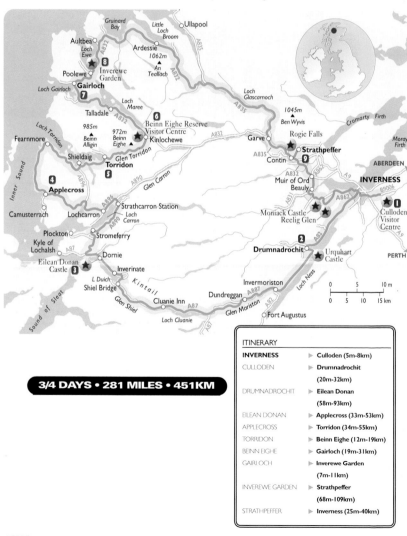

3/4 DAYS • 281 MILES • 451KM

ITINERARY		
INVERNESS	▶	**Culloden** (5m-8km)
CULLODEN	▶	**Drumnadrochit** (20m-32km)
DRUMNADROCHIT	▶	**Eilean Donan** (58m-93km)
EILEAN DONAN	▶	**Applecross** (33m-53km)
APPLECROSS	▶	**Torridon** (34m-55km)
TORRIDON	▶	**Beinn Eighe** (12m-19km)
BEINN EIGHE	▶	**Gairloch** (19m-31km)
GAIRLOCH	▶	**Inverewe Garden** (7m-11km)
INVEREWE GARDEN	▶	**Strathpeffer** (68m-109km)
STRATHPEFFER	▶	**Inverness** (25m-40km)

ⓘ *Castle Wynd, Inverness*

FOR CHILDREN

Before leaving Inverness, pay a visit to Whin Park, one of the finest children's play areas in the Highlands.

▶ *Leave Inverness on the **B9006** to the battlefield of Culloden.*

❶ Culloden, Highland
Cared for by the National Trust for Scotland, Culloden Moor is a place of sombre memories. It was here, on 16 April, 1746, that the Duke of Cumberland's army crushed the Jacobite rising led by Prince Charles. The battlefield is laid out with plaques showing the disposition of the opposing forces, and in the visitor centre you can follow the story of this last major battle on British soil. Displays illustrate the confusing political climate of the times, when there were Scots – and even different Highland clans – fighting on both sides. The bitter aftermath of the battle, when government

troops were sent on a murderous rampage through the glens, is also described.

▶ *Return to Inverness and leave on the **A82** as for Fort William.*

❷ Drumnadrochit, Highland
This is the site of the Loch Ness Centre, with its exhibition about the search for the world's most famous monster, said to lurk in the chill waters. You may arrive feeling sceptical, but you will almost certainly leave with the feeling that there is *something* here to be explained. Follow the 'Divach' sign off the A82 to the graceful Falls of Divach, and visit the striking lochside ruins of 13th-century Urquhart Castle, and the roadside monument to John Cobb, the land-speed record holder who was killed on Loch Ness in 1952 trying for the water-speed record.

ⓘ *Loch Ness Centre*

▶ *Continue on the **A82** to Invermoriston, then take the **A887** and go straight on along the **A87**. Continue through*

Eilean Donan Castle, built by Alexander II of Scotland in 1220

Inverinate and turn right up Carr Brae. Go into Dornie and turn left for Eilean Donan Castle.

❸ Eilean Donan, Highland
Probably the most photographed castle in Scotland, Eilean Donan was rebuilt on its splendid islet site between 1912 and 1932, after lying in ruins since the Jacobite Rising of 1719. The MacRaes have been its Constables since 1509. Principal apartments open to visitors are the barrel-vaulted billeting room and the small but impressive banqueting hall. In the hall, look for the letter from Bonnie Prince Charlie – 'Being fully persuaded of yr loyalty and zeal for the King's service…' – sent to clan chiefs on behalf of his father, seeking their support in the 1745 Rising.

▶ *Leave Dornie on the **A87** as for Kyle of Lochalsh, then turn right on to the **A890**, left on to the **A896** through Lochcarron and Kishorn, and left for Applecross.*

Loch Maree, one of Scotland's most beautiful inland lochs

FOR HISTORY BUFFS

Beside the A87 in wild Glenshiel a plaque describes the battle fought there during the short-lived Jacobite Rising of 1719. The defeated Jacobite army included a company of Spanish troops – the last foreign soldiers to fight on Scottish soil.

RECOMMENDED WALKS

Lochcarron Environmental Group publishes a guide to 15 hill, coast and forest walks. One climbs the Allt nan Carnan gorge above three waterfalls, with glorious views over Loch Carron and the Attadale hills.

❹ Applecross, Highland

If you don't like narrow mountain roads, skip Applecross; if you do you will find a beautifully located crofting village, facing the splendid skyline of the Cuillin Hills on Skye. St Maelrhuba is the local saint, and after his death in AD 722, villagers carried soil from his grave on long or perilous journeys. Potter southwards to the lovely rocky bay beyond Camusterrach and take a picnic behind the rippled sandbanks of Applecross Bay. On the lonely road north, look for the pathway which, until a generation ago, was the only land link between the scattered settlements of North Applecross.

ⓘ *Main Street, Lochcarron*

▶ *Leave Applecross following the 'Shieldaig' sign. Turn left at a T-junction to rejoin the A896.*

❺ Torridon, Highland

The Torridon landscape has no peers in mainland Scotland, with shapely Beinn Alligin and its outliers soaring from the sea-loch and, further east, Liathach's seven-peaked pinnacled ridge towering over Torridon village and glen. Both ranges are owned by the National Trust for Scotland, and a classic 9-mile (14km) walk on Trust ground explores the wild country behind Liathach. In summer, the Trust Visitor Centre explains the history, geology and wildlife of this glorious district, and there is an exhibition and audio-visual presentation on red deer near by.

ⓘ *NTS Visitor Centre*

▶ *Continue on the A896. Turn left on to the A832.*

❻ Beinn Eighe, Highland

This magnificent mountain range, with quartzite summit rocks which give the impression of a permanent dusting of snow, was Britain's first National Nature Reserve. The Visitor Centre on the A832 illustrates the fascinating wildlife of the mountain – warblers and redstarts in the birchwoods, crossbills among the pines, otters and black-throated divers on the margins of Loch Maree. Two waymarked trails – one to 1,700 feet (518m) – offer tremendous views over the loch.

ⓘ *Beinn Eighe Reserve Visitor Centre*

BACK TO NATURE

Beinn Eighe National Nature Reserve, near Kinlochewe, has some of the most dramatic scenery in Britain. Remnants of Caledonian pine forest harbour interesting plants such as creeping lady's tresses, lesser twayblade orchid, twinflower and chickweed wintergreen.

▶ *Continue on the A832 to Gairloch.*

❼ Gairloch, Highland

Gairloch is really a cluster of crofting settlements on the shores of an attractive sea-loch, which has become a resort with fine sands, a fishing harbour and one of the most beautifully located golf-courses in Scotland. Gairloch Heritage Museum has fishing boats in its courtyard, an old lighthouse tower installed at ground level, and indoor displays on the fishing, crofting and archaeological history of the heartland of the MacKenzies.

> [i] *Auchtercairn, Gairloch*

> ▶ *Continue through Poolewe.*

8 Inverewe Garden,
Highland
This is perhaps the most famous garden in the whole of Scotland. Its Victorian creator transformed a bare, windswept promontory into a pine-sheltered woodland where, helped by the benign effect of the Gulf Stream, a spectacular collection of rhododendrons, primulas, deep blue meconopsis and hundreds of other plants and flowering shrubs now flourishes.

FOR HISTORY BUFFS

Turn off the A832 into Aultbea and behind Pier Road is a board describing how, during World War II, the anchorage of Loch Ewe was the gathering-point for Arctic convoys to the Soviet port of Murmansk.

> ▶ *Continue on the A832, turn right on to the A835 then left at Contin on the A834.*

9 Strathpeffer, Highland
What was once Europe's most northerly spa remains a fine-looking resort centred on a gathering of sturdy Victorian hotels and villas in wooded grounds. Strathpeffer's redundant station has been restored to house craft shops, and in a pavilion in the square, you can sample some of the mineral-rich waters from local springs. Be prepared for a strong taste of sulphur! In the old days, spa visitors were expected to take vigorous exercise; so there is an excellent golf-course, as well as a network of paths in a pleasant pinewood and, on the southern hills patrolled by kestrels and sparrowhawks, to the commanding viewpoint summit of Knock Farril.

> [i] *The Square*

RECOMMENDED WALKS

Turn off the A835 after Tarvie for the Rogie Falls. Footpaths cross a bridge over the rock pools and rapids, and pass a salmon ladder built to allow fish to swim upstream in the spawning season.

FOR CHILDREN

At Strathpeffer, ask the children to find the street names in the Victorian heart of the town. Apart from 'The Square', there are none: in its heyday as a spa, house names were the only addresses.

> ▶ *Return to Contin and turn left on the A835. Turn right on the A832 then right on the A862 through Beauly. Turn right to Moniack and pass Moniack Castle. Turn right at a T-junction following the Rebeg sign, pass the start of the Reelig Glen forest walk, then continue over a bridge and uphill. Take the first tarred road left, past a house called Kilninver, turn left at a T-junction and immediately first right, then right at a Give Way sign to Inverness.*

SCENIC ROUTES

Down Glenshiel, the A87 slices through a landscape of steep green mountainsides. After Inverinate, Carr Brae leads to a wonderful viewpoint, and, later, the A890 opens up dramatic views around Loch Carron.

Inverness Castle: Macbeth is thought to have lived on the site of the first castle here

The Castles
of Mar

Aberdeen is the gateway to Royal Deeside and to the great spread of historic houses known as the Castles of Mar. The Royal Family's Scottish home is here, where pine and birchwoods line the riversides and heathery grouse moors rise to the skyline hills. Salmon and trout anglers fish the Dee and its companion river, the Don. Gliders soar above Aboyne and Dinnet, while older transport is the fascination at Alford.

ITINERARY

ABERDEEN	▶ **Crathes Castle** (17m-27km)
CRATHES CASTLE	▶ **Aboyne** (16m-26km)
ABOYNE	▶ **Ballater** (17m-27km)
BALLATER	▶ **Balmoral Castle** (8m-13km)
BALMORAL CASTLE	▶ **Kildrummy Castle** (27m-43km)
KILDRUMMY CASTLE	▶ **Alford** (10m-16km)
ALFORD	▶ **Craigievar** (7m-11km)
CRAIGIEVAR	▶ **Drum Castle** (22m-36km)
DRUM CASTLE	▶ **Aberdeen** (10m-16km)

3 DAYS • 134 MILES • 215KM

The Castles of Mar

TOUR 27

i *St Nicholas House, Broad Street, Aberdeen*

▶ *Leave Aberdeen on the B9077. Turn right on the A957, then left on the A93 to Crathes Castle.*

❶ Crathes Castle, Grampian
Sixteenth-century Crathes Castle was the home of generations of the Burnett family. It is a typical design by the Bells, master masons of Aberdeen and its hinterland, with a tower-like structure and an intriguing ornamented roofline. Look for the lovely painted ceiling of the Nine Nobles Room, and in the Green Lady's Room ponder the story of the Crathes ghost. There are eight splendid individual gardens, and one of their major attractions is the array of massive yew hedges, planted in 1702. Topiarists trim them into sweeping shapes, a task which takes three weeks every year.

FOR CHILDREN

Turn left off the B9077 for Storybook Glen, with its tableaux of children's stories, ranging from *Jack and the Beanstalk* and *Little Jack Horner* to the *Incredible Hulk* and *ET*.

▶ *Continue on the A93 to Aboyne.*

❷ Aboyne, Grampian
Built in Victorian times round a spacious green, Aboyne was previously a base for the 'floaters', the intrepid characters who made rafts of timber, cut up-river, and then steered them down the Dee to Aberdeen. There is a well-kept golf-course not far from the water-skiing centre at Aboyne Loch. Anglers fish the Dee, and there are pleasant riverside walks backed by banks of broom.

Aboyne Highland Games, held every August on the green, are among the most famous in Scotland.

RECOMMENDED WALKS

After Aboyne, turn left off the B976 at the grand gateway by the Bridge o' Ess into beautiful Glen Tanar.
Call in at the Glen Tanar Visitor Centre for information on the footpath routes beside the Water of Tanar and along part of the Firmounth road, one of the historic rights of way across the Grampians.

SPECIAL TO...

Aboyne is just one place which hosts annual Highland Games. Tossing the caber, shot-putting and hill races, as well as normal track events, are featured at Ballater and further up Royal Deeside. The Lonach Gathering at Bellabeg, on the A944 in Strathdon, is preceded by a march of the green-clad Lonach Highlanders.

▶ *Leave Aboyne to the south. Turn right on the B976, right on the A97 as far as Ordie. Turn left on to the B9119 and right on the A93 to Ballater.*

❸ Ballater, Grampian
Close to the Royal Family's Balmoral estate, this sturdy granite-built town has many shops showing the royal warrant. Golf, angling and walks by the Dee are favourite recreations here, but there are also enjoyable footpaths on Craigendarroch and Craig Coillich, the two wooded viewpoint hills which squeeze the town towards the river. In the now redundant railway station there is a display on the Deeside Line and its most celebrated passengers: the Royal Family used to arrive by train at Ballater and continue by road to Balmoral.

i *Station Square*

▶ *Leave Ballater to the south and turn right on the B976 to the car park for Balmoral Castle.*

SPECIAL TO...

Single malt whisky is a classic Highland product. Turn left off the B976 before Balmoral for a tour of Royal Lochnagar Distillery, which received its royal warrant after a visit from Queen Victoria.

Sixteenth-century Crathes Castle

Craigievar Castle rises six storeys high and is topped by turrets

4 Balmoral Castle,
Grampian
The Royal Family's Scottish home is their private property, and not one of the great state houses. Prince Albert collaborated closely with the architect commissioned to build the present castle in Scottish Baronial style. From May till the end of July, the beautiful grounds are generally open to visitors. The ballroom houses an exhibition on the history of the estate. Across the river from the car park, Crathie parish church is where the Royal Family worship when they are in residence at Balmoral.

▶ *Turn left on the* **A93**, *right on the* **B976**, *left on the* **A939**, *right on the* **A944**, *then straight on along the* **A97** *to Kildrummy Castle.*

5 Kildrummy Castle,
Grampian
Built in the 13th century, this was the first great stone fortress in the north of Scotland. Even in decay it remains an impressive place. Modern Kildrummy Castle, once a mansion house, is now a hotel. The quarry from which it was built was transformed in Victorian times into a Japanese-style rock and water-garden with woodlands, pools, waterfalls, shrubs and flower beds linked by paths and stairways in a narrow ravine.

FOR HISTORY BUFFS

Kildrummy Castle witnessed a gruesome deed in 1306, when its English besiegers promised to reward the blacksmith who betrayed it to them with gold. They kept their promise by melting the gold pieces and pouring them down his throat to kill him.

▶ *Continue on the* **A97**, *then right on the* **A944** *to Alford.*

6 Alford, Grampian
If it runs on wheels, Alford welcomes it. The Grampian Transport Museum houses a fine collection of cars, commercial and farm vehicles, models and transport memorabilia. Look for the *Craigievar Express*, a steam wagon built in the 1890s by a local postman; and a Sentinel steam lorry from a distillery, whose wares it advertises as most suitable for medicinal purposes.

Outside, the museum operates a little motor-racing circuit where sprints for modern and vintage cars are held. Close by, the old station has been restored as a railway museum.

ⓘ *Railway Museum*

FOR CHILDREN

From Alford station the narrow-gauge Alford Valley Railway runs into Haughton House Country Park, where there is an adventure playground in the birchwoods.

▶ *Return from Alford along the* **A944** *straight on along the* **A980**, *then right to Craigievar Castle.*

7 Craigievar Castle,
Grampian
Although they were not building for fairy-tales, the Bell family of master masons combined a firm grasp of technique with a glorious lightness of touch. With its profusion of towers and turrets, Craigievar demonstrates this very clearly. Built for 'Danzig Willie' Forbes, who made his fortune in the Baltic trade, it was completed in 1626. Craigievar's five floors of rooms include such features as a grand heraldic fireplace carved from granite, pine and oak panelling, intricate plaster ceilings and the first of the Craigievar gaming tables which had a vogue among 18th-century card players.

▶ *Continue on the* **A980** *and go straight on along the* **B977** *and the* **B9125**, *then immediately after Flora's Shop, turn right, following the 'Hopeton' sign. Turn right at a crossroads, avoiding a farm road straight ahead, then follow signs to Drum Castle.*

FOR HISTORY BUFFS

On the B977, look to the left for the granite monument to the Battle of Corrichie in 1562. Mary, Queen of Scots' army crushed the Gordons, the most powerful family in the northeast, in this battle. The Earl of Huntly, the head of the family, died in the battle, and his corpse was taken to Edinburgh to 'hear' the sentence that forfeited his lands and titles.

---

8 Drum Castle, Grampian
The Irvine family have been lairds at Drum Castle for 24 generations before giving the property to the National Trust for Scotland. They lived in a complex of linked buildings: a 13th-century keep, a Jacobean mansion and Victorian additions. Drum is well furnished with valuable pieces from different centuries. Among the portraits is one of Washington Irving, author of the classic *Rip van Winkle*, whose family left Scotland to live in America.

▶ *Rejoin the public road, then turn left on to the* **A93** *to return to Aberdeen.*

Exploring the
Tweed Valley

Hills are an important part of this tour, which visits the Pentlands, the Eildons and the Lammermuirs, and looks south to the Cheviots. But the valley of the River Tweed, one of Scotland's great trout and salmon waters, is the most significant element as the journey reaches the Border country.

2/3 DAYS • 134 MILES • 216KM

ITINERARY		
EDINBURGH	▶	**Hillend Country Park** (5m-8km)
HILLEND COUNTRY PARK	▶	**Peebles (18m-29km)**
PEEBLES	▶	**Traquair (8m-13km)**
TRAQUAIR	▶	**Innerleithen (2m-3km)**
INNERLEITHEN	▶	**Melrose (16m-26km)**
MELROSE	▶	**Kelso (14m-23km)**
KELSO	▶	**Coldstream (9m-14km)**
COLDSTREAM	▶	**Haddington (37m-60km)**
HADDINGTON	▶	**Aberlady (5m-8km)**
ABERLADY	▶	**Edinburgh (20m-32km)**

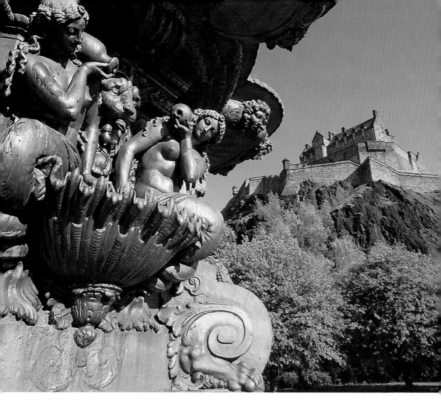

Edinburgh Castle perches on Castle Rock, possibly the site of an old Iron Age fort

i   *3 Princes Street, Edinburgh*

▶ *Leave Edinburgh on the A702 and turn right into Hillend Country Park, 5 miles (8km).*

❶ Hillend Country Park, Lothian

This is one of two similar parks in the exhilarating Pentland Hills, which rise directly from Edinburgh's southern suburbs. Footpaths climb steeply to the grassy viewpoint summits of Caerketton and Allermuir, the boyhood hills of Robert Louis Stevenson.

These paths link up with others across the rounded passes in the Pentlands, and alongside the many reservoirs which supply the city. Hillend Ski Centre, with its extensive artificial ski-slope, is a year-round mountain resort in miniature.

i   *Pentland Hills Ranger Service Office*

▶ *Continue on the A702, then straight on along the A703 and follow the A701 and B7026 through Auchendinny. Take the A6094 and the A703 again to Peebles.*

FOR CHILDREN

Hillend Ski Centre is the largest of its kind in Europe. Children's courses start for those aged six. On the return to Edinburgh, the Butterfly and Insect World on the A7 houses hundreds of exotic butterflies as well as scorpions, tarantulas and stick insects.

---

❷ Peebles, Borders

No development is allowed to encroach upon Peebles' tree-lined riverside walks by the Tweed, and the town itself has a traditional charm. The Tontine Hotel in the High Street retains the old front yard where stage-coaches used to sweep to a halt. There is a well-stocked Tweeddale Museum, and the Scottish Museum of Ornamental Plasterwork is close by, where you will be encouraged to don wellies and an apron, and try your hand at the craft. Peebles has extensive public parks and an interesting town walk.

Medieval Neidpath Castle stands dramatically above an up-river wooded curve of the Tweed, to the west of Peebles. Its walls still show signs of the bombardment in 1650 by Cromwell's artillery.

RECOMMENDED WALKS

The Sware Walk at Peebles heads west along the wooded riverbank below Neidpath Castle, crosses Manor Bridge and Old Manor Bridge, then climbs to the wide-ranging Tweeddale viewpoint at Manor Sware.

---

i   *High Street*

▶ *Leave Peebles on the B7062 and turn left for Traquair House.*

3 Traquair, Borders

Twenty generations of Stuart lairds made Traquair House their home, but it dates from well before their time – from 1107 at least – and is the oldest inhabited house in Scotland. Traquair retains mementoes of such famous Stuarts as Mary, Queen of Scots and Bonnie Prince Charlie. As well as having valuable collections of glass, porcelain and embroideries, it is famous for its one derelict 18th-century estate brew-house. The present laird restored the copper, the mash tun, the coolers and fermenters, and now brews the rare Traquair Ale in quantities of no more than 210 barrels every year.

▶ *Continue on the B7062 then turn left on the B709 to Innerleithen.*

4 Innerleithen, Borders

The founder of this little textile town had the idea of using London names so addresses here include The Strand and Bond Street. Cashmere cloth is still woven in Innerleithen's mills, and the National Trust for Scotland has completely restored Robert Smail's Printing Works, closed as a family business only in 1986. A tour of this fascinating place recalls the otherwise lost technology of planers, reglets, quoins and sidesticks, and you may be given the chance to hand-set some type

yourself. At a glorious viewpoint high in the town, the little blue-and-white spa pavilion of St Ronan's Wells can be found. The spring was originally known as the 'Doo Well' because of the number of wood pigeons which frequented the area.

St Ronan was thought to be a saint from France or Ireland and was adopted as patron saint of Innerleithen. The wells became famous when, in 1824, Sir Walter Scott used them as a setting for his novel *St Ronan's Well*.

▶ *Leave Innerleithen on the A72. Bear right on the A707, then left on the B7060. Turn right on the A7, left on the B6360, right on the A6091 as for Jedburgh, and left on the B6374 into Melrose.*

FOR HISTORY BUFFS

Abbotsford, on the way to Melrose, was the home of Sir Walter Scott, author of the *Waverley* novels. He bought the site on which he built Abbotsford between 1811 and 1822. It took a long time to complete as he kept adding on bits. The tour includes his impressive library and study.

Robert Smail's print shop was started in 1840, when the original press was water-powered

5 Melrose, Borders

One of the pleasantest of the Border towns, Melrose is notable for the mellow ruin of its abbey, where the heart of Robert the Bruce is buried, and for Priorwood Garden, in which something like the old monks' orchard has been revived. Harmony Garden is an attractive walled garden with magnificent views over Melrose Abbey and the Eildon Hills. Two walks explore the town, and the Southern Upland Way includes a lovely riverside stretch along the meadows by the Tweed.

[i] *Abbey House*

RECOMMENDED WALKS

Starting from the B6359 in Melrose, the waymarked Eildon Walk climbs to the 1,325-foot (404m) Eildon North Hill, a magnificent viewpoint where a Roman signal station overlooked the Dere Street route from the Cheviots to the Forth. Here is the legendary resting place of King Arthur and his knights, sleeping under a spell.

▶ *Leave Melrose on the A6091 as for Jedburgh. Turn right on to the A68 then left on the A699 and left on the A698 into Kelso.*

6 Kelso, Borders

Here is a Border market town with a ruined abbey, the oldest cricket club in Scotland, a racecourse and a reputation for providing some of the best angling beats on the Tweed. Kelso has an elegant Georgian centre, and its cobbled square retains a bull ring – a pattern of stones marking the place where bulls were tethered during livestock sales. Kelso Pottery is well worth a visit.

Outside the town, Floors Castle, home of the Duke of Roxburghe, is richly furnished with paintings, tapestries and

The Myreton Motor Museum at Aberlady

porcelain, and has a window for every day of the year. This huge mansion was built by William Adam between 1721 and 1725.

ⓘ *Town House, The Square*

▶ *Leave Kelso on the **A698** for Coldstream.*

7 Coldstream, Borders
This is the closest Scottish town to the English border. The Coldstream Guards, under an earlier name, were stationed in the town in 1660 when they marched south to assist in the restoration of King Charles II to the throne. There is a museum here dedicated to the regiment and its impressive heritage. Just outside Coldstream, the Hirsel estate has a comprehensive museum and a craft centre, several walks and a colourful collection of rhododendrons in Dundock Wood.

ⓘ *High Street*

▶ *Leave Coldstream on the **A6112** for Duns, then take the **A6105** as for Earlston. After leaving Duns, watch for the*

*right turn to Gifford. Turn right to Haddington on the **B6369** and **B6368**.*

SPECIAL TO...

In Newtown Street, Duns, the Jim Clark Memorial Room commemorates the great world race-driving champion who won 25 Grand Prix races and the Indianapolis 500.

FOR HISTORY BUFFS

Memorials at Gifford recall the Rev John Witherspoon, who signed the American Declaration of Independence and was president of the college which became Princeton university. Off the B6369, Lennoxlove House is the home of the Dukes of Hamilton. It contains many mementoes of Mary, Queen of Scots, including the ring which, on her way to the scaffold, she bequeathed to the Hamiltons.

8 Haddington, Lothian
Haddington is famous for the dozens of listed buildings along its streets, lanes and riverside walks. St Mary's Church contains the Lauderdale Aisle, scene of an annual ecumenical pilgrimage. Near by, St Mary's Pleasance is a garden laid out in an old Scottish style. Features to look for in Haddington include the town history display in Lady Kitty's Doocot (dovecote); Jane Welsh Carlyle's House, with its memories of the Victorian writer Thomas Carlyle; the Nungate Bridge; and the statue of two goats fighting. A goat eating grapes is Haddington's unusual coat of arms.

▶ *Leave Haddington on the **A6137** for Aberlady.*

9 Aberlady, Lothian
Once the trading seaport for Haddington, Aberlady is now a residential village with carefully

preserved buildings, including a medieval parish church with fine stained-glass windows, and attractive 18th- and 19th-century houses in the High Street. Aberlady's golf-course, Kilspindie, shared the ground with a rifle range when it was opened in 1898; hence the names of holes such as the Target and the Magazine. West of the village, Gosford House is the home of the Earl of Wemyss. The magnificent entrance hall houses Gosford's imposing portrait gallery.

BACK TO NATURE

The tidal inlet, saltmarsh and dunes at Aberlady Bay Nature Reserve, east of Aberlady, attract great numbers of waders. Regular reports are posted of bird observations: hundreds of sandwich terns, for instance, and godwits, dunlin and plover.

▶ *Leave Aberlady on the **A198** as for Edinburgh, then straight ahead on the **B1348**. Turn left on the **A199** then right on the **A6094** through Dalkeith. Turn right on the **A772** and return to Edinburgh.*

BACK TO NATURE

On the return towards Edinburgh, Dalkeith Park nature trails link the River North Esk and the South Esk through extensive estate woodlands.

SCENIC ROUTES

The B7062, past Kailzie Gardens, and the A72 follow the Tweed as it winds among woodlands, farms and hillside forests. You can follow a tree-lined road on the B7060 over the shoulder of a hill between two stretches of the Tweed.

Along the
Smugglers' Coast

Mountains, forests and beautiful stretches of coastline are the accompaniment to this tour from Dumfries. The huge Galloway Forest Park offers walks and trails, exhibitions, nature reserves and fishing waters. Along the coast, the Solway smugglers once brought contraband from the Isle of Man.

2/3 DAYS • 119 MILES • 191KM

ITINERARY		
DUMFRIES	▶	**New Abbey** (7m-11km)
NEW ABBEY	▶	**Kirkbean** (5m-8km)
KIRKBEAN	▶	**Rockcliffe** (10m-16km)
ROCKCLIFFE	▶	**Castle Douglas** (11m-18km)
CASTLE DOUGLAS	▶	**Kirkcudbright** (10m-16km)
KIRKCUDBRIGHT	▶	**Gatehouse of Fleet** (9m-14km)
GATEHOUSE OF FLEET	▶	**Kirroughtree** (16m-26km)
KIRROUGHTREE	▶	**The Queens Way** (9m-14km)
THE QUEENS WAY	▶	**Dumfries** (42m-68km)

i *Whitesands, Dumfries*

BACK TO NATURE

The Wildfowl Trust reserve at Caerlaverock, southeast of Dumfries, provides some of the best opportunities anywhere to observe wild barnacle geese and family parties of whooper swans in the winter. Both the sanctuary of the reserve and the supplementary supply of food attract these species along with wigeon, teal and many more. There is a charge for admission (except to members of the Wildfowl Trust).

New Abbey's 18th-century corn mill restored to working order

▶ *Leave Dumfries on the A710 to New Abbey.*

❶ New Abbey, Dumfries and Galloway

Here, 'new' is a relative term. It refers to the lovely ruined abbey of mellow red sandstone which stands on the south side of the village. This is Sweetheart Abbey, new in the 13th century when it was founded by the family which also endowed Balliol College at Oxford. New Abbey also has a splendidly restored 18th-century corn mill. Among the pinewoods at the entrance to the village, Shambellie House is the site of Scotland's Museum of Costume.

▶ *Continue on the A710 to Kirkbean.*

❷ Kirkbean, Dumfries and Galloway

American visitors often come to this attractive village in 'the garden of Galloway' to trace the roots of Paul Jones, organiser and first commander of the Navy, who was baptised John Paul in the parish church here. His birthplace cottage on the Arbigland estate is a museum of his life and exploits, which included raiding his home coast during the American War of Independence! Arbigland itself has attractive sheltered gardens stretching to the Solway shore, where Paul Jones' father was employed.

Also near Kirkbean, Carsethorn is a Solwayside village with salmon stake-nets out on the treacherous tidal sands. Facing the Cumbrian shore, it was built to house the men of a 19th-century coastguard station, in the days when the coastguards' preoccupation was stopping the smugglers.

▶ *Continue on the A710. Turn left off it, first to Rockcliffe and then to Kippford.*

❸ Rockcliffe and Kippford, Dumfries and Galloway

These are the principal villages of the Colvend coast, the most beautiful stretch of the Solway Firth. Rockcliffe, with its rock flakes in a curving bay, was a Victorian sea-bathing resort.

Kippford, near the mouth of the River Urr, used to make its living from boat-building and quarrying. Now it is the main sailing centre on the Solway. Almost all the land between the villages is owned by the National Trust for Scotland. Both offer outstanding views over the wooded peninsulas around Rough Firth.

Above Rockcliffe stands the Mote of Mark, site of a 6th-century settlement on a granite outcrop and now a glorious viewpoint.

i *Colvend Post Office, A710*

RECOMMENDED WALKS

For one of the most beautiful walks in Scotland, leave Rockcliffe by the Jubilee Path with its gorgeous views over the estuary.
At Kippford, turn left by the post office along the shore road, then return to Rockcliffe by grassy pathways.
Except in May and June when the terns and oystercatchers are nesting, you can extend the walk – with care – along the tidal causeway to Rough Island.

FOR CHILDREN

Take the children for a boat trip from the floating jetty at Kippford, and let their imaginations run riot as they sail the smugglers' waters around Rough Firth and Hestan Island, a place honeycombed with 'brandy holes' and contraband hideaways.

▶ *Continue on the A710, then follow signs for Castle Douglas on the A711 and A745. Turn left at a roundabout and go through the town centre, 11 miles (18km).*

❹ Castle Douglas, Dumfries and Galloway

A light and lively market town, Castle Douglas is lucky in having, as its principal public park, the land around Carlingwark Loch. Here you can hire a rowing boat to potter round the wooded islets and reed-beds where swans and great crested grebes nest and raise their young.

West of the loch, watch for the road on the left to Threave Garden. A property of the National Trust for Scotland, it features springtime daffodil displays as well as herbaceous borders, peat, woodland and rock gardens. Threave House is the Trust's School of Horticulture, and the whole 60 acres (24 hectares) are impeccably kept.

i Market Hill Car Park

FOR HISTORY BUFFS

At the roundabout after Castle Douglas, take the second exit for the walk and short ferry trip across the Dee to Threave Castle, the ruined island fortress of the Black Douglases, rebels against the crown, in the River Dee.

▶ *Turn left at a roundabout, go along the **A75**, then turn left on to the **A711** to Kirkcudbright.*

❺ Kirkcudbright, Dumfries and Galloway

Built as the county town, this is a place of elegantly proportioned and colour-washed Georgian houses. It attracted turn-of-the-century artists, and their successors still live and work here. Broughton House, an 18th-century mansion, was presented to the town by the painter E A Hornel. It hosts art exhibitions and is well furnished with a fine antiquarian library and features such as a 1920s-style laundry. Outside, you may be surprised to find a Japanese garden; Hornel was influenced by Oriental themes.

Maclellan's Castle, now an ancient monument, is the ruin of a grander and earlier town mansion. The Stewartry Museum holds a fascinating local collection, including a room devoted to Kirkcudbright shipping, in which Paul Jones features strongly.

i Harbour Square

▶ *Leave Kirkcudbright on the **A755** then follow the **B727** through Gatehouse of Fleet.*

The estuary of the Dee in Kirkcudbright at dusk

SPECIAL TO...

Phone Kirkcudbright 330114 to book a place on the tour – starting from Kirkcudbright – of Tongland power station, with its audio-visual presentation on the Galloway hydro-electric scheme, followed by visits to the spotless turbine hall and the salmon ladder in the ravine behind.

❻ Gatehouse of Fleet, Dumfries and Galloway

Gatehouse by the River Fleet is one of the most intriguing country towns in Scotland, full of restored buildings from its brief heyday – from 1790 onwards – as a cotton town. Robert Burns visited Gatehouse during the boom years, and it was in a room at the Murray Arms Hotel that he wrote what was to become Scotland's unofficial anthem, *Scots, wha hae*. The town is surrounded by delicious woodland country. Try the Fleet Oakwoods interpretative trail. A shorter open-ground stroll leads to the field-top viewpoint on Venniehill, which identifies the features of Gatehouse and its surroundings. Beyond

Grey Mare's Tail waterfall

Venniehill, Cardoness Castle is an imposingly situated 15th-century tower which was the home of the notoriously hot-tempered McCullochs.

[i] *The Car Park, High Street*

▶ *Turn right on to the A75 (heading west) and in Palnure watch for a right turn to Kirroughtree Visitor Centre.*

FOR HISTORY BUFFS

Turn right off the A75 for the standing stones of Cairn Holy, overlooking the Solway. On the return to Dumfries, Maxwelton House, on the B729, was the birthplace of the heroine of Scotland's famous love song, *Annie Laurie*.

7 Kirroughtree Forest,
Dumfries and Galloway
The oldest South of Scotland plantations of the Forestry Commission cover a landscape of hills and a river valley over-looked by the great bulk of Cairnsmore of Fleet. An audio-visual presentation explains the workings of the forest, and outdoor attractions include a forest garden with plots of more than 60 tree species, from redwoods and monkey puzzles to cypress and rarities such as the Englemann spruce. Four trails explore the upper parts of the forest, visiting hill lochs and viewpoints, and you should follow the separate Papy Ha'bird trail above the Palnure Burn, habitat of warblers, woodpeck-ers, dippers, goosanders, shel-duck, jays and ravens.

[i] *Visitor Centre*

▶ *Rejoin the A75, then go right on to the A712.*

8 The Queens Way,
Dumfries and Galloway
Several visitor areas of the Galloway Forest Park are concentrated along the stretch of A712 known as the Queens Way. The start is signalled by the hilltop obelisk at Talnotry commemorating Alexander Murray, a local shepherd's son who became the greatest Oriental linguist in early 19th-century Britain.
    Look for the Grey Mare's Tail waterfall, the wild goats and their kids in the roadside reserve at Craigdews Hill, the red deer range and the Galloway Deer Museum which is situated among a stand of pines above Clatteringshaws Loch.

[i] *Galloway Deer Museum*

RECOMMENDED
WALKS

At Talnotry, on the Queens Way, marked trails explore the steep forested hills. Do not be misled by the wide path at the start; much of this is roughish going. The trails go to viewpoints and an old lead mine, and follow the 'lost' 18th-century Edinburgh-Wigtown coach road.

FOR CHILDREN

Turn off the Queens Way after the red deer range for the Raiders Road forest drive, an old cattle-rustlers' trail which runs beside the Black Water of Dee. Children usually love the bronze otter sculpture at a picnic pool with rocky islets.

▶ *Continue on the A712 through New Galloway. Turn right on the A713, left on the A712, left on the B7075 and right on the A702 through Moniaive. In Kirkland, turn right on the B729 and return to Dumfries.*

SCENIC ROUTES

Beyond Dumfries, the A710 gradually comes within sight of the wide Solway sands and, across the water, the faraway Lakeland hills.
    After Gatehouse, the A75 offers beautiful high-level views over the bird-watcher's paradise of Wigtown Bay.
    After Moniaive, the A702 and B729 follow the Cairn Valley through a fine landscape of farms, woods and stone-dyked fields.

The Beautiful
Western Highlands

4 DAYS • 246 MILES • 396KM Some of the most striking seascapes, mountains, forests and moorland scenery in the West Highlands form the landscape of this tour, based on the firmly Lowland town of Dumbarton.

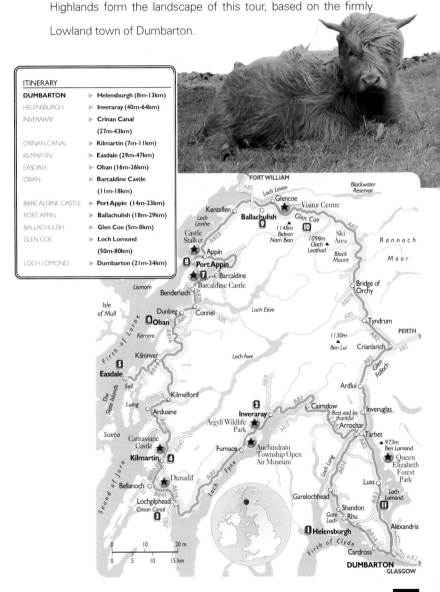

_i_ *Milton, by Dumbarton*

▶ *Leave Dumbarton on the A814 through Cardross, Helensburgh, Rhu and Shandon.*

❶ Helensburgh, Strathclyde
Think of this residential town rising from the estuary of the River Clyde when you switch on your television. John Logie Baird, the television pioneer, was born here in 1888. Another inventive Helensburgh man was Henry Bell, whose *Comet*, launched in 1812, was the world's first sea-going steamboat. Both men are commemorated in the town.

Charles Rennie Mackintosh, the most famous of Scotland's 20th-century architects, completed The Hill House in 1902. You may share the feelings of many visitors that the elegant interiors, showing Mackintosh's amazing attention to detail, seem to become more rather than less modern as the decades pass.

The cone-topped towers of Inveraray Castle

In summer, ferries sail across the Clyde from Helensburgh. There are sailing races, and dozens of yachts lie moored off Rhu – where the garden of Glenarn is an early-season attraction – and Shandon. After Shandon the road passes the Clyde Submarine Base, home port of Britain's nuclear fleet.

_i_ *The Clock Tower*

▶ *Take the third exit from the roundabout, follow the A814 to Arrochar and turn left on the A83. Ignore a left turn for the A815, bear left on an unclassified road through Cairndow, and rejoin the A83 for Inveraray.*

❷ Inveraray, Strathclyde
Once the county town of Argyll, this gem of 18th-century architecture is reflected in the waters of Loch Fyne near Inveraray Castle, home of the 12th Duke of Argyll. The castle's public rooms include an imposing armoury hall, a tapestry drawing room and a state dining room with elaborate plasterwork. In the grounds, Cherry Park houses

a Combined Operations Museum recalling how a quarter of a million troops were trained at Inveraray for seaborne landings of World War II. There are also pleasant woodland walks. If you are fit and sure-footed, try the steep climb through roe deer territory to the viewpoint summit of Dun na Cuaiche.

The town's 20th-century bell tower acts as the Clan Campbell war memorial; and Inveraray Gaol is one of the finest theme museums in Scotland. In the courtroom, sitting among lifelike figures of lawyers and jurymen, you can hear the tape-recorded transcript of an actual trial held in 1850.

FOR CHILDREN

South of Inveraray, Argyll Wildlife Park covers 60 acres (18 hectares) of open ground, forest and lochside. There are wildfowl pools as well as badgers, wildcats, foxes, pine martens and deer, and the residents of Owl Avenue stare imperiously down.

⊳ Continue on the **A83** to Lochgilphead. Turn right on the **A816**, bear left on the **B841** to cross the Crinan Canal, then go right at Bellanoch on the **B8025**.

| i | Front Street

FOR HISTORY BUFFS

Beside the A83, Auchindrain is a farming museum. In and around a cluster of restored cottages once lived in by MacCallums, MacCoshams, MacNicols and Munros you can see furnishings and displays of agricultural techniques of generations long gone by.

Crinan Canal was opened in 1801

8 Crinan Canal, Strathclyde
Built to save fishing boats and trading ships the risky journey round the Mull of Kintyre, this 9-mile (14m) waterway is now used mostly by yachts and motor cruisers. To the south of the summit level, spruce plantations clothe the hills where reservoirs store the canal's water supply. From the picnic site at Dunardry a forest walk looks down on the canal, its locks and towpath, and an attractive tree-backed lagoon.

⊳ Bear left on the **A816** to Kilmartin.

4 Kilmartin, Strathclyde
The lovely Kilmartin valley was the heartland of the 6th-century kingdom of Dalriada, which expanded to become the kingdom of Scotland. The valley also contains Bronze Age burial cairns and standing stones, some set out in a straight linear alignment.

Kilmartin church and churchyard house many medieval grave slabs, and Carnassarie Castle, high above the village, offers a magnificent view, unobtainable from road level, into the narrow canyon which swings down from Loch Awe.

⊳ Continue on the **A816**, then left on the **B844** and follow signs to Easdale.

FOR HISTORY BUFFS

Few places are as atmospheric, for Scots or descendants of Scots, as Dunadd, south of Kilmartin. With its lovely panoramic views, this hilltop fortress was the capital of the kingdom of Dalriada and the coronation site of the first Scottish kings.

---

5 Easdale, Strathclyde
The steeply-arched 'bridge over the Atlantic' to Seil joins one of Argyll's Slate Islands to the mainland. Easdale is the name both of the old quarry village on the west side of Seil, and of the smaller offshore island facing it. A deep quarry at Easdale village, breached by the sea during a ferocious storm in November 1881, survives as an open bay.

The village retains its rows of whitewashed quarriers' cottages. In contrast, high walls and a wooded cliff protect the garden of An Cala – with its gentle stream, ponds, herbaceous borders and flowering shrubs – from the salt-laden wind.

Across the narrow sound on Easdale Island, the workings of a now vanished trade and the way the quarry communities created their own lively social life are explained in a fascinating museum.

| i | Easdale Island Folk Museum

⊳ Return to the **A816** and turn left for Oban.

6 Oban, Strathclyde
Oban is a major car-ferry port and hosts several important yacht races. St Columba's, the 20th-century cathedral with carved oak panels showing scenes from the life of the famous Celtic saint, is the heart of the Roman Catholic diocese of Argyll and the Isles.

Elsewhere in the town you can watch glass-blowers and paper-weight-makers at work, and visit the distillery founded in the 18th century. Footpaths climb to outstanding viewpoints such as McCaig's Tower, built in the style of the Colosseum at Rome. Gallanach Road leads south to the little ferry slip for Kerrera, where you can enjoy an exhilarating island walk round a 7-mile (11km) circuit of paths and farm roads.

| i | Argyll Square

⊳ Leave Oban on the **A85**. At Connel, turn right on the **A828** as it swings over Connel Bridge.

7 Barcaldine Castle, Strathclyde
This 16th-century home of the Campbells of Barcaldine, set in magnificent scenery with views

Fishing boats at Oban harbour

FOR CHILDREN

A World in Miniature, on the North Pier at Oban, displays amazingly intricate ½ scale model scenes. Look for the pub with its tiny dartboard, the charming music room and the workshop where the miniaturised tools work like their full-scale counterparts.

---

towards Glencoe, is also known as the Black Castle because of the colour of the stone. It was built by Black Duncan, and is associated with the Appin Murder and Glencoe Massacre. The castle has secret passages and dungeons and you could even see a ghost!

▶ Continue on the **A828** into Appin village then turn left for Port Appin.

RECOMMENDED WALKS

The most spectacular of the Forestry Commission walks around Barcaldine on the A828 starts from Sutherland's Grove. Paths lead up Glen Dubh – the Dark Glen – to a footbridge over the ravine where the river rampages down.

---

8 Port Appin, Strathclyde
On one of the finest stretches of the coast of Argyll, this little village looks out to the long island of Lismore and, beyond it, to the lonely hills of Kingairloch. There is a peninsula walk past a natural archway in the cliffs, and another excursion could start with a ferry trip to the north end of Lismore. Walks there include one to the former limeworkers' village of Port Ramsay. North of Port Appin, look for Castle Stalker, romantically located on a tidal islet.

▶ Return to the **A828** and turn left. Pass Ballachulish Hotel and turn left on the **A82**.

9 Ballachulish, Strathclyde
The 'Village at the Narrows' used to be well-known for its ferry across Loch Leven, which has been replaced with a modern bridge. A flight of steps after the Ballachulish Hotel climbs to a memorial marking the site of the gibbet where, in 1755, James Stewart of the Glen was hanged for the murder – which he did not commit – of government agent Colin Campbell. After he was dead, Stewart's body was left hanging for three years. The mystery of who really did commit the Appin Murder is still discussed, and Robert Louis Stevenson made it the central theme of his novel *Kidnapped*.

Extensive landscaping has disguised the fact that between 1697 and 1955 Ballachulish was a major centre of the slate industry. A comprehensive display in the visitor centre describes its rise and decline.

i Albert Road

SPECIAL TO...

Railway enthusiasts often trace the old line from Oban via Connel Bridge to Ballachulish. It features handsome turn-of-the-century stations, one of which is the Holly Tree Hotel at Kentallen.

▶ Continue on the **A82**, diverting left into Glencoe village, then return to the main road for Glen Coe itself.

10 Glen Coe and the Black Mount, Strathclyde
Now the tour heads into its most dramatic phase. At the village of Glencoe the informative local museum recalls how, one night

in February 1692, the MacDonalds of Glencoe were slaughtered in their homes by troops billeted on them – an atrocity which has never been forgotten. The story of the massacre is retold in a National Trust for Scotland Visitor Centre a little way up the glen. It also features the wildlife and geology of the district. The northern wall of Glen Coe is a forbidding mountain ridge, while a glorious succession of towers, buttresses, gullies and hanging valleys marches along its southern side. Beyond the isolated Kings House Hotel, desolate Rannoch Moor stretches away to the left.

Further on there are tremendous views into the corries of the Black Mount.

i   National Trust for Scotland Visitor Centre, A82

▶ Continue on the **A82**.

⑪ Loch Lomond,
Strathclyde
Having swooped down Glen Falloch, the route reaches Ardlui at the head of Loch Lomond. In the north, the loch fills a narrow glacial trough between crammed-in mountains. Luss, with its low sandstone cottages and fine Victorian church, lies where Loch Lomond broadens out to become part of a gentler Lowland scene with lovely wooded islands. Like Ardlui, Inveruglas, Tarbet, Inverbeg and Balloch, Luss is a port of call for ferries. You can cruise through the islands or cross the loch, walk on the West Highland Way through spruce, larch, birch and oakwoods under the shoulder of Ben Lomond, and sail back to the western shore.

Glen Coe, the most infamous glen in Scotland

i   Main Street, Tarbet

SPECIAL TO...

The most famous but most elusive fish for Loch Lomond anglers is the powan, unique to Scotland. This freshwater herring had to adapt to life away from the sea after glacial debris blocked out the tidal waters.

▶ Continue on the **A82** and return to Dumbarton.

BACK TO NATURE

Queen Elizabeth Forest Park, near to Loch Lomond, harbours woodland birds, including woodcock and wood warbler, while on the higher ground of Ben Lomond there are golden eagles, ptarmigan and mountain flowers.

RECOMMENDED WALKS

After the river bridge at Glencoe village, turn left for the Lochan Trail, which circles an ornamental lake backed by Corsican pines. On a calm day it reflects like a mirror the striking outline of Ben Vair – the Peak of the Thunderbolt.

ACCIDENTS

In the event of an accident, move the vehicle off the carriageway wherever possible. If it is fitted with hazard warning lights, they should be used and, if available, a red triangle should be placed on the same side of the road at least 165ft (50m) before the vehicle.

If damage or injury is caused to any other person or vehicle you must stop, give your own and the vehicle owner's name and address and the registration number of the vehicle to anyone who has reasonable grounds for having them. If you do not do this, report the accident to the police as soon as reasonably practicable, and in any case within 24 hours.

BREAKDOWNS

Visitors who are members of a recognised automobile club may benefit from the services prov-ided free by the AA. Car rental companies normally provide cover with one of the major motoring organisations. On motorways there are emergency telephones located beside the hard shoulder every mile (1.6km).

In the event of a breakdown, see **accidents** above.

CARAVANS
Brakes

Check that the caravan braking mechanism is correctly adjusted. If it has a breakaway safety mechanism, the cable between the car and caravan must be firmly anchored to ensure that the trailer brakes act immediately if the two part company.

Caravan and luggage trailers

A towed vehicle should be readily identifiable by a plate in an accessible position showing the name of the make of the vehicle and the production and serial number.

MOTORING IN GREAT BRITAIN

Lights

Make sure that <u>all</u> the lights are working, and check that the flasher rate is 60–120 times a minute.

Tyres

Both tyres on the caravan should be of the same size and type. Inspect them carefully: if you think they are likely to be more than three-quarters worn before you get back, replace them before you leave. If you notice uneven wear, scuffed treads or damaged walls, get expert advice on whether the tyres are suitable for further use. Find out the recommended tyre pressures from the caravan manufacturer.

CAR HIRE AND FLY/DRIVE

Drivers must have a valid national licence held for at least one year, or an International Driving Permit.

The minimum age for hiring a car ranges from 18 to 25, depending on the model of car. With some companies, there is a maximum age limit of 70. You can arrange to pick up your car in one town and return it in another.

A fly/drive package often represents the best value.

CHILDREN

The following restrictions apply to children travelling in private motor vehicles:

Children under 3 years: front seat – appropriate child restraint must be worn; rear seats – appropriate child restraint must be worn if available.

Child aged 3 to 11 and under 1.5 metres tall: front seat — appropriate child restraint must be worn if available. If not, adult seat belt must be worn.

Child aged 12 or 13 or younger child 1.5 metres or more in height: front and rear seats – adult seat belt must be worn if available. Note: under no circumstances should a rear-facing restraint be used in a seat with an airbag.

CRASH (SAFETY) HELMETS

Visiting motorcyclists and their passengers must wear crash or safety helmets.

DOCUMENTS

You must have a valid driver's licence or an International Driving Permit. Holders of permits written in a foreign language are advised to obtain an official translation from an embassy or recognised automobile association. Non-EC nationals must have Green Card insurance.

DRINKING AND DRIVING

The laws regarding drinking and driving are strict and the penalties severe. If you drink don't drive.

DRIVING CONDITIONS

Traffic drives on the left (it goes clockwise at roundabouts [traffic circles], of which there are many). Speed-limit and destination signs use miles (one kilometre is roughly ⅝ of a mile). Motorways link most major cities; service areas are indicated well in advance. On some motorway stretches, however, there aren't many stopping-places, eg the M25 (London's busy orbital route), the M11, M20 and M40.

Tolls are levied on certain bridges and tunnels. Roads in parts of Wales and in the north-west of Scotland are sometimes narrow.

On single-track roads, pull into passing places only if they are on your left. Stop level with those on your right – oncoming traffic will make the detour.

FUEL

Petrol and diesel are widely available, and outlets for LPG are increasing. Unleaded petrol has a minimum octane rating of 95; super octane has around 98. Leaded petrol has been replaced by LPR (Lead Replacement Petrol). Petrol stations are plentiful on motorways and major roads. Those on motorways, and some on busy major roads and in large towns, are open 24 hours, or at least until late at night. Most accept credit cards.

INSURANCE

Fully comprehensive insurance covering some of the expenses incurred after a breakdown or an accident, is advisable.

LIGHTS

Front and rear side lights and rear registration plate lights must be lit at night. Headlights must be used when visibility is poor and at night on unlit roads and those where the street lights are more than 185m (600 feet) apart.

ROADS

Roads in Britain are generally very good, but busy. Try to travel outside the main rush hours of 8–9.30am and 4.30–6pm, especially in built-up areas.

ROUTE DIRECTIONS

These abbreviations are used for British roads:
A - main roads
B - local roads
unclassified roads - minor roads.

SEAT BELTS

Seat belts are compulsory for drivers and front seat passenger, and for those in rear seats where belts are fitted.

SPEED LIMITS

Speed limits for cars are: motorways and dual carriageways 70mph (112kph); other roads 60mph (96kph); built-up areas 30mph (48kph), unless otherwise indicated.

TOLLS

Tolls are levied on certain bridges and tunnels.

WARNING TRIANGLE/ HAZARD WARNING LIGHTS

If the vehicle has hazard warning lights, they should be used in the event of a breakdown or accident. If available, a red triangle should be placed on the road at least 55 yards (50m) before the obstruction and on the same side of the road.

ACCOMMODATION

Listed below is a selection of hotels which can be found along the routes of each tour.

The AA booking service is exclusively for AA personal members, and provides a free, fast and easy way to find a place to stay. With your AA membership number to hand, call the number below and let us know your requiremets. Our knowledgeable staff will help you make the right choice and book the accommodation for you. 0990 050505.

Full listings of the British and Irish hotels and B&Bs available through the service can be found and booked at the AA's Internet site: www.theAA.co.uk.hotels

Prices

Hotel charges are divided into three price brackets based on a nightly rate for a double room with breakfast:
Expensive £££ – £110 or more
Moderate ££ – between £60 and £110
Budget £ – up to £60

TOUR 1
PENZANCE Cornwall
The Sea & Horses £
Seafront, 6 Alexandra Terrace, TR18 4NX (tel: 01736 361961)

TRURO Cornwall
Carlton £
Falmouth Road, TR1 2HL
(tel: 01872 272450)

TOUR 2
BODMIN Cornwall
Westberry £
Rhind Street, PL31 2EL
(tel: 01208 72772)

OKEHAMPTON Devon
White Hart £
Fore Street, EX20 1HD
(tel: 01837 52730)

TOUR 3
MINEHEAD Somerset
Periton Park ££
Middlecombe TA24 8SN (tel: 01643 706885). Closed January

BIDEFORD Devon
Yeoldon Country House ££
Durrant Lane, Northam, EX39 2RL (tel: 01237 474400)

TOUR 4
TAUNTON Somerset
Falcon £
Henlade TA3 5DH (tel: 01823 442502)

TOUR 5
SALISBURY Wiltshire
Howard's House £
Teffont Evias SP3 5RJ
(tel: 01722 716392)

TOUR 6
TUNBRIDGE WELLS Kent
Swan ££
The Pantiles TN2 5TD
(tel: 01892 541450)

TOUR 7
CANTERBURY Kent
Canterbury ££
71 New Dover Road CT1 3DZ
(tel: 01227 450551)

DEAL Kent
Royal Hotel ££
Beach Street, CT14 6JD
(tel: 01304 375555)

TOUR 8
SOUTHAMPTON Hampshire
Elizabeth House £
43–44 The Avenue SO17 1XP
(tel: 023 80224327)

TOUR 9
BROCKENHURST Hampshire
Cloud ££
Meerut Road SO42 7TD
(tel: 01590 622165)

RINGWOOD Hampshire
Moortown Lodge Hotel £
244 Christchurch Road, BH24 3AS (tel: 01425 471404). Closed Christmas–mid-Jan.

TOUR 10
BRECON Powys
Castle of Brecon £
Castle Square LD3 9DB
(tel: 01874 624611)

TOUR 11
TENBY Pembrokeshire
Esplanade £
The Esplanade SA70 7DU
(tel: 01834 842760)

ST DAVID'S Pembrokeshire
Old Cross ££
Cross Square, SA62 6SP
(tel: 01437 720387). Closed
Christmas–1 Mar.

TOUR 12
ABERYSYWYTH Ceredigion
Four Seasons ££
50–54 Portland Street SY23 2DX
(tel: 01970 612120)

TOUR 13
BALA Gwynedd
Plas Coch ££
High Street LL23 7AB
(tel: 01678 520309)

TOUR 14
CAERNARFON Gwynedd
Menai Bank £
North Road LL55 1BD
(tel: 01286 673297)

CONWY Conwy
Castle Bank £
Mount Pleasant LL32 8NY
(tel: 01492 593888)

TOUR 15
WOODHALL SPA
Lincolnshire
Eagle Lodge £
The Broadway LN10 6ST
(tel: 01526 353231)

TOUR 16
FAKENHAM Norfolk
Crown ££
Market Place NR21 9BP
(tel: 01328 851418)

TOUR 17
IPSWICH Suffolk
Claydon Country House ££
16–18 Ipswich Road, Claydon
IP6 0AR (tel: 01473 830382)

LAVENHAM Suffolk
Angel ££

Market Place CO10 9QZ (tel:
01787 247388)

TOUR 18
OXFORD Oxfordshire
Victoria ££
180 Abingdon Road OX1 4RA
(tel: 01865 724536)

CHIPPING NORTON
Oxfordshire
The White Hart £
16 High Street OX7 5AD
(tel: 01608 642572)

TOUR 19
GREAT MALVERN
Worcestershire
Great Malvern ££
Garham Road WR14 2HN
(tel: 01684 563411)

TOUR 20
BRIDGNORTH Shropshire
Parlors Hall £
Mill Street WV15 5AL
(tel: 01746 761931)

CHURCH STRETTON
Shropshire
Mynd House ££
Ludlow Road, Little Stretton
SY6 6RB (tel: 01694 722212).
Closed 6–31 Jan.

TOUR 21
KESWICK Cumbria
Chaucer House £
Derwentwater Place CA12 4DR
(tel: 017687 72318)

TOUR 22
RICHMOND North Yorkshire
King's Head ££
Market Place DL10 4HS
(tel: 01748 850220)

TOUR 23
LANCASTER Lancashire
Hampson House £
Hampson Lane, Hampson
Green LA2 0JB (tel: 01524
751158)

KIRKBY LONSDALE Cumbria
Pheasant Inn ££
LA6 2RX (tel: 015242 71230)

TOUR 24
BAKEWELL Derbyshire
Croft Country House ££
Great Longstone DE45 1TF

(tel: 01629 640278). Closed
2 Jan–10 Feb.

BUXTON Derbyshire
**Portland Hotel and Park
Restaurant ££**
32 St John's Road SK17 6XQ
(tel: 01298 71493)

TOUR 25
YORK North Yorkshire
Elmbank ££
The Mount YO24 1GE
(tel: 01904 610653)

TOUR 26
INVERNESS Highland
Windsor Town House ££
22 Ness Bank IV2 4SF
(tel: 01463 715535)

GAIRLOCH Highland
Myrtle Bank ££
Low Road IV21 2BS (tel: 01445
712004)

TOUR 27
ABOYNE Aberdeenshire
Birse Lodge £
20 Charleston Road AB34 5EL
(tel: 013398 86253)

TOUR 28
EDINBURGH
Iona £
Strathearn Place EH9 2AL
(tel: 0131 4476264)

TOUR 29
CASTLE DOUGLAS
Dumfries & Galloway
Douglas Arms ££
King Street DG7 1DB
(tel: 01556 502231)

KIRKCUDBRIGHT Dumfries
& Galloway
Royal £
St Cuthbert Street DG6 4DY
(tel: 01557 331213)

TOUR 30
OBAN Argyll & Bute
Foxholes £
Cologin, Lerags PA34 4SE
(tel: 01631 564982)

DUMBARTON West
Dumbartonshire
Dumbuck House ££
Glasgow Road G82 1EG
(tel: 01389 734336)

TOUR INFORMATION
The addresses, telephone numbers and opening times of the attractions mentioned in the tours, including the telephone numbers of the Tourist Information Centres are listed below tour by tour.

TOUR 1

i Station Road, Penzance. Tel: 01736 362207.

i The Guildhall, Street-an-Pol, St Ives. Tel: 01736 796297.

i Municipal Buildings, Boscawen Street, Truro. Tel: 01872 274555.

i 28 Killigrew Street, Falmouth. Tel: 01326 312300.

1 Newlyn
Newlyn Art Gallery
Newlyn, Penzance. Tel: 01736 363715.
Open all year, Mon–Sat.

3 Porthcurno
The Minack
Porthcurno, Penzance. Tel: 01736 810181/810471.
Open all year, daily.

4 Land's End
Last Labyrinth
Land's End, Sennen. Tel: 01736 871220.
Open all year, daily.

5 St Just
Geevor Tin Mine
Pendeen, Penzance. Tel: 01736 788662.
Open all year, daily.

6 Zennor
Wayside Folk Museum
Zennor. Tel: 01736 796945.
Open Apr–Sep, daily, Oct, Sun–Fri.

7 St Ives
Barbara Hepworth Museum
Barnoon Hill, St Ives. Tel: 01736 796226.
Open Jul–Aug, daily, Sep–Jun, Tue–Sun.

Leach Pottery
Higher Stennack, St Ives. Tel: 01736 796398.
Open Easter–Oct, Mon–Sat, Nov–Easter, Mon–Fri.

8 Lelant
Merlin's Magic Land
Lelant, St Ives. Tel: 01736 752885.
Open Apr–Oct, daily.

9 Hayle
Paradise Park
Hayle, near St Ives. Tel: 01736 757407.
Open all year, daily.

12 Truro
Royal Cornwall Museum
River Street, Truro. Tel: 01872 272205.
Open all year, Mon–Sat.

13 St Mawes
St Mawes Castle
St Mawes. Tel: 01326 270526.
Open 1 Apr–1 Nov, daily, 2 Nov–31 Mar, Fri–Tue.

Trelissick Garden
Feock, Truro. Tel: 01872 862090.
Open 19 Feb–29 Oct, Mon–Sat and Sun afternoon.

14 Penryn
Pendennis Castle
Castle Drive, Falmouth. Tel: 01326 316594.
Open all year daily.

15 Gweek
The National Seal Sanctuary
Gweek, near Helston. Tel: 01326 221874.
Open all year, daily.

16 Cadgwith
Lizard Point Lighthouse
Lizard Point. Tel: 01326 290431.
Open May–Oct, daily pm.

18 Helston
Flambards Village Theme Park
Clodgey Lane, Helston. Tel: 01326 573404.
Open 15 Apr–29 Oct.

19 Marazion
St Michael's Mount
The Manor Office, Marazion. Tel: 01736 710507.
Open Apr–Oct, Mon–Fri,

TOUR 2

i Bypass Service Station, St Austell. Tel: 01726 76333.

i Shire House, Mount Folly Square, Bodmin. Tel: 01208 76616.

i North Cornwall Museum, The Cleave, Camelford. Tel: 01840 212954.

i Market House Arcade, Market Street, Launceston. Tel: 01566 772321/772333.

i 3 West Street, Okehampton. Tel: 01837 53020.

i Town Hall, Bedford Square, Tavistock. Tel: 01822 612938.

i Lostwithiel Community Centre, Liddicoat Road, Lostwithiel. Tel: 01208 872207.

1 Bodmin
Pencarrow House
Pencarrow, Bodmin. Tel: 01208 841369.
Open Easter–15 Oct, Sun–Thu.

2 Camelford
North Cornwall Museum
The Cleave, Camelford. Tel: 01840 212954.
Open Apr–Sep, Mon–Fri.

3 Tintagel
Tintagel Castle
Tintagel Head. Tel: 01840 770328.
Open all year, daily.

Old Post Office
Tintagel. Tel: 01840 770024.
Open 1 Apr–1 Nov, daily.

5 Launceston
Launceston Steam Railway
Newport, Launceston. Tel: 01566 775665.
Open May–Sep, Sun–Fri, Oct–May, Sun and Tue.

Tamar Otter Park and Wild Wood
North Petherwin, Launceston. Tel: 01566 785646.
Open Apr–Oct, daily.

7 Okehampton
The Museum of Dartmoor Life
West Street, Okehampton. Tel: 01837 52295.
Open Easter–May and Oct, Mon–Sat; Jun–Sep, daily; Nov–Easter, weekdays.

8 Moretonhampstead
Castle Drogo
Drewsteignton. Tel: 01647 433306.
Open 27 Mar–Oct, Sat–Thu.

9 Princetown
The Miniature Pony Stud
Moretonhampstead. Tel: 01647 432400.
Open 1 Apr–1 Nov, daily.

12 Liskeard
Paul Corin's Magnificent Music Machines
St Keyne Station, Liskeard. Tel: 01579 343108/342925.
Open Easter–Oct.

13 Dobwalls
Dobwalls Family Adventure Park
Dobwalls. Tel: 01579 320325/321129.
Open Easter–Sep, daily, Oct weekends.

14 Lostwithiel
Restormel Castle
Lostwithiel. Tel: 01208 872687.
Open 1 Apr–Nov, daily.

Shipwreck and Heritage Centre
Quay Road, Charlestown, St Austell. Tel: 01726 69897.
Open Mar–Oct, daily.

Wheal Martyn China Clay Heritage Centre
Carthew. Tel: 01726 850362.
Open Apr–Oct, daily.

TOUR 3

i Town Hall, Lee Road, Lynton. Tel: 01598 752225.

i 17 Friday Street, Minehead. Tel: 01643 702624.

i 1 East Street, South Molton. Tel: 01769 574122.

i Castle Hill, Great

[i] Tourist Information Centre

[12] Number on tour

Torrington. Tel: 01805
623302.

[i] The Quay, Kingsley
Road, Bideford. Tel: 01237
477676.

[i] 36 Boutport Street,
Barnstaple. Tel: 01271
375000.

[3] Porlock
Exmoor Falconry and
Animal Farm
Allerford, near Porlock. Tel:
01643 862816.
*Open 1 Mar–30 Jun and 1
Sep–31 Oct, Sun–Fri; 1
Jul–31 Aug, daily.*

[5] Minehead
West Somerset Railway
The Station, Minehead. Tel:
01643 704996.
Open Mar–Dec, daily.

Butlin's Somerwest
World
Minehead. Tel: 01643
703331.
Open 18 Feb–Nov, daily.

Dunster Castle and
Garden
Minehead. Tel: 01643
821314.
*Open Castle, 30 Mar–Oct,
Sat–Wed; Gardens daily.*

[6] Watchet
Tropiquaria
Washford Cross, Watchet.
Tel: 01984 640688.
*Open Easter–Oct, daily;
winter, weekends and school
holidays.*

Cleeve Abbey
Abbey Road, Washford,
near Watchet. Tel: 01984
640377.
*Open Apr–Octr, daily,
Nov–Mar, Wed–Sun.*

Combe Sydenham
Country Park
Monksilver, Watchet. Tel:
01984 656284.
Open Apr–Sep, daily.

[10] South Molton
Cobbaton Combat
Collection
Chittlehampton, Umber-
leigh, near Barnstaple. Tel:
01769 540740.
Open Easter–Oct, daily.

[11] Great Torrington
Dartington Crystal
School Lane, Great

Torrington. Tel: 01805
626266.
Open all year, daily.

Rosemoor Garden
Great Torrington. Tel:
01805 624067.
Open all year, daily.

The Gnome Reserve
West Putford, near
Bradworthy. Tel: 01409
241435.
Open 21 Mar–31 Oct, daily.

[12] Bideford
Tapeley Park
Instow. Tel: 01271
860528/342371.
Open Easter–Oct, Sun–Fri.

The Big Sheep
Bideford. Tel: 01237
477916.
Open all year, daily.

North Devon Maritime
Museum
Odun Road, Appledore.
Tel: 01237 422064.
*Open May–30 Sep, Mon–Fri
and weekend afternoons;
Easter–May and Oct after-
noons.*

[13] Barnstaple
Museum of Barnstaple
and North Devon
The Square, Barnstaple. Tel:
01271 346747.
Open Tue–Sat.

[14] Arlington
Arlington Court
Arlington, Barnstaple. Tel:
01271 850296.
Open 28 Mar–Oct, Sun–Fri.

[15] Blackmoor Gate
Exmoor Zoological Park
South Stowford, Bratton
Fleming, near Barnstaple.
Tel: 01598 763352.
Open all year, daily.

TOUR 4

[i] 50 High Street,
Bridgwater. Tel: 01278
427652.

[i] Paul Street, Taunton. Tel:
01823 336344.

[i] Shudrick Lane,
Ilminster. Tel: 01460 57294.

[i] The Guildhall, Fore
Street, Chard. Tel: 01460
67463.

[i] 32 South Street,
Bridport. Tel: 01308
424901.

[i] Unit 11, Antelope
Walk, Dorchester. Tel:
01305 267992.

[i] 3 Tilton Court, Digby
Road, Sherborne. Tel:
01935 815341.

[i] Petter's House, Petter's
Way, Yeovil. Tel: 01935
471279.

[1] Taunton
County Museum
Taunton Castle, Taunton.
Tel: 01823 320201.
Open all year, Tue–Sat.

Somerset Cricket
Museum
7 Priory Avenue, Taunton.
Tel: 01823 275893.
Open Apr–Nov, Mon–Fri.

West Somerset Railway
The Station, Minehead. Tel:
01643 704996.
*Open 12 Mar–Oct, most
days, Dec–11 Mar occa-
sional opening.*

[2] Ilminster
Perry's Cider Mills
Dowlish Wake, near
Ilminster. Tel: 01460 52681.
Open all year, daily.

Barrington Court
Barrington, near Ilminster.
Tel: 01460 241938.
Open Apr–Oct, Sat–Thu.

[3] Chard
Chard Museum
Godworthy House, High
Street, Chard. Tel: 01460
65091.
*Open May–Oct, Mon–Sat;
Jul and Aug, daily.*

Cricket St Thomas
Near Chard. Tel: 01460
30111.
Open all year, daily.

[5] Beaminster
Parnham House
Near Beaminster. Tel:
01308 862204.
*Open Apr–Oct, Sun, Tue,
Wed, Thu, Bank Holidays.*

[7] Abbotsbury
Abbotsbury Swannery
Abbotsbury. Tel: 01305
871858.
Open Mar–Oct.

[8] Dorchester
Dinosaur Museum
Icen Way, Dorchester. Tel:
01305 269880.
Open all year, daily.

The Keep Military
Museum
Bridport Road,
Dorchester. Tel: 01305
264066.
*Open Sep–Jun, Mon–Sat; Jul
and Aug, daily.*

Dorset County
Museum
High West Street,
Dorchester. Tel: 01305
262735.
*Open Sep–Jun, Mon–Sat; Jul
and Aug, daily.*

[10] Sherborne
Sherborne Old Castle
Sherborne. Tel: 01935
812730.
*Open Apr–1 Nov, daily; 2
Nov–31 Mar, Wed–Sun.*

Worldlife
Compton House, near
Sherborne. Tel: 01935
474608.
Open Easter–Sep, daily.

[12] Montacute
Montacute House
Montacute. Tel: 01935
823289.
*Open 1 Apr–1 Nov,
Wed–Mon afternoons.*

Tintinhull House
Near Yeovil. Tel: 01935
822545.
Open Apr–Sep, Wed–Sun.

TOUR 5

[i] Fish Row, Salisbury. Tel:
01722 334956.

[i] Central Car Park,
Warminster. Tel: 01985
218548.

[i] The Round Tower,
Justice Lane, Frome. Tel:
01373 467271.

[i] Town Hall, Market
Place, Wells. Tel: 01749
672552.

[i] The Gorge, Cheddar.
Tel: 01934 744071.

[i] The Tribunal, 9 High
Street, Glastonbury. Tel:
01458 832954.

ⓘ Tourist Information Centre
🄓 Number on tour

ⓘ 8 Bell Street,
Shaftesbury. Tel: 01747
853514.

❸ Warminster
Longleat House and Safari
Park
Longleat, Warminster. Tel:
01985 844400.
Open House, all year, daily;
Safari Park, 13 Mar–31 Oct.

❺ Wells
Wookey Hole Caves
Wookey Hole, Wells. Tel:
01749 672243.
Open all year, daily.

❻ Cheddar
Gough's and Cox's Caves
Cheddar. Tel: 01934
742343.
Open all year, daily.

King John's Hunting Lodge
The Square, Axbridge. Tel:
01934 732012.
Open Easter–Sep, after-
noons.

❼ Glastonbury
Somerset Rural Life
Museum
Chilkwell Street,
Glastonbury. Tel: 01458
831197.
Open Easter–Oct, Tue–Fri
and weekend afternoons;
Nov–Easter, Tue–Sat.

❾ Stourhead
Stourhead Garden and
House
Stourton, Warminster. Tel:
01747 841152.
Open Garden, all year, daily.
House, 28 Mar–1 Nov,
Sat–Wed, afternoons.

❿ Shaftesbury
Shaftesbury Town
Museum
Gold Hill, Shaftesbury. Tel:
01747 852910.
Open Easter– Sep, daily.

⓫ Wilton
Wilton House
Estate Office, Wilton,
Salisbury. Tel: 01722
746720.
Open 15 Apr–29 Oct, daily.

TOUR 6

ⓘ The Old Fish Market,
The Pantiles, Royal
Tunbridge Wells. Tel: 01892
515675.

ⓘ Buckhurst Lane,
Sevenoaks. Tel: 01732
450305.

ⓘ Vestry Hall, Stone
Street, Cranbrook. Tel:
01580 712538.

ⓘ Town Hall, High Street,
Tenterden. Tel: 01580
763572.

❶ Penshurst
Penshurst Place and
Gardens
Penshurst, Tonbridge. Tel:
01892 870307.
Open 27 Feb–26 Mar,
weekends; 27 Mar–Oct,
daily.

❷ Hever
Hever Castle and
Gardens
Hever, Edenbridge. Tel:
01732 865224.
Open Mar–Nov, daily.

Chiddingstone Castle
Chiddingstone, Edenbridge.
Tel: 01892 870347.
Open Apr–May and Oct,
Sun and Bank Holidays;
Jun–Sep, Wed–Fri after-
noons and Sun and Bank
Holidays.

Haxted Watermill
Riverside
Haxted Road, Haxted,
Edenbridge. Tel: 01732
862914.
Under renovation; expected
to reopen in 2001.

❸ Limpsfield
Quebec House
Westerham. Tel: 01892
890651.
Open 28 Mar–26 Oct, Tue
and Sun afternoons.

Squerryes Court
Westerham. Tel: 01959
562345.
Open Apr–Sep, Wed, Sat and
Sun afternoons.

Chartwell
Westerham. Tel: 01732
866368.
Open 1 Apr–1 Nov,
Wed–Sun, Jul and Aug, Tue
also.

❹ Sevenoaks
Knole
Sevenoaks. Tel: 01732
450608.
Open 27 Mar–Oct,

Wed–Sat afternoons; daily
at Easter.

❺ Ightham
Ightham Mote
Ivy Hatch, Sevenoaks. Tel:
01732 810378.
Open 1 Apr–1 Nov, Mon,
Wed, Thu, Fri and Sun.

❻ Mereworth
Hop Farm Country Park
Beltring, Tonbridge. Tel:
01622 872068.
Open daily.

❼ Lamberhurst
Owl House Gardens
Mount Pleasant,
Lamberhurst, Royal
Tunbridge Wells. Tel: 01892
890230.
Open all year, daily.

Bayham Abbey
Lamberhurst, Royal
Tunbridge Wells. Tel: 01892
890381.
Open winter weekends;
Apr–Oct, daily.

Scotney Castle Garden
Lamberhurst, Royal
Tunbridge Wells. Tel: 01892
891081.
Open 27 Mar–Oct, Wed–Fri
and weekend afternoons.

❽ Cranbrook
Cranbrook Union
Windmill
The Hill, Cranbrook. Tel:
01580 712256.
Open Easter–Sep, Sat pm;
mid-Jul–Aug, also Sun pm.

Sissinghurst Castle
Sissinghurst, Cranbrook. Tel:
01580 715330.
Open 1 Apr–15 Oct, Tue–Fri
afternoons and weekends.

Bedgebury National
Pinetum
Goudhurst, Cranbrook. Tel:
01580 211044.
Open all year, daily.

❾ Tenterden
Smallhythe Place
Ellen Terry Memorial
Museum, Small Hythe,
Tenterden. Tel: 01580
762334.
Open 1 Apr–28 Oct,
Sat–Wed afternoons.

Kent and East Sussex
Railway
Town Station, Tenterden.

Tel: 01580 765155.
Open Apr–Sep, daily; other
times throughout year.

❿ Northiam
Great Dixter House and
Gardens
Northiam, Rye. Tel: 01797
252878.
Open Apr–Oct, Tue–Sun
afternoons.

⓫ Bodiam
Bodiam Castle
Bodiam, Robertsbridge. Tel:
01580 830436.
Open all year, daily.

⓬ Burwash
Bateman's
Burwash, Etchingham. Tel:
01435 882302.
Open 27 Mar–Oct
Sat–Wed.

TOUR 7

ⓘ 34 St Margaret's Street,
Canterbury. Tel: 01227
766567.

ⓘ 18 The Churchyard,
Ashford. Tel: 01233
629165.

ⓘ The Heritage Centre,
Strand Quay, Rye. Tel:
01797 226696.

ⓘ Town Hall, 35 High
Street, New Romney. Tel:
01797 364044.

ⓘ En Route Travel, Red
Lion Square, Hythe. Tel:
01303 267799.

ⓘ Harbour Street,
Folkestone. Tel: 01303
258594.

ⓘ Townwall Street,
Dover. Tel: 01304 205108.

ⓘ Town Hall, High
Street, Deal. Tel: 01304
369576.

ⓘ The Guildhall, Market
Square, Sandwich. Tel:
01304 613565

❺ New Romney
Romney, Hythe and
Dymchurch Railway
New Romney Station,
New Romney. Tel: 01797
362353.
Open Mar and Oct, week-
ends; Easter–Sep, daily.

Practical Information

⑥ Lympne
Lympne Castle
Lympne. Tel: 01303 267571.
Closed during 2000.

Port Lympne Wild Animal Park
Port Lympne, Lympne. Tel: 01303 264647.
Open all year, daily.

⑦ Folkestone
Museum and Art Gallery
2 Grace Hill, Folkestone. Tel: 01303 850123.
Open all year, Mon–Sat.

The Russian Submarine
South Quay, Folkestone Harbour. Tel: 01303 240400.
Open all year, daily.

Rotunda Amusement Park
The Sea Front, Folkestone. Tel: 01303 245245.
Open all year, daily.

⑧ Hawkinge
Kent Battle of Britain Museum
Hawkinge Airfield, Hawkinge, Folkestone. Tel: 01303 893140.
Open Apr–Oct, daily.

⑨ Dover
Roman Painted House
New Street, Dover. Tel: 01304 203279.
Open Ap–Jun and Sep, Tue–Sun; Jul–Aug, daily.

Old Town Gaol
Town Hall, High Street, Dover. Tel: 01304 242766.
Open all year, Tue–Sat and Sun afternoons.

Dover Castle
Dover. Tel: 01304 201628.
Open all year, daily.

⑩ St Margaret's at Cliffe
Pines Garden
Beach Road, St Margaret's Bay, Dover. Tel: 01304 852764.
Open all year, daily.

⑪ Walmer
Walmer Castle
Kingsdown Road, Walmer, Deal. Tel: 01304 364288.
Open Apr–Oct, daily; Nov–Mar, Wed–Sun.

Deal Castle
Victoria Road, Deal. Tel:

01304 372762.
Open Apr–Oct, daily; Nov–Mar, Wed–Sun.

Time Ball Tower
Victoria Parade, Deal. Tel: 01304 201200.
Open Jul–Aug, Tue–Sun.

Deal Maritime and Local History Museum
St George's Road, Deal. Tel: 01304 381344.
Open Apr–Sep, daily pm.

⑫ Sandwich
White Mill and Folk Museum
Ash Road, Sandwich. Tel: 01304 612076.
Open Easter–mid-Sep afternoons; Fri and Sun mornings all year.

Royal St George's Golf Club
Sandwich. Tel: 01304 613090.
Open all year, daily.

⑬ Wingham
Wingham Bird Park
Rusham Road, Wingham, Canterbury. Tel: 01227 720836.
Open all year, daily.

TOUR 8

ℹ The Guildhall, The Broadway, Winchester. Tel: 01962 840500/848180.

ℹ 1 Latimer Street, Romsey. Tel: 01794 512987.

ℹ Marwell Zoological Park (see ⑤)

ℹ Queen Elizabeth Country Park (see ⑨)

❶ Stockbridge
Andover Museum (Museum of Iron Age)
6 Church Close, Andover. Tel: 01264 366283.
Open Apr–Sep, Tue–Sun daily.

❷ Middle Wallop
Museum of Army Flying
Middle Wallop. Tel: 01980 674421.
Open all year, daily.

❸ Mottisfont Abbey
Mottisfont Abbey
Mottisfont, Romsey. Tel: 01794 340757.

Open 27 Mar–Oct, Sat–Wed afternoons; 12–27 Jun, daily.

❹ Romsey
Broadlands
Romsey. Tel: 01794 505010.
Open 12 Jun–1 Sep, afternoons.

The Sir Harold Hillier Gardens and Arboretum
Jermyns House, Jermyns Lane, Ampfield, Romsey. Tel: 01794 368787.
Open all year, daily.

Paultons Park
Ower, Romsey. Tel: 023 8081 4455.
Open mid-Mar–Oct, daily.

❺ Marwell Zoo
Marwell Zoological Park, Colden Common, Winchester. Tel: 01962 777407.
Open all year, daily.

❻ Bishop's Waltham
Bishop's Waltham Museum
Brook Street, Bishop's Waltham, Southampton. Tel: 01489 892460.
Open by special arrangement.

❾ Queen Elizabeth Country Park
Queen Elizabeth Country Park
Gravel Hill, Horndean, Waterlooville. Tel: 023 9259 5040.
Open all year, daily.

Butser Ancient Farm
Horndean. Tel: 023 9259 8838.
Open all year, daily.

❿ New Alresford
Watercress Line
Alresford Station, Alresford. Tel: 01962 733810.
Open weekends, except Nov and Jan. Also some weekdays.

TOUR 9

ℹ Westover Road, Bournemouth. Tel: 0906 802 0234.

ℹ 23 High Street, Christchurch. Tel: 01202 471780.

ℹ The Furlong, Ringwood. Tel: 01425 470896.

ℹ St Barb Museum and Visitor Centre, New Street, Lymington. Tel: 01590 689000.

ℹ John Montague Building, Beaulieu, Brockenhurst. Tel: 01590 612345.

ℹ New Forest Museum and Visitor Centre, Main Car Park, Lyndhurst. Tel: 023 8028 2269.

ℹ 29 High Street, Wimborne Minster. Tel: 01202 886116.

❶ Christchurch
Place Mill
Quay, Christchurch. Tel: 01202 487626.
Open Apr–May, weekends; Jun–Sep, daily.

❻ Bucklers Hard
Bucklers Hard Village and Maritime Museum
Beaulieu, Brockenhurst. Tel: 01590 616203.
Open all year, daily.

❼ Exbury
Exbury Gardens
Exbury Estate Office, Exbury, Southampton. Tel: 023 8089 1203.
Open 27 Febr–Oct, daily.

Lepe Country Park
Lepe, Exbury, Southampton. Tel: 023 8089 9108.
Open all year, daily.

Hurst Castle
Keyhaven, Lymington. Tel: 01590 642344.
Open Apr–Oct, daily.

❽ Beaulieu
National Motor Museum
John Montagu Building, Beaulieu, Brockenhurst. Tel: 01590 612345.
Open all year, daily.

❾ Lyndhurst
New Forest Museum
High Street, Lyndhurst. Tel: 023 8028 3914.
Open all year, daily.

⓫ Wimborne Minster
Rockbourne Roman Villa
Rockbourne,

Fordingbridge. Tel: 01725 518541.
Open Apr–Oct, Mon–Fri pm, Sat , Sun; Jul and Aug, daily.

TOUR 10

⚑ The Castle Car Park, Bridge Street, Chepstow. Tel: 01291 623772.

⚑ Shire Hall, Agincourt Square, Monmouth. Tel: 01600 713899.

⚑ Swan House, Edde Cross Street, Ross-on-Wye. Tel: 01989 562768.

⚑ Oxford Road, Hay-on-Wye. Tel: 01497 820144.

⚑ Cattle Market Car Park, Brecon. Tel: 01874 622485.

⚑ Swan Meadow, Monmouth Road, Abergavenny. Tel: 01873 857588.

❶ Monmouth
The Castle and Regimental Museum
The Castle, Monmouth. Tel: 01600 772175.
Open Apr–Oct, daily afternoons; Nov–Mar, weekend afternoons.

Tintern Abbey
Tintern, near Chepstow. Tel: 01291 689251.
Open all year, daily.

❷ Symonds Yat
Museum of Mazes
Jubilee Park, Symonds Yat West, Ross-on-Wye. Tel: 01600 890360.
Open Easter–Sep, daily; weekends and half-term holidays in winter.

❸ Goodrich
Goodrich Castle
Goodrich, near Ross-on-Wye. Tel: 01600 890538.
Open all year, daily.

❼ Hay-on-Wye
Hay Cinema Bookshop
The Old Cinema, Castle Street, Hay-on-Wye, via Hereford. Tel: 01497 820071.
Open all year, daily.

❾ Brecon
The Brecknock Museum
Captain's Walk, Brecon. Tel:

01874 624121.
Open Mar–3 Nov, Mon–Sat; Apr–Sep, Sun also.

South Wales Borderers Army Museum
The Barracks, The Watton, Brecon. Tel: 01874 613310.
Open Apr–Sep, daily; Oct–Mar, Mon–Fri.

The Mountain Centre
Libanus, Brecon. Tel: 01874 623366.
Open all year, daily.

🔟 Pontsticill
Brecon Mountain Railway
Pant Station, Merthyr Tydfil. Tel: 01685 722988.
Open 28 Mar–29 Oct, most days.

⓮ Raglan
Raglan Castle
Raglan. Tel: 01291 690228.
Open all year, daily.

⓯ Usk
Gwent Rural Life Museum
The Malt Barn, New Market Street, Usk. Tel: 01291 673777.
Open Apr–Oct, daily; winter by arrangement.

⓰ Caerleon
Caerleon Fortress Baths, Amphitheatre and Barracks
High Street, Caerleon, Newport. Tel: 01633 422518.
Open all year, daily

Legionary Museum
High Street, Caerleon, Newport. Tel: 01633 423134.
Open all year, Mon–Sat and Sun afternoons.

⓱ Penhow
Penhow Castle
Penhow. Tel: 01633 400800.
Open Easter–Sep, Wed–Sun, Bank Holidays; Aug daily; Oct–Dec and Mar, Wed, and Sun afternoons.

Caldicot Castle, Museum and Countryside Park
Caldicot. Tel: 01291 420241.
Open Mar–Oct, Mon–Sat and Sun afternoons.

TOUR 11

⚑ The Croft, Tenby. Tel: 01834 842402.

⚑ Visitor Centre, Commons Road, Pembroke. Tel: 01646 622388.

⚑ Old Bridge, Haverfordwest. Tel: 01437 763110.

⚑ City Hall, St David's. Tel: 01437 720392.

⚑ The Square, Fishguard. Tel: 01348 873484.

⚑ Theatre Mwldan, Bath House Road, Cardigan. Tel: 01239 613230.

⚑ Lammas Street, Carmarthen. Tel: 01267 231557.

⚑ The Barbecue, Harbour Car Park, Saundersfoot. Tel: 01834 813672.

❶ Manorbier
Manorbier Castle
Near Tenby. Tel: 01834 871394.
Open Easter–Sep, daily.

❷ Lamphey
Bishop's Palace
Lamphey. Tel: 01646 672224.
Open all year, daily.

❸ Pembroke
Pembroke Castle
Main Street, Pembroke. Tel: 01646 681510.
Open all year, daily.

Museum of the Home
7 Westgate Hill, Pembroke. Tel: 01646 681200.
Open May–Sep, Mon–Thu.

❹ Haverfordwest
Town Museum
Castle House, Haverfordwest Castle, Haverfordwest. Tel: 01437 763087.
Open Easter–Oct Mon–Sat.

Scolton Manor
Haverfordwest. Tel: 01437 731328.
Open all year, daily.

❺ Solva
Middle Mill
The Woollen Mill, Middle

Mill, Solva, Haverfordwest. Tel: 01437 721112.
Open Easter–Sep, Mon–Sat and Sun afternoons; Sep–Easter, Mon–Fri.

❻ St David's
St David's Cathedral
The Close, St David's. Tel: 01437 720202.
Open all year, daily.

Bishop's Palace
St David's. Tel: 01437 720517.
Open late Mar–late Oct, daily; late Oct–late Mar, Mon–Fri and Sun pm.

Oceanarium
42 New Street, St David's. Tel: 01437 720453.
Open all year, daily.

Marine Life Centre
Feidr Pant-y-Bryn, St David's. Tel: 01437 721665.
Open Mar–Oct, daily.

St David's Farm Park and Rare Breeds Centre
St David's Park, St David's. Tel: 01437 721601.
Open Apr–Oct, daily.

❽ Fishguard
Tregwynt Woollen Mill
Castle Morris, Haverfordwest. Tel: 01348 891225.
Open all year, Mon–Sat.

❾ Newport
Pembrokeshire Candle Centre
Trefelin, Cilgwyn, Newport. Tel: 01239 820470.
Open Easter–Oct, daily, Winter, ring for times.

Pentre Ifan Cromlech
Newport. Tel: 029 2050 0200.
Open all year, daily.

🔟 Cardigan
Cilgerran Castle
Cilgerran. Tel: 01239 615007.
Open all year, daily.

Welsh Wildlife Centre
Cilgerran, Cardigan. Tel: 01239 621600.
Open Apr–Oct, daily.

National Coracle Centre and Cenarth Mill
Cenarth, Cardigan. Tel: 01239 710980/710507.
Open Easter–Oct, Sun–Fri.

i Tourist Information Centre
12 Number on tour

Dre-fach and Felindre

Teifi Valley Railway
Henllan Station, Henllan, near Newcastle Emlyn. Tel: 01559 371077.
Open Easter–Oct most days.

Museum of the Welsh Woollen Industry
Dre-Fach Felindre, Llandysul. Tel: 01559 370929.
Open Apr–Sep, Mon–Sat; Oct–Mar, Mon–Fri.

Carmarthen

Gwili Steam Railway
Bronwydd Arms Station, Bronwydd. Tel: 01267 230666.
Open Apr–Oct and Dec, various days.

Laugharne

Dylan Thomas' Boat House
Dylans Walk, Laugharne. Tel: 01994 427420.
Open all year, daily.

Laugharne Castle
King Street, Laugharne. Tel: 01994 427906.
Open May–Sep, daily.

TOUR 12

i Terrace Road, Aberystwyth. Tel: 01970 612125.

i Canolfan Owain Glyndwr, Machynlleth. Tel: 01654 702401.

i Town Hall, Great Oak Street, Llanidloes. Tel: 01686 412605.

i The Leisure Centre, North Street, Rhayader. Tel: 01597 810591.

i Groe Car Park, Builth Wells. Tel: 01982 553307.

Borth

Brynllys Farm
Dol-y-bont, Aberystwyth. Tel: 01970 871489.
Open all year.

Machynlleth

Centre for Alternative Technology
Machynlleth. Tel: 01654 702400.
Open all year, daily.

Furnace
The Furnace, Eglwysfach. Tel: 029 2082 6185.
Open all year.

Rhayader

Welsh Royal Crystal Glass Factory
5 Brynberth, Rhayader. Tel: 01597 811005.
Open all year, daily.

Gigrin Farm
South Street, Rhayader. Tel: 01597 810243.
Open all year, daily.

Elan Valley Visitor Centre
Ellen Valley, Rhayader. Tel: 01597 810898/810880.
Open Mar–Oct, daily.

Builth Wells

Wyeside Arts Centre
Castle Street, Builth Wells. Tel: 01982 552555.
Open all year, Mon–Sat.

Tregaron

Cors Caron
Countryside Council for Wales, Neuaddlas. Tel: 01974 298480:

Kite Centre
Dewi Road. Tel: 01974 298977.
Open Apr–Sep, Mon–Sat

Pontrhydygroes

Strata Florida Abbey
Pontrhydfendigaid, Tregaron. Tel: 01222 500200.
Open all year, daily.

Devil's Bridge

Vale of Rheidol Railway
Park Avenue, Aberystwyth. Tel: 01970 625819.
Open Easter–Oct.

Ponterwyd

Llywernog Silver Lead Mining Museum and Caverns
Llywernog Mine, Ponterwyd. Tel: 01970 890620.
Open Easter–Oct, daily; Nov–Dec, by appointment.

Nant-yr-Arian Visitor Centre
Ponterwyd. Tel: 01970 890694.

TOUR 13

i The Old Library,

Station Road, Barmouth. Tel: 01341 280787.

i Gwyddfor House, High Street, Harlech. Tel: 01766 780658.

i Penllyn, Pensarn Road, Bala. Tel: 01678 521021.

i Craft Centre, Corris. Tel: 01654 761244.

i The Wharf Gardens, Aberdyfi. Tel: 01654 767321.

i High Street, Tywyn. Tel: 01654 710070.

i Ty Meirion, Eldon Square, Dolgellau. Tel: 01341 422888.

Llanbedr

Charwel Hên Llanfair Slate Caverns
Llanfair, near Harlech. Tel: 01766 780247.
Open Easter–Oct, daily.

Harlech

Harlech Castle
Harlech. Tel: 01766 780552.
Open all year, daily.

Trawsfynydd

Rhiw Goch Ski Centre
Bronaber, Trawsfynydd. Tel: 01766 540578.
Open all year, daily.

Bala

Bala Lake Railway
The Station, Llanuwchllyn. Tel: 01678 540666.
Open Easter–3 Oct

Lake Vyrnwy

Vyrnwy Visitor Centre and RSPB
Bryn Awel, Llanwddyn, Oswestry. Tel: 01691 870278.
Open 1 Apr–24 Dec, daily; Jan–Mar, weekends.

Corris

Corris Craft Centre
Machynlleth. Tel: 01654 761584.
Open all year, daily.

King Arthur's Labyrinth
Tel: 01654 761584.
Open all year, daily.

Tywyn

Talyllyn Railway
Wharf Station, Tywyn. Tel: 01654 710472.
Open Easter, Mar–Oct.

Fairbourne

Fairbourne Railway
Beach Road, Fairbourne, Dolgellau. Tel: 01341 250362.
Open Easter–Nov.

Dolgellau

Abergwynant Trekking Centre
Abergwynant Farm, Penmaenpool, Dolgellau. Tel: 01341 422377.
Open all year, daily.

TOUR 14

i Town Hall, Deiniol Road, Bangor. Tel: 01248 352786.

i Oriel Pendeitsh, Castle Street, Caernarfon. Tel: 01286 672232.

i 41a High Street, Llanberis. Tel: 01286 870765.

i Tourist Association, Ael-y-Bryn, Beddgelert. Tel: 01766 890310.

i Station Yard, Porthmadog. Tel: 01766 512981.

i Unit 3, High Street, Blaenau Ffestiniog. Tel: 01766 830360.

i Royal Oak Stables, Betws-y-Coed. Tel: 01690 710426.

i Prince's Drive, Colwyn Bay. Tel: 01492 530478.

i 1–2 Chapel Street, Llandudno. Tel: 01492 876413.

i Conwy Castle Visitor Centre, Castle Street, Conwy. Tel: 01492 592248.

Menai Bridge

Tegfryn Art Gallery
Tegfryn, Cadnant Road, Menai Bridge, Anglesey. Tel: 01248 712437.
Open Mar–Dec, Tue–Sun.

Caernarfon

Caernarfon Air World
Dinas Dinlle, Caernarfon. Tel: 01286 830800.
Open Apr–2 Nov, daily.

Caernarfon Castle
Caernarfon.

i Tourist Information Centre
12 Number on tour

Tel: 01286 677617.
Open all year, daily.

Segontium Roman Fort and Museum
Bedgelert Road, Caernarfon. Tel: 01286 675625.
Open all year, Mon–Sat and Sun afternoons.

3 Llanrug
Bryn Bras Castle and Gardens
Llanrug, near Llanberis. Tel: 01286 870210.
Open by appointment only.

4 Llanberis
Llanberis Lake Railway
Llanberis. Tel: 01286 870549.
Open Easter–Oct.

Padarn Country Park
The Quarry Hospital, Llanberis, Caernarfon. Tel: 01286 870892.
Open all year, daily.

Electric Mountain
Dinorwig, Llanberis. Tel: 01286 870636.
Open Easter–23 Dec, daily; 8 Jan–Easter, Thu–Sun.

Dolbadarn Castle
Llanberis. Tel: 01286 870253.
Open all year, daily.

Snowdon Mountain Railway
Llanberis. Tel: 01286 870223.
Open 15 Mar–1 Nov, daily.

Welsh Slate Museum
Gilfach Ddu, Padarn Country Park, Llanberis. Tel: 01286 870630.
Open Easter–Oct, daily; Nov–Mar, Sun–Fri.

5 Beddgelert
Sygun Copper Mine
Beddgelert. Tel: 01766 510100.
Open all year, daily.

6 Porthmadog
Ffestiniog Railway
Harbour Station, Porthmadog. Tel: 01766 512340.
Open late Mar–early Nov, daily; Nov–Dec, most days; Feb and Mar, limited service.

Welsh Highland Railway
Tremadog Road, Porthmadog.

Tel: 01766 513402.
Open Apr–Oct, most days.

Madog Motor Museum
Snowdon Street, Porthmadog. Tel: 01758 713618.
Open May–Sep, Mon–Fri.

Porthmadog Pottery
Porthmadog.
Open Mon–Fri and weekends during summer.

7 Portmeirion
Portmeirion Village
Minffordd. Tel: 01766 770228.
Open all year, daily.

8 Blaenau Ffestiniog
Llechwedd Slate Caverns
Blaenau Ffestiniog. Tel: 01766 830306.
Open all year, daily.

Ffestiniog Visitor Centre
Tan-y-Grisiau, Blaenau Ffestiniog. Tel: 01766 830310.
Open Easter–Oct, Sun–Fri.

Rhiw Goch Ski Centre
Bronaber, Trawsfynydd. Tel: 01766 540578.
Open all year, daily.

9 Betws-y-Coed
Motor Museum
Betws-y-Coed. Tel: 01690 710760.
Open Easter–Oct, daily.

10 Llanrwst
Trefriw Wells Roman Spa
Trefriw. Tel: 01492 640057.
Open Easter–Oct, daily; Nov–Easter, Mon–Sat and Sun afternoons.

Trefriw Woollen Mills
Trefriw. Tel: 01492 640462.
Open Easter–Oct, Mon–Fri.

11 Tal-y-Cafn
Bodnant Garden
Tal-y-Cafn, Colwyn Bay, Conwy. Tel: 01492 650460.
Open mid-Mar–Oct, daily.

12 Colwyn Bay
Welsh Mountain Zoo
Colwyn Bay. Tel: 01492 532938.
Open all year, daily.

Dinosaur World
Eirias Park, Colwyn Bay. Tel: 01492 518111.
Open Easter–Sep, daily.

13 Llandudno
The Great Orme
Llandudno. Tel: 01492 870870/870447.
Open Apr–Oct.

Alice in Wonderland Visitor Centre, The Rabbit Hole
3 and 4 Trinity Square, Llandudno. Tel: 01492 860082.
Open all year, daily.

14 Conwy
Conwy Castle
Conwy. Tel: 01492 592358.
Open all year, daily.

Conwy Butterfly House
Bodlondeb Gardens, Conwy. Tel: 01492 593149.
Open Apr–Oct.

TOUR 15

i 9 Castle Hill, Lincoln. Tel: 01522 529828.

i Pearoom Craft Centre, Heckington (see 3)

i Money's Yard, Carre Street, Sleaford. Tel: 01529 414294.

i The Gilstrap Centre, Castlegate, Newark-on-Trent. Tel: 01636 678962.

i Sherwood Visitor Centre, Edwinstowe. Tel: 01623 823202.

2 Woodhall Spa
Tattershall Castle
Tattershall, Lincoln. Tel: 01526 342543.
Open 1 Apr–1 Nov, Sat–Wed; 7 Nov–20 Dec, Sat and Sun afternoons.

Dogdyke Pumping Station
Bridge Farm, Tattershall, Lincoln. Tel: 01526 342352.
Open Apr–Oct, occasional Sunday afternoons.

3 Heckington
Heckington Windmill
Hale Road, Heckington, Sleaford. Tel: 01529 461919.
Open 22 Sep–12 Apr, Sun pm; 13 Apr–24 Jul, Thu–Sun pm; 25 Jul–21 Sep, Mon–Sat, daily, Sun pm.

Pearoom Craft Centre
Station Yard, Heckington,

Sleaford. Tel: 01529 460765.
Open all year, daily.

8 Edwinstowe
Sherwood Forest Country Park and Visitor Centre
Edwinstowe. Tel: 01623 823202/824490.
Open all year, daily.

9 North Leverton
Sundown Adventureland
Treswell Road, Rampton, Retford. Tel: 01777 248274.
Open all year, daily.

TOUR 16

i The Custom House, Purfleet Quay, King's Lynn. Tel: 01553 763044.

i 2–3 Bridge Street, Wisbech. Tel: 01945 583263.

i Oliver Cromwell's House, 29 St Mary's Street, Ely. Tel: 01353 662062.

i Red Lion House, Market Place, Fakenham. Tel: 01328 851981.

i Shire Hall Museum, Common Place, Little Walsingham. Tel: 01328 820510.

i Staithe Street, Wells-next-the-Sea. Tel: 01328 710885.

i Town Hall, The Green, Hunstanton. Tel: 01485 532610.

1 Wisbech
Wisbech and Fenland Museum
Museum Square, Wisbech. Tel: 01945 583817.
Open all year, Tue–Sat.

Aviation Museum
Old Lynn Road, West Walton, Wisbech. Tel: 01945 585946.
Open Mar–Sep, weekends.

Peckover House
North Brink, Wisbech. Tel: 01945 583463.
Open 29 Mar–2 Nov, House, Wed, Sat, Sun pm; Gardens, Mon and Tue pm.

5 Thetford
Euston Hall
Thetford.

Tel: 01842 766366.
*Open Jun–Sep, occasional
Thu and Sun afternoons.*

Ancient House Museum
White Hart Street, Thetford. Tel: 01842 752599.
*Open 2 Jan–30 May,
Mon–Sat; 31 May–Aug,
daily; 29 Sep–31 Dec,
Mon–Sat.*

6 Dereham
Bishop Bonner's Cottage Museum
St Withburga Lane, Dereham. Tel: 01362 850293.
*Open 1 May–1 Oct, Tue,
Thu–Sat afternoons.*

Norfolk Rural Life Museum and Union Farm
Beech House, Gressenhall, Dereham. Tel: 01362 860563.
Open 5 Apr–1 Nov, daily.

7 Fakenham
Fakenham Museum of Gas and Local History
Hempton Road, Fakenham. Tel: 01328 863150.
Open 6 Aug–17 Sep, Thu.

Pensthorpe Waterfowl Park
Pensthorpe, Fakenham. Tel: 01328 851465. *Open daily.*

9 Wells-next-the-Sea
Wells & Walsingham Railway
Stiffkey Road, Wells-next-the-Sea. Tel: 01328 710631.
Open 10 Apr–30 Sep, daily.

Cley Marshes Nature Reserve
Coast Road, Cley-next-the-Sea, Holt. Tel: 01263 740008.
*Open 25 Mar–13 Dec,
Tue–Sun.*

10 Holkham
Holkham Hall and Bygones Museum
Wells-next-the-Sea. Tel: 01328 710227.
*Open 28 May–28 Sep,
Sun–Thu pms and Bank
Holidays.*

12 Hunstanton
Sea Life Centre
Southern Promenade, Hunstanton. Tel: 01485 533576.
Open all year, daily.

Norfolk Lavender
Caley Mill, Heacham, King's Lynn. Tel: 01485 570384.
Open all year, daily.

Oasis Leisure Centre
Central Promenade, Hunstanton. Tel: 01485 534227.
Open Feb–Nov.

13 Sandringham
Sandringham Estate
Sandringham, King's Lynn. Tel: 01553 772675.
*Open 15 Apr–mid-Jul (not
Good Fri), Aug–8 Oct, daily.*

Castle Rising
Castle Rising, King's Lynn. Tel: 01553 631330.
*Open 1 Nov–21 Mar, Wed–
Sun, 22 Mar–31 Oct, daily.*

TOUR 17

[i] St Stephen's Church, St Stephen's Lane, Ipswich. Tel: 01473 258070.

[i] Town Hall, Market Hill, Sudbury. Tel: 01787 881320.

[i] 1 Market Place, Saffron Walden. Tel: 01799 510444.

[i] Wheeler Street, Cambridge. Tel: 01223 322640.

[i] Lady Street, Lavenham. Tel: 01787 248207.

[i] Toppesfield Hall, Hadleigh. Tel: 01473 822922.

1 East Bergholt
Flatford Mill
East Bergholt, Colchester. Tel: 01206 298260.
*Open Mar–Apr, Wed–Sun;
May–Sep, daily; Oct–Nov,
Wed–Sun.*

Dedham Art and Craft Centre
High Street, Dedham, Colchester. Tel: 01206 322666.
*Open Jan–Mar, Tue–Sun;
Apr–Dec, daily.*

2 Sudbury
Gainsborough's House
46 Gainsborough Street, Sudbury. Tel: 01787 372958.
*Open all year, Tue–Sat and
Sun afternoons.*

Quay Theatre
Quay Lane, Sudbury. Tel: 01787 374745.
Open all year, daily.

3 Castle Hedingham
Hedingham Castle
Castle Hedingham, Halstead. Tel: 01787 460261.
Open Easter–Oct, daily.

Colne Valley Railway
Yeldham Road, Castle Hedingham. Tel: 01787 461174.
Open Mar–Dec, daily.

5 Thaxted
John Webb's Windmill
Mill Row, Thaxted. Tel: 01371 830285.
*Open May–Sep, weekends
and Bank Holidays.*

Thaxted Guildhall
Town Street, Thaxted. Tel: 01371 831339.
Open 28 Mar–Sep, weekends and Bank Holidays.

6 Saffron Walden
Saffron Walden Museum
Museum Street, Saffron Walden. Tel: 01799 510333.
*Open all year, Mon–Sat, Sun
afternoons and Bank
Holidays.*

Audley End House
Saffron Walden. Tel: 01799 522399.
*Open Apr–Oct, Wed–
Sun and Bank Holidays.*

Linton Zoo
Hadstock Road, Linton. Tel: 01223 891308.
Open all year, daily.

7 Duxford
Imperial War Museum
Duxford Airfield, Duxford. Tel: 01223 835000.
Open all year, daily.

9 Cambridge
Fitzwilliam Museum
Trumpington Street, Cambridge. Tel: 01223 332900.
*Open all year, Tue–Sat and
Bank Holidays, Sun afternoons.*

Fowlmere Nature Reserve
Manor Farm, High Street, Fowlmere. Tel: 01763 208978.
Open all year, daily.

10 Lode
Anglesey Abbey, Gardens and Lode Mill
Lode, Cambridge. Tel: 01223 811200.
Open Mar–Nov, most days.

11 Newmarket
National Stud
Newmarket. Tel: 01638 663464.
Open Mar–Aug, by appointment.

National Horse Racing Museum
99 High Street, Newmarket. Tel: 01638 667333.
*Open Easter–Oct, Tue–Sat,
also Bank Holiday Mon;
Jul–Aug, Mon–Sat.*

12 Clare
Clare Castle Country Park
Malting Lane, Clare, Sudbury. Tel: 01787 277491.
Open all year, daily.

13 Long Melford
Melford Hall
Long Melford, Sudbury. Tel: 01787 880286.
*Open Apr and Oct weekend
afternoons; May–Sep,
Wed–Sun, Bank Holidays.*

Kentwell Hall
Long Melford, Sudbury. Tel: 01787 310207.
*Open Mar–Oct, most Sun
afternoons; 12 Jul–20 Jul,
daily.*

14 Lavenham
Lavenham Guildhall
Market Place, Lavenham. Tel: 01787 247646.
Open 28 Mar–1 Nov, daily.

15 Hadleigh
Guildhall
Market Place, Hadleigh. Tel: 01473 823884.
*Open 4 Jun–13 Sep, Thu and
Sun afternoons.*

TOUR 18

[i] The Old School, Gloucester Green, Oxford. Tel: 01865 726871.

[i] Park Street, Woodstock. Tel: 01993 813276.

[i] The Guildhall, Chipping Norton. Tel: 01608 644379.

ℹ Banbury Museum, 8 Horsefair, Banbury. Tel: 01295 259855.

❶ Woodstock
Blenheim Palace
Woodstock. Tel: 01993 811091/811325.
Open Mar–Oct, daily.

Oxfordshire County Museum
Fletcher's House, Woodstock. Tel: 01993 811456.
Open all year, Tue–Sat and Sun afternoons.

❹ Broughton
Broughton Castle
Banbury. Tel: 01295 262624.
Open Easter and 20 May–13 Sep, Wed and Sun; also Thu in Jul and Aug.

❻ Sulgrave
Sulgrave Manor
Manor Road, Sulgrave. Tel: 01295 760205.
Open Apr–Oct, weekends, Mon, Tue, Thu, Fri pm; Mar, Nov, Dec, weekends only.

❼ Aynho
Aynho Park
Aynho. Tel: 01869 810636.
Open May–Sep, Wed and Thu afternoons.

❾ Steeple Aston
Rousham House
Near Steeple Aston. Tel: 01869 347110.
Open Apr–Sep, Wed and Sun afternoons.

TOUR 19

ℹ 28 Southgate Street, Gloucester. Tel: 01452 421188.

ℹ 3 The Homend, Ledbury. Tel: 01531 636147.

ℹ 21 Church Street, Great Malvern. Tel: 01684 892289.

ℹ 64 Barton Street, Tewkesbury. Tel: 01684 295027.

ℹ The Almonry, Abbey Gate, Evesham. Tel: 01386 446944.

ℹ Bridgefoot, Stratford-upon-Avon. Tel: 01789 293127.

ℹ 2 Rosery Court, Chipping Campden. Tel: 01386 841206.

ℹ Town Hall, High Street, Winchcombe. Tel: 01242 602925.

ℹ 77 Promenade, Cheltenham. Tel: 01242 522878.

ℹ Painswick Library, Stroud Road, Painswick. Tel: 01452 812569.

❶ Ledbury
Eastnor Castle
Eastnor, Ledbury. Tel: 01531 6331160/632302.
Open Easter–Jun and Sep, Sun; Jul and Aug, Sun–Fri.

❷ Great Malvern
Priory Church of St Mary and St Michael
Church Street, Malvern.
Open all year, daily.

Malvern Museum
Abbey Road, Malvern. Tel: 01684 567811.
Open Easter–Oct, Thu–Tue.

❻ Alcester
Coughton Court
Alcester. Tel: 01789 762435.
Open Mar–Apr, weekends Apr–Sep, Wed–Sun; Oct, Fri and Sat.

Ragley Hall
Alcester. Tel: 01789 762090.
Open 13 Apr–10 Oct, Thu–Sun; Jul and Aug, daily.

❼ Wilmcote
Mary Arden's House and the Shakespeare Countryside Museum
Station Road, Wilmcote, Stratford-upon-Avon. Tel: 01789 204016.
Open all year, daily.

❽ Stratford-upon-Avon
Shakespeare's Birthplace
Henley Street, Stratford-upon-Avon. Tel: 01789 204016. *Open all year, daily.*

Royal Shakespeare Company Collection
Royal Shakespeare Theatre, Waterside, Stratford-upon-Avon. Tel: 01789 296655.
Open all year, daily.

Harvard House
High Street, Stratford-upon-Avon. Tel: 01789 204016.
Open 20 May–22 Sep, daily.

The Teddy Bear Museum
19 Greenhill Street, Stratford-upon-Avon. Tel: 01789 293160.
Open all year, daily.

Anne Hathaway's Cottage
Cottage Lane, Shottery, Stratford-upon-Avon. Tel: 01789 204016.
Open all year, daily.

New Place
Chapel Street, Stratford-upon-Avon. Tel: 01789 204016.
Open all year, daily.

❾ Chipping Campden
Hidcote Manor Garden
Chipping Campden. Tel: 01386 438333.
Open Apr–1 Nov, Mon, Wed, Thu, Sat and Sun; Jun and Jul, Tue also.

❿ Buckland
GWR Steam Railway Centre
The Railway Station, Toddington. Tel: 01242 621405.
Open various days throughout year.

Hailes Abbey
Near Winchcombe, Cheltenham. Tel: 01242 602398.
Open Apr–Oct, daily, weekends in winter.

Broadway Tower Country Park
off A44, Broadway. Tel: 01386 852390.
Open Apr–Oct, daily.

⓫ Winchcombe
Winchcombe Railway Museum
23 Gloucester Street, Winchcombe. Tel: 01242 620641.
Open Easter–Oct, weekends and bank holidays, daily during school holidays.

Winchcombe Folk and Police Museum
Town Hall, High Street, Winchcombe. Tel: 01242 602925.
Open Apr–Oct, Mon–Sat.

Sudeley Castle and Gardens
Winchcombe. Tel: 01242 603197/602308.
Open Apr–Oct, daily.

⓬ Cheltenham
Pittville Pump Room
Pittville, Cheltenham. Tel: 01242 523852.
Open May–Sep, daily; Oct–Apr, Wed–Mon.

Holst Birthplace Museum
4 Clarence Road, Pittville, Cheltenham. Tel: 01242 524846/237431.
Open all year, Tue–Sat.

TOUR 20

ℹ The Music Hall, The Square, Shrewsbury. Tel: 01743 350761.

ℹ Castle Street, Ludlow. Tel: 01584 875053.

ℹ Bewdley Museum, Load Street, Bewdley. Tel: 01299 404740.

ℹ The Library, Listley Street, Bridgnorth. Tel: 01746 763257.

ℹ The Museum, High Street, Much Wenlock. Tel: 01952 727679.

ℹ The Wharfage, Ironbridge. Tel: 01952 432166.

❶ Acton Burnell
Acton Burnell Castle
Acton Burnell, Shrewsbury.
Open all reasonable times.

❷ Church Stretton
Acton Scott Historic Working Farm
Wenlock Lodge, Acton Scott. Tel: 01694 781306/781307.
Open 28 Mar–29 Oct, Tue–Sun.

❸ Craven Arms
Stokesay Castle
Craven Arms. Tel: 01588 672544.
Open Apr–Oct, daily; Nov–Mar, Wed–Sun.

❹ Ludlow
Ludlow Castle
Castle Square, Ludlow. Tel: 01584 873355.
Open Feb–Dec, daily and Jan weekends.

i Tourist Information Centre

12 Number on tour

Ludlow Museum
Castle Street, Ludlow. Tel: 01584 875384.
Open daily in summer, weekdays only in winter.

6 Bewdley
Severn Valley Railway
The Railway Station, Bewdley. Tel: 01299 403816, 01746 764361.
Open May–Sep, daily, weekends other times.

West Midlands Safari and Leisure Park
Spring Grove, Bewdley. Tel: 01299 402114.
Open Apr–Oct, daily.

7 Bridgnorth
Bridgnorth Castle
West Castle Street, Bridgnorth. Tel: 01746 762231.
Open all year, daily.

8 Shipton
Shipton Hall
Shipton. Tel: 01746 785225.
Open Apr–Sep, Thu pm.

9 Much Wenlock
Benthall Hall
Broseley. Tel: 01952 882159.
Open Apr–Sep, Wed and Sun afternoons.

10 Ironbridge
Ironbridge Gorge Museums
Ironbridge. Tel: 01952 433522/432166.
Open all year, daily.

Buildwas Abbey
Ironbridge. Tel: 01952 433274.
Open Apr–Oct, daily.

11 Wroxeter
Wroxeter Roman Town
Wroxeter. Tel: 01743 761330.
Open Apr–Oct, daily; Nov–Mar, Wed–Sun.

Attingham Park
Atcham. Tel: 01743 708123.
Open Gardens, all year, daily; House, 24 Mar–Oct, Fri–Tue afternoons.

TOUR 21

i Carlisle Visitor Centre, Old Town Hall, Green Market, Carlisle. Tel: 01228 512444.

i Moot Hall, Market Square, Keswick. Tel: 017687 72645.

i Redbank Road, Grasmere. Tel: 015394 35245.

i Central Buildings, Market Cross, Ambleside. Tel: 015394 32582.

i Ruskin Avenue, Coniston. Tel: 015394 41533.

i Glebe Road, Bowness-on-Windermere. Tel: 015394 42895.

i Victoria Street, Windermere. Tel: 015394 46499.

i Main Car Park, Glenridding. Tel: 01768 482414.

i Robinson's School, Middlegate, Penrith. Tel: 01768 867466.

i Railway Station, Station Road, Haltwhistle. Tel: 01434 322002.

3 Buttermere
Whinlatter Forest Park Visitor Centre
Braithwaite, Keswick. Tel: 017687 78469.
Open all year, daily.

4 Keswick
Cumberland Pencil Museum
Southey Works, Keswick. Tel: 017687 73626.
Open all year, daily.

5 Grasmere
Dove Cottage and the Wordsworth Museum
Grasmere. Tel: 015394 35544/35547.
Open all year, daily.

Rydal Mount and Gardens
Ambleside. Tel: 015394 33002.
Open Mar–Oct, daily; Nov–Feb, Wed–Mon.

6 Ambleside
Stagshaw Gardens
Stagshaw, Ambleside. Tel: 015394 35599.
Open Apr–Jun, daily.

7 Coniston
Beatrix Potter Gallery
Main Street, Hawkshead, Ambleside.

Tel: 015394 36355.
Open Apr–Oct, Sun–Thu.

Hill Top
Near Sawrey, Hawkshead, Ambleside. Tel: 015394 36269.
Open Apr–Oct, Sat–Wed.

8 Bowness and Windermere
Windermere Steamboat Museum
Rayrigg Road, Bowness-on-Windermere. Tel: 015394 45565.
Open 18 Mar–29 Oct, daily.

Lake District National Park Visitor Centre
Brockhole, Windermere. Tel: 015394 46601.
Open Easter–early Nov, daily.

10 Penrith
Lowther Leisure and Wildlife Park
Hackthorpe, Penrith. Tel: 01931 712523.
Open 15 Apr–1 May, weekends; 27 May–10 Sep, daily.

11 Haltwhistle
South Tynedale Railway
Railway Station, Alston. Tel: 01434 381696.
Open Easter–Oct, daily; other occasional days and Santa specials.

Housesteads Fort
Bardon Mills, Hexham. Tel: 01434 344363.
Open all year, daily.

Roman Army Museum
Greenhead. Tel: 016977 47485.
Open Feb–Nov, daily.

TOUR 22

i Minster Road, Ripon. Tel: 01765 604625.

i Central Chambers, Railway Street, Leyburn. Tel: 01969 623069/622773.

i Friary Gardens, Victoria Road, Richmond. Tel: 01748 850252.

i Woodleigh, Flatts Road, Barnard Castle. Tel: 01833 690909/630272.

i 72 Main Street, Sedbergh. Tel: 015396 20125.

i Dales Countryside Museum (see **8**)

i National Park Centre, Hebden Road, Grassington. Tel: 01756 752774.

i 18 High Street, Pateley Bridge. Tel: 01423 711147.

1 Masham
Jervaulx Abbey
Masham. Tel: 01677 460226.
Open all year, daily.

2 Middleham
Middleham Castle
Middleham. Tel: 01969 623899.
Open Apr–Oct, daily; Nov–Mar, Wed–Sun.

4 Richmond
Richmond Castle
Richmond. Tel: 01748 822493.
Open all year, daily.

Georgian Theatre Royal
Richmond. Tel: 01748 823710.
Open Museum Easter–Oct, daily; Theatre Mar–Dec, daily.

Green Howards Museum
Trinity Church Square, Market Place, Richmond. Tel: 01748 822133.
Open Feb–Nov, most days.

5 Barnard Castle
Barnard Castle
Barnard Castle. Tel: 01833 38212.
Open Apr–1 Nov, daily; 2 Nov–Mar, Wed–Sun.

Bowes Museum
Barnard Castle. Tel: 01833 690606.
Open all year, daily.

7 Sedbergh
National Park Centre
72 Main Street, Sedbergh. Tel: 015396 20125.
Open Apr–Nov, daily.

8 Hawes
Dales Countryside Museum
Station Yard, Hawes. Tel: 01969 667450.
Open daily.

10 Buckden
Kilnsey Park
Buckden. Tel: 01756 752150.
Open all year, daily.

i Tourist Information Centre
12 Number on tour

12 Pateley Bridge
Nidderdale Museum
Pateley Bridge. Tel: 01423 711225.
Open Easter–Oct, daily afternoons; Nov–Apr, weekend afternoons.

13 Fountains Abbey and Studley Royal
Fountains Abbey. Tel: 01765 608888.
Open all year, daily.

TOUR 23

i Old Station Buildings, Marine Road, Morecambe. Tel: 01524 582808/9.

i 24 Main Street, Kirkby Lonsdale. Tel: 015242 71437.

i Community Centre Car Park, Ingleton Via Carnforth. Tel: 015242 41049.

i Town Hall, Cheapside, Settle. Tel: 01729 825192.

i Craven Court, Skipton. Tel: 01756 792809.

i 12–14 Market Place, Clitheroe. Tel: 01200 425566.

i 1 Clifton Street, Blackpool. Tel: 01253 478222.

i Blackpool Pleasure Beach, Unit 11, Ocean Boulevard, Blackpool. Tel: 01253 403223.

i 29 Castle Hill, Lancaster. Tel: 01524 32878.

2 Warton
Leighton Hall
Carnforth. Tel: 01524 734474.
Open May–Sep, daily.

8 Skipton
Skipton Castle
Skipton. Tel: 01756 792442.
Open all year, daily.

Craven Museum
Skipton. Tel: 01756 706407.
Open all year, most days.

Embsay and Bolton Abbey Steam Railway
Skipton. Tel: 01756 794727.
Open all year, weekends.

9 Clitheroe
Clitheroe Castle Museum

Castle Hill, Clitheroe. Tel: 01200 424635.
Open all year, most days.

Browsholme Hall
Clitheroe. Tel: 01254 826719.
Open 10–13 Apr, 23–25 May; Aug weekends, 31 Aug.

11 Ribchester
Ribchester Roman Museum
Riverside, Ribchester. Tel: 01254 878261.
Open all year, daily.

12 Blackpool
Blackpool Tower
The Promenade, Blackpool. Tel: 01253 622242.
Open all year, weekends only Nov–Mar.

Blackpool Pleasure Beach
525 Ocean Boulevard, Festival Coast, Blackpool. Tel: 0870 444 5566.
Open Mar weekends; Apr–Nov daily.

Sandcastle
Promenade, Blackpool. Tel: 01253 343602.
Open all year, most days.

Blackpool Sea Life Centre
The Promenade, Blackpool. Tel: 01253 622445.
Open all year, daily.

Blackpool Zoo
off East Park Drive, Blackpool. Tel: 01253 830830.
Open all year, daily.

13 Lancaster
Lancaster Maritime Museum
Custom Housem St George's Quay, Lancaster. Tel: 01524 64637.
Open all year, Easter–Oct. daily, Nov–Mar afternons.

Lancaster Castle
Shire Hall, Castle Parade, Lancaster. Tel: 01524 64998.
Open 15 Mar–19 Dec, most days.

Lancaster City Museum
Market Square, Lancaster. Tel: 01524 64637.
Open all year, Mon–Sat.

Judges' Lodgings Museum
Church Street, Lancaster.

Tel: 01524 32808.
Open Apr–Oct, most days.

TOUR 24

i Town Hall, Macclesfield. Tel: 01625 504114/5

i The Pavillion, Matlock Bath. Tel: 01629 55082.

i Old Market Hall, Bridge Street, Bakewell. Tel: 01629 813227.

i The Crescent, Buxton. Tel: 01298 25106.

1 Castleton
Peveril Castle
Market Place, Castleton. Tel: 01433 620613.
Open Apr–1 Nov, daily; 2 Nov–Mar, Wed–Sun.

Peak Cavern
Castleton. Tel: 01433 620285.
Open Easter–Oct, daily; Nov–Easter, weekends.

Treak Cliff Cavern
Castleton. Tel: 01433 620571.
Open all year, daily.

Speedwell Cavern
Winnats Pass, Castleton. Tel: 01433 620512.
Open all year, daily.

Blue John Cavern and Mine
Buxton Road, Castleton. Tel: 01433 620638/620642.
Open all year, daily.

3 Chatsworth
Chatsworth House
Chatsworth. Tel: 01246 582204.
Open 18 Mar–1 Nov, daily.

4 Matlock and Matlock Bath
Riber Castle Wildlife Park
Riber, Matlock. Tel: 01629 582073.
Open all year, daily.

Heights of Abraham
Matlock Bath. Tel: 01629 582365.
Open Easter–Oct, daily.

National Tramway Museum
Crich. Tel: 01773 852565.
Open Apr–Oct, daily; winter, Sun.

5 Bakewell
Old House Museum
Cunningham Place, Bakewell. Tel: 01629 813165.
Open Apr–Oct, afternoons; Jul and Aug, mornings also.

Haddon Hall
Bakewell. Tel: 01629 812855.
Open Apr–Sep, daily; Oct, Mon–Thu.

7 Buxton
Buxton Spa Water Swimming Pool
St John's Road, Buxton. Tel: 01298 26548.
Open all year, daily.

Buxton Opera House
Water Street, Buxton. Tel: 01298 72190.
Open all year for shows.

Pavilion Gardens
St John's Road, Buxton. Tel: 01298 23114.
Open all year, daily.

TOUR 25

i York Railway Station, York. Tel: 01904 621756.

i 58 Market Place, Malton. Tel: 01653 600048.

i Eastgate Car Park, Pickering. Tel: 01751 473791.

i The Moors Centre, Danby Lodge, Lodge Lane, Danby. Tel: 01287 660654.

i Rydale Folk Museum, Hutton-le-Hole. Tel: 01751 417367.

i Town Hall, Market Place, Helmsley. Tel: 01439 770173.

1 Malton
Malton Museum
Old Town Hall, Market Place, Malton. Tel: 01653 695136.
Open Easter Sat–Oct, Mon–Sat.

Eden Camp Modern History Museum
Eden Camp. Tel: 01653 697777.
Open 12 Jan–13 Feb, Mon–Fri; 14 Feb–23 Dec, daily.

Practical Information

i Tourist Information Centre
12 Number on tour

Castle Howard
Castle Howard. Tel: 01653 648333/648444.
Open Mar–Oct, daily.

Flamingo Land Theme Park and Zoo
Kirby Misperton, Malton.
Tel: 01653 668287.
Open 28 Mar–26 Sep, daily; Oct, weekends only.

2 Pickering
North Yorkshire Moors Railway
Pickering Station, Pickering.
Tel: 01751 472508.
Open 20 Mar–Oct, daily.

Pickering Castle
Pickering. Tel: 01751 474989.
Open Apr–Octr, daily; Nov–Mar, Wed–Sun.

Beck Isle Museum of Rural Life
Pickering. Tel: 01751 473653.
Open Mar–Oct, daily.

5 Danby
The Moors Centre
Lodge Lane, Danby. Tel: 01287 660654.
Open Mar–Dec, daily; Jan–Feb, weekends.

7 Hutton-le-Hole
Rydale Folk Museum
Hutton-le-Hole. Tel: 01751 417367.
Open 12 Mar–5 Nov, daily.

9 Helmsley
Helmsley Castle
Helmsley. Tel: 01439 770442.
Open Apr–Oct, daily; Nov–mid-Mar, Wed–Sun.

Rievaulx Abbey
Helmsley. Tel: 01439 798228.
Open all year, daily.

10 Coxwold
Shandy Hall
Coxwold. Tel: 01347 868465.
Open House May–Sep, Wed and Sun afternoons; Gardens May–Sep, daily.

Newburgh Priory
Coxwold. Tel: 01347 868435.
Open Apr–Jun, Wed, Sun afternoons.

13 Sutton-on-the-Forest
Sutton Park
Sutton-on-the-Forest. Tel: 01347 811239.
Open Easter–Sep, daily.

TOUR 26
---

i Castle Wynd, Inverness.
Tel: 01463 234353.

i Loch Ness Centre (see 2).

i Main Street, Lochcarron. Tel: 01520 722357.

i NTS Visitor Centre, Torridon. Tel: 01445 791221.

i Beinn Eighe Reserve Visitor Centre, near Kinlochewe. Tel: 01445 760258.

i Achtercairn, Gairloch.
Tel: 01445 712130.

i The Square, Strathpeffer. Tel: 01997 421415.

1 Culloden
Culloden Visitor Centre
Culloden Moor, Inverness.
Tel: 01463 790607.
Open all year, daily.

2 Drumnadrochit
The Official Loch Ness Monster Exhibition
The Drumnadrochit Hotel, Drumnadrochit. Tel: 01456 450573.
Open all year, daily.

3 Eilean Donan
Eilean Donan Castle
Dornie, Kyle of Lochalsh.
Tel: 01599 555202.
Open 23 Mar–1 Nov, daily.

7 Gairloch
Gairloch Heritage Museum
Achtercairn, Gairloch. Tel: 01445 712287.
Open Easter–Oct, Mon–Sat.

TOUR 27
---

i St Nicholas House, Broad Street, Aberdeen.
Tel: 01224 632727.

i Station Square, Ballater.
Tel: 013397 55306.

i Railway Museum, Station Yard, Alford. Tel: 019755 62052.

1 Crathes Castle
Crathes Castle
Banchory. Tel: 01330 844525.
Open Apr–Oct, daily.

Storybook Glen
Maryculter, Aberdeen. Tel: 01224 732941.
Open Mar–Oct, daily; Nov–Feb, weekends.

3 Ballater
Royal Lochnagar Distillery
Crathie, Ballater. Tel: 013397 42273.
Open 7 Apr–Jul, Mon–Sat.

4 Balmoral Castle
Balmoral Castle
Balmoral, Ballater. Tel: 013397 42334/5.
Open 7 Apr–Jul, Mon–Sat.

5 Kildrummy Castle
Kildrummy Castle Gardens
Kildrummy, Alford. Tel: 019755 71277/71203.
Open Apr–Oct, daily.

6 Alford
Grampian Transport Museum
Alford. Tel: 019755 62292.
Open 28 Mar–Oct, daily.

Alford Valley Railway
Dunnideer, Kingsford Road, Alford. Tel: 019755 62326/62811.
Open Apr–May and Sep, weekends; Jun–Aug, daily.

8 Drum Castle
Drum Castle
Drumoak, Banchory. Tel: 01330 811204.
Open Easter and 1 May–30 Sep, daily afternoons; Oct, weekend afternoons.

TOUR 28
---

i 3 Princes Street, Edinburgh. Tel: 0131 4733800.

i Pentland Hills Ranger Service Office, Hillend Country Park, Edinburgh.
Tel: 01968 677879.

i High Street, Peebles.
Tel: 01721 720138.

i Abbey House, Melrose.
Tel: 01896 822555.

i Town House, The Square, Kelso. Tel: 01573 223464.

i High Street, Coldstream. Tel: 01890 882607.

1 Hillend Country Park
Midlothian Ski Centre
Hillend, near Edinburgh. Tel: 0131 4454433.
Open all year, daily.

Edinburgh Butterfly and Insect World
Dobbies Garden World, Lasswade. Tel: 0131 6634932.
Open all year, daily.

2 Peebles
Tweeddale Museum
Chambers Institute, High Street, Peebles. Tel: 01721 724820.
Open Mar–Dec, Mon–Fri; Easter–Oct, also Sat.

Scottish Museum of Ornamental Plaster-work
Innerleithen Road, Peebles.
Tel: 01721 720212.
Open all year, daily.

Neidpath Castle
Peebles. Tel: 01721 720333.
Open Easter–Sep, Mon–Sat and Sun afternoons.

3 Traquair
Traquair House
Innerleithen. Tel: 01896 830323.
Open Easter–May and Sep, daily afternoons; Jun–Aug, daily; Oct, Fri–Sun afternoons.

4 Innerleithen
Robert Smail's Printing Works
7–9 High Street, Innerleithen. Tel: 01896 830206.
Open May–Sep, Mon–Sat and Sun afternoons; Oct, weekends.

St Ronan's Wells Interpretive Centre
Wells Brae, Innerleithen.
Tel: 01896 830660.
Open Easter–Sep, pm only.

ⓘ Tourist Information Centre
⓬ Number on tour

Abbotsford House
Melrose. Tel: 01896 752043.
Open Mar–Oct, daily.

⑤ Melrose
Harmony Garden
St Mary's Road, Melrose. Tel: 01721 722502.
Open Apr–Sep, Mon–Sat and Sun afternoons.

⑥ Kelso
Kelso Pottery
The Knowes, Kelso. Tel: 01573 224027.
Open all year, Mon–Sat.

Floors Castle
Kelso. Tel: 01573 223333.
Open 2 Apr–Oct, daily.

⑦ Coldstream
Coldstream Museum
12 Market Square, Coldstream. Tel: 01890 882630.
Open Apr–Sep, daily and Sun pm; Oct, Mon–Sat.

Hirsel Estate
Estate Office, The Hirsel. Tel: 01890 882834/ 882965.
Open all year, daily.

⑧ Haddington
Lennoxlove House
Lennoxlove Estate, Haddington. Tel: 01620 823720.
Open Easter–Oct, Wed and Thu and some Sat and Sun afternoons.

Jane Welsh Carlyle Museum
2 Lodge Street, Haddington. Tel: 01620 823738.
Open Apr–Sep, Wed–Sat afternoons.

⑨ Aberlady
Gosford House
Longniddry. Tel: 01875 870201.
Open 8 Jul–11 Aug, Wed, Sat and Sun, afternoons.

Dalkeith Country Park
Dalkeith. Tel: 0131 654 1666.
Open Apr–Oct, daily.

TOUR 29
ⓘ Whitesands, Dumfries. Tel: 01387 253862.

ⓘ Jean's Shop, Colvend Post Office, Colvend. Tel: 01556 630228.

ⓘ Market Hill Car Park, Castle Douglas. Tel: 01556 502611.

ⓘ Harbour Square, Kirkcudbright. Tel: 01557 330494.

ⓘ The Car Park, High Street, Gatehouse of Fleet. Tel: 01557 814212.

ⓘ Kirroughtree Visitor Centre, Palnure. Tel: 01671 402165.

ⓘ Galloway Forest Park Clatteringshaws Wildlife Centre, Castle Douglas. Tel: 01644 420285.

① New Abbey
Shambellie House Museum of Costume
New Abbey, Dumfries. Tel: 01387 850375.
Open Easter–Oct, daily.

② Kirkbean
John Paul Jones Birthplace Museum
Arbigland, Kirkbean, Dumfries. Tel: 01387 880613.
Open Apr–Sep, Tue–Sun afternoons.

④ Castle Douglas
Threave Garden and Estate
Castle Douglas, Dumfries. Tel: 01556 502575.
Open all year, daily.

Threave Castle
Castle Douglas, Dumfries. Tel: 01831 168512.
Open Apr–Sep, Mon–Sat and Sun afternoons.

⑤ Kirkcudbright
Broughton House and Garden
12 High Street, Kirkcudbright. Tel: 01557 330437.
Open Apr–Oct, afternoons.

The Stewartry Museum
St Mary Street, Kirkcudbright. Tel: 01557 331643.
Open all year, Mon–Sat; Jun–Sep, Sun afternoons.

⑥ Gatehouse of Fleet
Cardoness Castle
Gatehouse of Fleet. Tel: 01557 814427.
Open Apr–Sep, Mon–Sat, Sun pm; Oct–Mar weekends.

Maxwelton House
Moniaive, Thornhill. Tel: 01848 200385.
Open last Sun in May–Sep, Sun–Fri.

⑦ Kirroughtree Forest
Kirroughtree Forest Visitor Centre
Stronord, Palnure, Newton Stewart. Tel: 01671 402165.
Open Easter–Sep, daily pm.

⑧ The Queens Way
Clatterinsgshaws Red Deer Range and Wild Goat Park
New Galloway, Castle Douglas. Tel: 0860 853351.
Open Jun–Sep, Tues, Thu, Sun.

Galloway Deer Museum,
New Galloway, Castle Douglas. Tel: 01644 420285.
Open Easter–Oct, daily.

TOUR 30
ⓘ Milton, Dumbarton. Tel: 01389 742306.

ⓘ The Clock Tower, Helensburgh. Tel: 01436 672642.

ⓘ Front Street, Inveraray. Tel: 01499 302063.

ⓘ Easdale Island Folk Museum, Easdale. Tel: 01852 300370.

ⓘ Argyll Square, Oban. Tel: 01631 563122.

ⓘ Albert Road, Ballachulish (see ⑨)

ⓘ National Trust for Scotland Visitor Centre, A82, Glencoe. Tel: 01855 811307.

ⓘ Main Street, Tarbet. Tel: 01301 702260.

① Helensburgh
The Hill House
Upper Colquhoun Street, Helensburgh. Tel: 01436 673900.
Open Apr–Oct, afternoons.

② Inveraray
Inveraray Castle
Inveraray. Tel: 01499 302203.
Open Apr–mid-Oct.

Inveraray Gaol
Church Square, Inveraray. Tel: 01499 302381.
Open all year, daily.

Argyll Wildlife Park
Inveraray. Tel: 01499 302455.
Open all year, daily.

Auchindrain
Inveraray. Tel: 01499 500235.
Open Apr–Sep, daily.

④ Kilmartin
Carnassarie Castle
Kilmartin. Tel: 0131 6688800.
Open all reasonable times.

⑤ Easdale
Easdale Island Folk Museum
Easdale Island, Oban. Tel: 01852 300370.
Open Apr–Sep, daily.

⑥ Oban
Oban Distillery
Stafford Street, Oban. Tel: 01631 572004.
Open all year, Mon–Fri.

A World in Miniature
Kilninver, Oban. Tel: 01852 316272/202.
Open Easter–Oct, Mon–Sat and Sun afternoons.

⑦ Barcaldine Castle
Barcaldine Connel, Oban. Tel: 01631 720598.
Open Easter–Sep, daily (closed Sat in Jun and Sep).

⑨ Ballachulish
Ballachulish Visitor Centre, Albert Road, Ballaculish. Tel: 01855 811296.
Open Apr–Oct, Mon–Sat afternoons.

⑩ Glen Coe and the Black Mount
Glencoe and North Lorn Folk Museum
Glencoe. Tel: 01855 811314.
Open Easter–Sep, Mon–Sat.

⑪ Loch Lomond
Queen Elizabeth Forest Park
Aberfoyle. Tel: 01877 382258.
Open Easter–Oct, daily; Nov, weekends.

INDEX

Index & Acknowledgements

The Automobile Association

would like to thank the following photographers and libraries for their assistance in the preparation of this book.
PICTURES COLOUR LIBRARY LTD 5, 7, 52/3; WOOLSACK COMMITTEE 2.

All remaining pictures are held in the Association's own library (AA PHOTO LIBRARY)
with contributions from the following photographers:
P AITHIE 77; M ALLWOOD-COPPIN 64, 69; A BAKER 89, 110/1, 137; P BAKER 13, 16/7, 19a, 19b, 25, 26, 32, 44, 86/7, 90/1, 130/1; J BEAZLEY 124, 147, 149, 150, 155; A W BESLEY 10; M BIRKITT 84, 85a, 85b, 88, 94, 95, 96, 97, 129; E A BOWNESS 113, 114, 115; P BROWN 40; I BURGUM 58/9, 65, 66, 66/7, 72, 107; D CORRANCE 146, 148; D CROUCHER 50, 57, 76, 81; S L DAY 24, 29, 99, 103, 106, 116, 127, 153; E ELLINGTON 140/1, 165; P ENTICKNAP 49; D FORSS 33, 35, 42, 46, 47, 48, 51, 54, 55; J GRAVEL 63; S GREGORY 135; J HENDERSON 139, 141; A J HOPKINS 59, 71, 128; C JONES 56, 78, 80, 109; A LAWSON 8, 12, 18; S & O MATHEWS 34, 45, 91, 92, 151; E MEACHER 28/9, 70; C & A MOLYNEUX 60, 61; J MORRISON 120/1, 123, 126; R MOSS 11, 15; J MOTTERSHAW 134; R NEWTON 22, 130, 132; D NOBLE 36, 37, 38, 39, 41, 43; K PATERSON 145, 154; N RAY 9, 23, 100/1; P SHARPE 117, 156, 156/7; M SHORT 102, 111; R SURMAN 83; D TARN 112, 119, 122b, 125; M TAYLOR 136; T TEEGAN 14a, 14b; T D TIMMS 73, 74, 75, 79; W VOYSEY 30, 31, 93; R WEIR 142/3, 144; J WELSH 104, 105; L WHITWAM 82, 122a; H WILLIAMS 6, 152; J WYAND 27.

Contributors
Copy editor: Penny Phenix **Indexer:** Marie Lorimer
Thanks also to **Vic Bates** for his updating work on this book.